Teach® Yourself

Be a Great Dad
Andrew Watson

For UK order enquiries: please contact Bookpoint Ltd,
130 Milton Park, Abingdon, Oxon OX14 4SB.
Telephone: +44 (0) 1235 827720. *Fax:* +44 (0) 1235 400454.
Lines are open 09.00–17.00, Monday to Saturday, with a 24-hour
message answering service. Details about our titles and how to
order are available at www.teachyourself.com

Long renowned as the authoritative source for self-guided
learning – with more than 50 million copies sold worldwide –
the **Teach Yourself** series includes over 500 titles in the fields of
languages, crafts, hobbies, business, computing and education.

British Library Cataloguing in Publication Data: a catalogue record
for this title is available from the British Library.

First published in UK 2010 by Hodder Education, part of
Hachette Livre UK, 338 Euston Road, London, NW1 3BH.

The **Teach Yourself** name is a registered trade mark of
Hodder Headline.

Typeset by MPS Limited, a Macmillan Company.

Printed in Great Britain for Hodder Education, an Hachette UK
Company, 338 Euston Road, London NW1 3BH, by CPI Cox &
Wyman, Reading, Berkshire RG1 8EX.

The publisher has used its best endeavours to ensure that the URLs
for external websites referred to in this book are correct and active
at the time of going to press. However, the publisher and the
author have no responsibility for the websites and can make no
guarantee that a site will remain live or that the content will remain
relevant, decent or appropriate.

Hachette UK's policy is to use papers that are natural, renewable
and recyclable products and made from wood grown in sustainable
forests. The logging and manufacturing processes are expected to
conform to the environmental regulations of the country of origin.

Impression number   10 9 8 7 6 5 4 3 2 1
Year   2014 2013 2012 2011 2010

This book is dedicated to my own parents, role models difficult to match, and to my wife Zoë, for giving me the opportunity to try.

Acknowledgements

A big thank you to my agent, Sallyanne Sweeney, and to my editor, Victoria Roddam. And special thanks to all those who shared their experiences of fatherhood so openly.

_____

Image credits

Front cover: © Warren Millar – Fotolia.com

Back cover: © Jakub Semeniuk/iStockphoto.com, © Royalty-Free/Corbis, © agencyby/iStockphoto.com, © Andy Cook/iStockphoto.com, © Christopher Ewing/iStockphoto.com, © zebicho – Fotolia.com, © Geoffrey Holman/iStockphoto.com, © Photodisc/Getty Images, © James C. Pruitt/iStockphoto.com, © Mohamed Saber – Fotolia.com

Contents

Meet the author

It seems to me that learning about fatherhood from a book is a bit like learning about sex from a book – as my teenage self will testify, no amount of reading can prepare you for the real thing. But that never stopped me doing my homework.

When my wife first fell pregnant, she soon built up a pile of well-thumbed, pastel-coloured parenting books by her bedside. But when I went looking for advice specific to me as a dad-to-be, I found – with very few exceptions – either unisex and uniformly dry reference books that gave no sense of the actual experience, or larger-print manuals that seemed to assume I'd really rather be down the pub than involved with my child.

That's not to disparage the reference books – I'd recommend having at least one of those weighty bibles on your shelf. They're informative, comprehensive and authoritative, and can be hugely reassuring at almost every stage of the pregnancy and beyond (see *Taking it further* at the back for some suggestions).

But while I needed to know the facts about fatherhood – how to bath a baby, deal with toddler tantrums and spot a chickenpox rash at 50 paces – I also wanted some idea of how I might *feel* about being a dad. Because, for pretty obvious reasons, I figured my experience of fatherhood would be predominantly emotional rather than physical. And I wanted to hear about those emotions from someone who credited me with the ability to read a page of text without needing a desperate gag in every paragraph to hold my attention. Did I really want to learn about something so subjective as feelings, I wondered, from an author who assumed I lacked the maturity to work a washing machine?

I needed a book that spanned the abyss, that taught me the facts while also being not only comfortable with the idea of a father really wanting to be involved, but actually *based* on that assumption. That an abyss existed between the two – between objective knowledge and subjective experience – was becoming increasingly clear as my wife slipped further and further into it. Because despite being a doctor in possession of all the dry facts, within minutes of falling pregnant she'd morphed from seasoned medic into terrified, first-time mum. And that was months before our daughter even arrived.

Search as I might, I couldn't find a book that effectively straddled that divide. Now, thanks first to my daughter and then my son, I've had the chance to experience fatherhood first-hand. And thanks to this book I've had the opportunity to talk to many other dads, and to share our experiences, while hopefully adding a few of the facts at the same time. A lot of it is common sense but, at three in the morning, when you're tearing your hair out with frustration and worry, common sense can be understandably lacking.

Raising a child is an immensely personal experience, with infinite variables impacting on everyone's circumstances – there is no one way to be a great dad. So the chances are you won't agree with everything you read here. And because the role of father is so infinitely diverse, I can't ever cover all there is to cover. Instead, my aim is a book that leaves you with a little more confidence and sufficient information – or at least advice over where to find sufficient information – to make up your *own* mind.

As I said at the start, it's not easy to communicate what being a dad is actually like. As with sex, theory is no substitute for experience. All I can hope is that – as with sex – you're soon too busy enjoying yourself to worry too much about whether or not you're doing it right.

Andrew Watson
London, 2010

Only got a minute?

▶ As a father, you'll be your child's principal male role model, and fundamental in forming the type of person they'll become. So consider carefully the values you're demonstrating in your every action.

▶ Given the chance, you're no less capable than your partner in caring for your child, and your contribution is of crucial and distinct importance. So take every opportunity to be actively involved as much as possible, right from the start.

▶ A large part of your role, especially early on, will be to support your partner in any way you can. No one is better placed or better equipped to offer her the comfort and reassurance she'll need.

- Don't be timid in your dealings with health professionals – if you're ever concerned about something or in doubt, ask.
- There's no one right way to raise a child. Sift through the mass of advice and apply a little common sense in taking whatever works for you.
- Be practical about your finances – recognize the difference between want and need, and communicate with your partner.
- Discipline should be founded on love, and is about the enforcing of clear and consistent boundaries established for your child's benefit, not yours.
- Parenting can be tough, so be forgiving of yourself and your partner.
- You will be tired, physically and emotionally, but you'll also surprise yourself with strengths you never knew you had.

- As much as you'll want to protect them, your child has to live in the real world, so be wary of bolstering them with false praise, or sheltering them from failure.

- Avoid the temptation to compare your child's development to others' – most children progress at hugely varying rates but soon end up much the same.

- There are few jobs on this earth more important than raising a child, so it's natural to be apprehensive. But there are few jobs that can offer so much in return.

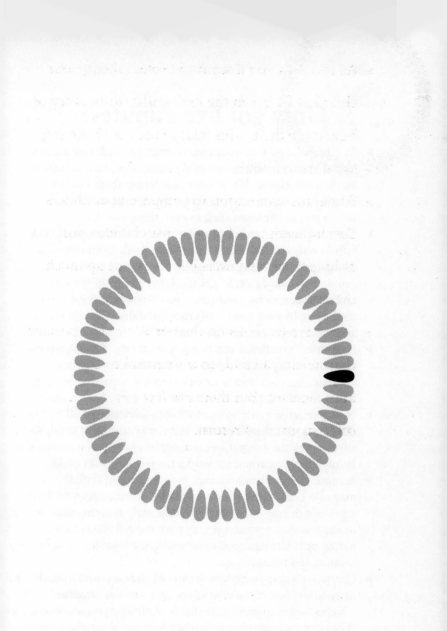

5 Only got five minutes?

▶ As a father, you'll be your child's principal male role model. Your behaviour will be one of the most important influences on their behaviour. It's no good just *telling* them how to behave – you need to *show* them. So consider carefully the values you're demonstrating in everything you do.

▶ The traditional – and outdated – roles of mothers and fathers only exist if you let them exist. Aside from actually giving birth and breastfeeding, there's nothing your partner can do that you can't. So get stuck in right from the start, and set a pattern for your future involvement. Your role in the raising of your child is of crucial and distinct importance, and you'll never get this time back.

▶ First-time parenthood can be nerve-wracking. Complications can arise at any stage. So never feel embarrassed about approaching your doctor or health visitor for advice – it's a large part of what they're there for.

▶ New parents are often swamped with advice from all directions. But there's no one 'right' way to raise a child, so sift through the suggestions and apply a little common sense before adopting whatever works for you and your child.

▶ Because your partner's journey is so hugely physical, she may also be far more emotional as well. Your principal role, especially through pregnancy and the early months, must be to support her in whatever way you can. No one is better placed or better equipped to recognize and meet her need for comfort and reassurance.

▶ Carry out a comprehensive review of your finances as early as possible, and make yourselves aware of the range of benefits and entitlements available. And when it comes to shopping, recognize the difference between want and need. Don't let your natural desire to provide your child with the best push you into overspending. You needn't fork out a fortune to provide your child with the basics.

- ▶ Children come hand in hand with worry. Parenthood requires an element of fatalism, even before they're born – without invasive and potentially risky tests during pregnancy, you can't rule out every possible abnormality. And you can't wrap them in cotton wool once they're out. After a certain point, all you can do is limit the risks, and hope for the best.
- ▶ Avoid the temptation to compare your child's development to others', or to push your child to progress. There's no research to suggest that the early achievement of learning milestones is linked to future success. Most children develop at hugely varying rates but soon end up much the same.
- ▶ Discipline should be founded on love, and is about the setting and enforcing of clear and consistent boundaries established for your child's benefit, not yours. And punishment should be a last resort, used only when the other more positive disciplinary techniques have proved unsuccessful.
- ▶ Praise can be a valuable means of encouraging and guiding your child, but it should be grounded in substance. The real world won't prop up their self-esteem with false praise, or shelter them from failure.
- ▶ There'll be times when you and your partner will be exhausted, physically and emotionally, but you'll also surprise yourself with strengths you never knew you had. And while life will be different, it'll soon settle down, and then you'll find you wouldn't want it any other way.
- ▶ Being a dad is one of the most responsible roles anyone could have – it's natural to be worried about what lies ahead. But it's a learning experience – you're allowed to get things wrong. So be forgiving of yourself. And recognize that the hardest challenges really are the most rewarding. Nothing else has the potential to offer you so much joy and satisfaction as being a dad.

10 Only got ten minutes?

▶ You will always be the principal male role model in your child's life, and representative of half the world's population. Your behaviour will be one of the most fundamental influences on your child's behaviour. And it's no good just *telling* them how to behave – you need to *show* them. Your actions demonstrate your values – how you treat others, your attitude to work and money, the priority you put on time as a family, etc. So consider carefully the values you're modelling in everything you do.

▶ Parenting styles are not hard-wired according to gender, but adapt according to context. As in everything, practice makes perfect, so unless you get involved from the start, you'll risk conforming to the outdated roles of father as provider and mother as carer. Given the same opportunities to develop childcaring skills, men are no less capable than women, and no less nurturing. Aside from giving birth and breastfeeding, there's nothing your partner can do that you can't.

▶ By being actively involved in your child's life, you give them the best possible chance of a healthy, balanced, happy future. So consider your priorities and seize every opportunity to get stuck in, right from the start – you're setting a pattern of involvement now for all the years ahead. You can never reclaim the passing minutes, and your child won't be a child forever.

▶ Pregnancy and childbirth is an unavoidably physical process, with endless opportunities for worry. And even the healthiest of babies or young children will pick up bugs with gruelling regularity. So never feel embarrassed about approaching your doctor or health visitor for advice – it's a large part of what they're there for.

▶ It's easy as a new parent to be overwhelmed by the mass of advice thrown out by friends, family and the media, whether it's about the benefits of routine, the use of a dummy, or what type of nappy to use. But there's no one 'right' way to raise a child, so sift through the suggestions and apply a little common sense before adopting whatever works for you and your child.

▶ While your journey into parenthood will be predominantly emotional, your partner's will be hugely physical as well. And her physical state, whether in labour, breastfeeding, or recovering from the birth, will only further disrupt her emotions. Your principal role, especially through pregnancy and the early months, must be to support her and encourage her in whatever way you can. Your involvement can make an enormous contribution to her experience of motherhood, and no one is better placed or better equipped than you to recognize and meet her need for comfort and reassurance.

▶ Carry out a comprehensive review of your finances as early as possible, and make yourselves aware of the range of benefits and entitlements available. Consider the many cutbacks possible that won't impact on your lifestyle. Make a will and, if you haven't got one yet, start a pension. And keep communicating with your partner – don't imagine finances are your sole domain any more than nappy changes are hers.

▶ When it comes to spending money on your baby, recognize the difference between want and need. Despite what the brand-sponsored 'experts' might say, you don't need to fork out a fortune to provide your child with the basics, so don't let your natural desire to provide your child with the best be exploited. An ability to spend money doesn't make you a good parent.

▶ Children come hand in hand with worry. Parenthood requires an element of fatalism, even before they're born – without invasive and potentially risky tests during pregnancy, you can never rule out every possible abnormality. Nor can you wrap them in cotton wool once they're out. After a certain point, all you can do is limit the risks, and hope for the best. The reward for your worry is to watch them develop into independent, self-sufficient individuals.

▶ Avoid the temptation to compare your child's development to others', or to push your child to progress. There's no research to suggest that the early achievement of learning milestones is linked to future success, only that pushing children too hard can backfire. Most progress at hugely varying rates but soon end up much the same.

▶ Discipline is founded on love – clear and consistent boundaries provide certainty and security. Still struggling to make sense of the world around them, children will naturally push against restraints. When they do, it's our job as parents to let them know that those boundaries – established for their benefit, not ours – can be relied upon.

▶ The best way to avoid bad behaviour is to encourage good behaviour, through praise, consistency and modelling. And when the inevitable bad behaviour emerges, there are a number of techniques available for dealing with it, from distraction to compromise. Punishment should be a last resort, used only when the other more positive techniques have proved unsuccessful.

▶ Praise can be a valuable means of encouraging and guiding your child, but it should be grounded in substance. After all, you're raising them to live in the real world, a world that won't prop up their self-esteem with false praise or shelter them from failure.

▶ Your childcarer's influence will be enormous, so treat their role with the respect it deserves and do your homework. Find someone who can provide love, security and stability. And stay involved – you will always remain your child's principal teacher.

▶ There will be times when you and your partner are exhausted, physically and emotionally, perhaps more than ever before. But you'll also surprise yourselves with strengths you never knew you had. And while life will be different, you will regain a sense of equilibrium, by which point you are unlikely to want things any other way.

▶ Being a parent is one of the most important and responsible roles anyone could have. Neither of you has done anything like it before, so it's only natural to be worried about what lies ahead – that in itself is recognition that you're taking the responsibility seriously. But like any learning experience, you're allowed to get things wrong – as long as you deal with those mistakes in the right way. So be forgiving of yourself and your partner, and look after each other.

▶ Fatherhood is about growth – not losing who you were, but building upon it. And it doesn't mean you're doing anything wrong or not up to the task if you find it difficult at times. It's the enormity of the challenge that makes it one of the most rewarding roles you could ever have. Nothing else in life has the potential to offer you so much joy and satisfaction.

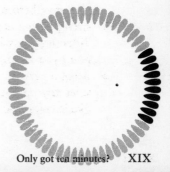

1

....

What being a father really means

In this chapter you will learn:
* *how to demonstrate the sort of person you want your child to be, rather than simply tell them*
* *how to be realistic in your expectations*
* *how to sift through the mass of parenting advice without guilt.*

Responsibilities and qualities

Ask me to list a father's typical responsibilities and I'd probably suggest a few pretty general duties, from the obligation to protect, maintain and discipline, to the need to make decisions about education, religion and medical treatment. But ask me to say what *qualities* are required to meet those responsibilities, and my answer wouldn't be quite so obvious.

> *The fundamental quality I associate with my dad is acceptance. He's always been there for me, no matter what.*
>
> Michael, father to Amy and Tom

Every day, consciously or not, our idea of what it means to be a father, already instilled in us by upbringing and education, is further shaped by the many examples to which we're exposed, be it by friends, the wider family, the television or other media. Each one impacts on our assumptions of what qualities are required.

But without doubt the greatest contributor to a man's sense of fatherhood is his own dad.

Insight

Whether you want to emulate him or do all you can to avoid turning into him, your own dad will influence your notion of fatherhood more than anyone else.

It took me a long time to realize it, but my dad was actually quite manipulative. He used guilt to enforce discipline.

Christian, father to Adrian, Kelly and Alice

For more on your legal responsibilities as a dad, go to www.direct.gov.uk/en/Parents/ParentsRights/DG_4002954.

Role model

There's no escaping, then, the obvious point: for better or for worse, you as a dad are going to be the first and principal male in your child's life. How you behave will be one of the fundamental influences on what sort of person they become. Our children learn to be adults from us.

Insight

To instil the values in your child that you think important, you have to demonstrate them every day. It's no good merely telling them how to behave – you have to show them.

If you have a son, he's going to at least start off by seeing you as the wisest and strongest man in the world. He's going to do all he can to imitate not just your mannerisms, but the way you interact with everyone else around you.

If you have a daughter, your relationship with her will be the most profound influence on her future relationship with the male sex. You'll be her reference point against which to judge other men.

And who better than her father to teach her that she's lovable and to be valued for who she is, regardless of what she looks like?

How you respond to strangers, how you treat women, how quick you are to argue and how willing you are to apologize – your behaviour exhibits your values, and is central to the development of your child's character. In all things, all the time, you have to strive to act as you would wish them to act when they become adults.

> *It never fails to amaze me, the parents I see who shout at their children to stop shouting...*
>
> Dan, father to Tricia and Miles

What type of person are you?

So at the risk of getting too psychoanalytical, this might be a good time to consider the values you've adopted, and work out which ones you admire and which ones you'd rather not pass on. For example:

- *Are you a glass half full sort of person, or always noting the negative?*
- *Are you affectionate, or uncomfortable displaying emotion?*
- *Are you spontaneous, or do you like your days to be regulated?*
- *Do you get energized from socializing, or prefer being alone?*
- *Are you always stressing about money?*
- *Do you worry about the future, or live more in the present?*
- *Are you outspoken about your opinions, or reserved?*

A greater awareness of your own character and qualities will allow you to work on those aspects you'd rather improve, and limit any possible negative impact on your child.

> *I had a tough childhood, and I wonder if I'm overprotective of Adam as a result.*
>
> James, father to Adam

Shared values and new values

I knew when I married my wife that we shared similar values. But becoming parents exposed us to new circumstances that, in turn, exposed slight differences.

Jess is far more particular about what Nathan watches on TV, while I'm always the one reminding him to say please and thank you.

Oliver, father to Nathan

It's difficult to know in advance how you'll feel about some aspects of fatherhood, especially as some of your values may well change when you become a dad. You may start to look at things differently and develop new attitudes. Similarly, you may re-evaluate old qualities in light of your new responsibility, and judge yourself according to new criteria. I guess that could be part of what they call growing up.

Ella used to ridicule my tendency to worry about money, despite us both having reasonably well-paid jobs. Now she's glad I'm more cautious than spendthrift.

Conor, father-to-be

Me, a dad?!

Those lofty preconceptions of what qualities are necessary to be a father can be difficult to live up to. Add to that the thought that your every action is under scrutiny and contributing directly to your child's development, and it's no wonder that the responsibility of fatherhood can terrify. Who ever really feels ready, or suitably qualified?

> *There's no way I feel old enough or wise enough to be a dad.*
>
> Winston, father to Joel and Anita

But the truth is, of course, that no adult truly feels as mature or knowledgeable or all-powerful as we as children imagined adults to be. There's no magic moment when life clicks into place and you're able to face each day with unwavering confidence. Unfortunately, our fears grow with us.

Be realistic

There is good news, though – you're allowed to get things wrong. In fact, it's important for your child to see that you *can* be wrong. After all, you're raising a human being, not a god, and they're going to make mistakes in life as well, from the minor and everyday to the major and life altering. What's important is that they learn from you how to deal with those mistakes, how to take responsibility, how to apologize where necessary, and how to move on.

Insight

You're allowed to get things wrong, as long as you deal with those mistakes in the right way.

Whether it's through making up after an argument with your partner, saying sorry to the neighbour after overreacting to the dog crap in your garden, or acknowledging that you forced your kid to wear that top only because your mum was coming to stay, by dealing with your negatives in a positive way, you're equipping your child with a blueprint for dealing with similar mistakes in their own lives.

That's not an excuse to expose them to your every fault, but your child will benefit from experiencing these dynamics in the safety of their home before they have to deal with them in the wider world.

The avalanche of advice

Telling people with kids that you're about to have one yourself is taken by some as an invitation to smother you with titbits of what they'll consider hard-won wisdom – whether you want their opinions or not.

> *My mother-in-law seems to think it's her job to dispense advice whenever she sees me. I think I could live with that, if most of the time she didn't turn out to be right.*
>
> Callum, father to Jack and Sam

On top of the unsolicited recommendations, there's the endless wave of warnings and opinions available through books, newspapers, magazines and the internet. And almost every week there's a new survey or study trumpeting the discovery of the definitive parenting method. The sheer diversity of information can be overwhelming, especially as it's so often conflicting or changing from one day to the next.

Insight
The internet is a fantastic resource, offering more access to information than ever before. But always bear in mind the difficulty of guaranteeing a website's credibility. Especially when dealing with medical issues, it's always best to see your own doctor or health visitor.

We all need a little support now and then, especially if we're exhausted and feeling the strain. Sometimes it can be a relief to offload responsibility onto a routine or technique that you can be confident won't harm your baby but will get you through the night.

And sometimes, amongst the cacophony of information, you'll find something that will really help.

Insight

I'm not suggesting you ignore all the advice thrown your way, merely that you question its source and sift and pick judiciously. Read or listen with an open mind and a healthy scepticism and then, from amongst the mass, adopt whatever works for you and your child.

Whether you believe it yet or not, when it comes to your own child, you'll soon be an expert as well. So choose whatever techniques or methods work – as long as your decisions are based on love and respect, they'll be the right decisions for your family.

The 'perfect' father

While it's always good to strive to be a better person, it's just as important to recognize that no one's perfect, neither you, your own dad or – whatever your partner may say – your child. Unfortunately, the ability to get a woman pregnant is no guarantee of an infallible sense of judgement, omniscience, or the ability to get by on three hours' sleep.

Insight

Parenting is a learning experience. At times you'll wonder what to do, and frequently you'll be just too exhausted to give your child or partner the attention they deserve or demand. But you don't have to be perfect – just good enough.

Don't set yourself up with unrealistic expectations, or writhe in a lather of guilt if you fail to adhere to every recommendation. There is no one 'right way' to parent. Be content to do things *your* way and recognize that, even with the best will in the world, at times you'll fall short of your ideal and get things wrong.

Inevitably, as in all things, there'll be moments when you'll look back and realize that you could've done better. And that's when it'll be a comfort to know that you acted according to your best judgement, not simply *re*acted according to received wisdom, expectation or the memory of how things were done to you.

Insight

We all have different strengths and weaknesses, and limited time and resources with which we can only do our best. It's important to acknowledge that, and to teach our children the same. Don't reproach yourself or each other with the benefit of hindsight.

Time

In today's world, where children are exposed to so much so young, your guiding influence as a parent is needed more than ever. Yet because of that world we live in, you're likely to have less time than ever before.

That's become one of the hardest things to accept, knowing that the best thing I can give my girls is my time, yet having so little of it to spare.

Harry, father to Paige and Taylor

Insight

In the years ahead, time will become your greatest ally and your worst enemy – it'll flash by fast enough to comfort and console when things are tough, and obstinately refuse to slow when you want to savour every minute.

As a result of a world that refuses to stop just because you have a baby, you may soon find yourself forced to achieve a greater level of efficiency at home and at work than ever before.

I can't believe how wasteful I was of my days before Becky came along. Now I'm ruthless over anything that risks stealing me of my time with her.

Sean, father to Becky

It's been said that we spend two years of our lives just looking for things. So the more organized you can become, the less time you'll spend down the back of the sofa and the more you'll have to enjoy being a dad.

The irreversible change

Making the most of the time that you have also means recognizing that life will never be the same. Faced with even more to do and less time to do it, an ability to compromise and prioritize becomes essential.

And from a life focused on yourself and your partner, everything will now revolve around the new arrival as you find yourselves redefined.

Even the clothes I wore changed. No more designer jeans, but an old pair that were soon through at the knees, and didn't matter if they were crusted in milky yack.

Dan, father to Tricia and Miles

Yes, at times you'll feel pulled in all directions. And yes, you'll be forced again and again to relegate your own needs beneath those of your partner and baby. Don't underestimate what's required.

But the more you throw yourself in and participate, in both the good and the bad, the more confidence you'll gain, and the more you'll get out of your new role as you and your child grow ever closer.

*I loved my life before we had kids. Every day was my own,
with no real worries. But now that I'm a dad, I wish I'd got
round to starting a family sooner.*

Michael, father to Amy and Tom

Modern parenthood

As the traditional roles of men and women change for the better,
there's a corresponding blurring of expectation and subsequent loss
of stability in the home that's yet to be replaced. The majority of
fathers still assume the role of main provider but, as many women
put in long hours themselves, men are also increasingly required to
be hands-on dads.

The result can be a status quo in which more and more mothers
and fathers struggle to achieve a balance between work and family,
leading to a sense of persistent compromise and often soul-sapping
guilt.

Fortunately, though, these changes are being driven not just by
women in the workplace, but by a growing recognition of the
importance of fathers. Society now offers dads more opportunities
than ever before to be directly involved in the raising of their sons
and daughters. And the more you grasp those opportunities, the
faster the world will turn towards a working – and fulfilling –
equilibrium.

As I hope this book will show, the potential benefits – for you and
your child – are enormous.

10 THINGS TO REMEMBER

1 *Your own father will be the greatest influence on your idea of what it means to be a dad.*

2 *You'll be the principal male role model in your child's life, and they'll learn from your actions how to be the adult they'll become.*

3 *It's no good just telling your child how to behave – you've got to show them.*

4 *Be aware of the type of person you are and how that can impact – positively and negatively – on your child.*

5 *The responsibility is huge – it's quite normal to feel unprepared.*

6 *You and your partner are allowed to get things wrong, so don't expect too much of yourselves, and don't beat yourselves up over mistakes with the benefit of hindsight.*

7 *Don't get intimidated by the inevitable barrage of parenting advice – when it comes to your own child, you're an expert too.*

8 *When times are tough, or as happy as you could hope for, remember that all things must pass.*

9 *More and more, society is recognizing the importance of your role in the raising of your child, and providing opportunities to be directly involved.*

10 *Parenting is tough, but it has the potential to offer more happiness and fulfilment than you ever knew was possible.*

2

Fathers and mothers

In this chapter you will learn:
- *that children with actively involved fathers live happier, more balanced lives*
- *that mothers and fathers both have important and complementary roles to play in raising their children*
- *that men are no less capable than women in caring for children.*

The myth of equality?

More than ever before, men and women are playing an increasingly equal role, both in the office and at home. But strive as we may for true equality, some think we'll inevitably fall short, not just because of the obvious physical discrepancies, but because men and women are intrinsically different in thought and action.

We've all heard those clichéd generalizations according to which women can't read maps or parallel park and are prone to smother with advice, while men hear that advice only as criticism, hate shopping, and will never stop to ask for directions.

These differences are thought to overflow into our parenting styles as well. To repeat a few oft-cited examples:

Encouraging independence
A mother might rush to pick up a fallen toddler, while fathers are more likely to wait to see if the toddler can get back up without help.

Playing
Fathers are more likely to get physical, while mothers tend to engage in a more structured way.

Communicating
Fathers often use more complex speech patterns, while mothers tend to simplify and slow down their speech.

Lifting
Fathers tend to lift babies in a far less predictable manner than mothers, who generally employ the same posture, rhythm and movement each time.

Comforting
A father might let a baby cry a little longer in the hope they'll settle themselves, while a mother might hurry to comfort them.

Perhaps she has some invisible bond after carrying the kids inside her for so long, or maybe it's just a lower threshold, but Sarah's always reacted far more emotionally to the sound of our daughters' crying.

Dominic, father to Millie and Tamsin

YOUR CHILD'S DIFFERING RESPONSES

According to the same theory, not only will you and your partner parent differently, but your baby's response will be gender-oriented as well. In one study, babies tended to relax when approached by their mothers, but grew more animated when approached by their fathers, seeming to reinforce the generalization that they look to their mothers for comfort but to their fathers for stimulation.

Certainly, my experience conforms to this theory – when our daughter wants someone to tickle her and roll around with, she comes to me, but when she hurts herself and wants a cuddle, it's her mum almost every time.

The importance of your involvement

Obviously having two involved parents is hugely beneficial for a child, from the advantages of their mutual support to the increased exposure to differing interests, skills and opportunities.

But on top of that – and as a result of these differences – experts can now list the many specific benefits that arise from greater paternal involvement. In other words, you as a father are capable of influencing your child to enormous advantage in a way that no one else can.

Research shows that children who grow up with an actively involved father:

▶ *are less likely to break the law*
▶ *are less likely to abuse drugs*
▶ *are more emotionally balanced*
▶ *have greater curiosity about the world around them*
▶ *are less likely to behave antisocially*
▶ *have higher self-esteem*
▶ *are better able to form happy, long-lasting adult relationships*
▶ *do better at school*
▶ *have higher life satisfaction*
▶ *are more compassionate.*

THE NATURE OF YOUR INVOLVEMENT

Chapter 8 looks at ways to get involved in your child's life, but here are a few examples of the direct impact of that involvement:

▶ *While mothers tend to reassure frustrated toddlers, fathers encourage them to manage that frustration, thereby teaching them early on how to deal with stress.*

► *Fathers give their children that little bit more space to solve problems for themselves and explore their own limits by taking risks.*
► *The more help that children – and especially girls – receive from their fathers with their maths homework, the better their quantitative reasoning.*
► *The more a father spends time reading to his child, the higher their verbal intelligence.*

And paternal influence is irrespective of income. While poverty is often blamed as the main instigator of antisocial behaviour or violent crime, studies confirm that your active involvement has a far greater role to play.

Your input during the early years of your child's life is crucial in every way, and lays the groundwork for your child's later years. By building a strong and positive relationship, you're giving them the best chance you can of a happy life, establishing a bond that will support them through the difficulties of adolescence and into life beyond.

Insight

Whatever type of father you may be – biological or step-, living at home or living apart, confident or terrified, rich or poor – you matter, and have a distinct and hugely important part to play in your child's development.

Unfortunately, while in a position to impact on your child's life to such a positive extent, you're obviously similarly placed to have a negative influence. So the message is clear – you have to take responsibility for your child by playing an active role in their life.

YOUR OWN HEALTH

Given the potential offered by parenthood for satisfaction – to say nothing of running around the garden, or pirouetting across the living room to dodge dropped toys – it's perhaps not surprising that studies also suggest a link between active fathering and increased health.

The influence of context

It's important to recognize, however, that – even if the above generalizations hold true – that doesn't mean that this gender differential is innate. Parenting styles are dictated to a very large extent by social conditioning, the context in which men and women find themselves interacting with their children.

For example, it could be that fathers are looked on as more playful simply because the time they spend with their kids is more likely to be recreational. Or they're less actively engaged because, by the time they get home, they're too exhausted or it's too close to bedtime to do more than sit with their child in front of the telly.

Maybe fathers simplify their language less than mothers because they spend less one-on-one time with their children, and so fail to speak at an appropriate level. Perhaps they aren't so predictable when lifting babies because, being so frequently sidelined early on, they fail to establish an optimum pattern or are unconsciously expressing a desire to be recognized as different to the mother.

The influence of expectation

As well as context, there's the influence of expectation. Although the world is changing and men today are increasingly involved in caring for their children, there remain at least the unavoidable residual expectations instilled by generations of men who went out to work and women who stayed at home. And while the work environment has changed considerably to incorporate women, the home environment still lags behind.

As men, we're expected to behave in certain ways and to demonstrate certain strengths and weaknesses. And it can be surprisingly easy to reinforce those expectations.

> *Chloe seemed to overreact to Darren's slightest slip, so much so that I could see him making a big issue out of every small event just to gain that same level of attention. I then found myself compensating by making light of each little hurt, which only prompted Chloe to fuss more and made me feel uncomfortable, like an old-fashioned, stiff-upper-lip kind of dad.*
>
> Seb, father to Darren

The erosion of distinct parenting styles

To some extent, then, fathers are pushed into – and bound within – a distinct parenting style by context and expectation. But studies show again and again that the more experience you gain in caring for your child, the more that differential erodes.

Specifically, the more time you spend alone with your child as the main carer and the greater level of responsibility you have for their daily routine, the more the traditional roles of mother and father converge.

Similarly, when parenting alone, mothers and fathers drift towards a middle way, as though to compensate for the lack of other. And when parenting as a couple with equal input, those traditional styles become interchangeable.

You are no less capable

Were we able to unshackle ourselves from the influence of social conditioning, we men and women might find ourselves – reproductive systems aside – surprisingly equally prepared for the principal childcaring role.

When given the opportunity, fathers learn to care for their children at much the same rate as mothers. And around the birth of their children, new fathers show similar hormonal changes to those experienced by women, from decreased testosterone and oestradiol to increased levels of prolactin and cortisol.

What's more, psychologists confirm that – as long as a child gets sufficient quality attention – they don't notice the gender of their carer.

If traditionally raising a child has been looked upon as a mother's role, it's not due to a biological inability in men but because, having been pushed into (or gratefully adopted?) a support role, men approach their part in parenting with less confidence, having less opportunity to practise. Not only that, but they receive far less support from health professionals, society, family and friends.

As women are increasingly offered the chance to compete as equals in the workplace, they are proving themselves just as proficient. And when fathers defy expectation and claim the same opportunities to be involved with their children, they're proving themselves just as nurturing, just as sensitive, just as attached, and just as capable.

Fortunately, Sara allowed me as much right to make mistakes as her, and was very good about not hovering ready to swoop at the first sign of trouble. Now, apart from actually giving birth and breastfeeding, there's nothing she can do that I can't.

Chris, father to Rowen and Holly

Insight

Men are just as capable of caring for children. Lack of breasts aside, there's nothing to stop you being every bit as involved and proficient as your partner at caring for your child.

10 THINGS TO REMEMBER

1 *The recognized differences in the way that men and women act and react is reflected in their differing parenting styles.*

2 *Where differences exist, they are complementary.*

3 *Fathers have an enormous and direct impact on their child's physical, cognitive, emotional and behavioural development.*

4 *Your input during your child's early years is crucial, and lays the foundation for your relationship throughout their life.*

5 *Studies suggest that actively involved fathers are healthier.*

6 *It's possible to attribute the differences in parenting styles not to gender, but to context – the circumstances in which men and women interact with their children.*

7 *Many of those differences can similarly be explained by traditional expectations of the mothering and fathering roles.*

8 *The more time a father spends alone with his child and the more responsibility he has for their daily routine, the more those parenting differences disappear.*

9 *Fathers have traditionally been viewed as supplementary to mothers because they've lacked the opportunities to develop the same childcaring skills.*

10 *Given those same opportunities, men are no less capable of caring for their children.*

3

The pregnancy: first thoughts

In this chapter you will learn:
- *how to react to the news of impending fatherhood*
- *how to allay any initial fears your partner may have*
- *how to share the news of the pregnancy*
- *how to get involved from the start.*

Reacting to the news

Even if it was planned, confirmation that your partner's pregnant can still come as a shock and generate any range of emotions, from elation to despair, trepidation to panic. Or perhaps you felt nothing, having no visible sign that anything's changed and no concept of what lies ahead.

Insight

While there's no correct emotion to feel, there is an optimum way to react. Because whatever your emotions, you're now on the path to fatherhood, and that means doing what's best for your partner and baby. She'll find pregnancy demanding enough without having to worry about the commitment of the one person she's likely to rely on most.

So don't give her any reason to suspect you're anything other than blissfully happy. If she's terrified, smother her fears in your joy. If she's ecstatic, match her delight. If she leaps headfirst into making plans, nod in happy agreement with everything she says, safe in the knowledge that you can always discuss it properly later on, when the initial shock has subsided.

Possible thoughts

'Thank God I'm not shooting blanks.'
That sense of pride, or perhaps relief, might provide a welcome antidote to other concerns, so go ahead and swagger. While you can.

'We'll never be able to leave the house again.'
Fear of social death is normal, from the moment your partner refuses to shift off the sofa to the increased restrictions when the baby arrives, at which point you face either the guilt of going out alone or enormous babysitter bills. You may even worry about slipping beneath the social radar entirely.

Likewise, you may mourn the freedom to be spontaneous. Suddenly you're no longer free to jack it all in and jump on the next plane to Rio – however much that may seem like a good idea right now.

> *Having Becky is restrictive, of course. But as we've both got more confident, we've found that she's surprisingly portable. Life just requires a little more planning.*
>
> Sean, father to Becky

So make the most of the time you have now. Go to the cinema and out for dinner, meet up with friends – all those things that will require extra planning and expense when the baby arrives. And when that time comes, you may discover you're actually quite happy turning down invitations in favour of staying at home with your new family.

> *I was worried that I'd lose touch with my friends who didn't have kids, but it just takes a bit more effort. And for those*

few who have slipped off the radar, I've made loads more through my kids.

Dominic, father to Millie and Tamsin

'There's no way we can afford this.'
Concerns over the cost of a child are a totally valid and justified expression of your new responsibility. Chapter 10 offers some suggestions to soften the blow.

'What's this going to do to our relationship?'
You might be worried that, with the arrival of a baby, your partner will no longer be focused on you. Perhaps her belly is already stealing attention that was previously yours.

But this is no time to be jealous – it's a time to feel proud and protective, and to take delight in the growing and hugely important relationship between your partner and your baby. Putting the needs of your partner and your baby before your own is the first step towards committing to your family.

Just the realization that we were going to become parents pulled Chloe and me together, as we shared an incredible secret that was ours alone.

Seb, father to Darren

'Our lifestyle's not suitable for a child.'
If this is a consideration, then you already know what you've got to change. Throw out the cigarettes, give up the drugs, think twice about throwing yourself out of planes in the name of recreation. Instead, go out and get fit, experiment with home cooking, and fill the freezer in preparation for the big day. You'll appreciate it later.

'There's nothing I can do – it's all happening to her.'
Most fathers-to-be come to this realization with a mixture of gratitude and helplessness. After all, pregnancy is unavoidably her cross to bear. But either way, there *is* plenty you can do – you may not be the lead figure in this story but, as this book hopes to make clear, your role is still enormously important.

'This flat's tiny – where are we going to put a baby?'
If you don't have a spare bedroom and can afford it, consider
upsizing. It's not easy working all day and then sharing a room
with a baby at night, and it's helpful to have somewhere for
family to stay over and lend a hand. Likewise, if you're facing the
prospect of dragging a pram up four flights of stairs, think about
relocating. And do it sooner rather than later – the stress of moving
home while heavily pregnant is something you want to avoid.

'How can I ever be as good a dad as mine was?'
It's natural at this time to reflect on your own childhood and your
own parents – perhaps so far your only frame of reference when it
comes to being a dad. But even within one generation, the role has
changed enormously, so don't overdo the comparisons. That said,
it's no bad thing to have high aspirations.

'I hope I'll be a better dad than mine was.'
If you're starting off with an awareness of a parenting style that
you want to avoid, you're already ahead of the game.

'I'm just not ready for this.'
It's as near as scientifically proven that no man is ready for
fatherhood. In one test monitoring pupil dilation as a register of
emotional response, every single woman reacted positively to the
sight of a beautiful baby, whether they had children of their own
or not. And men who were already fathers had the same response.
By contrast, the pupils of the men who *didn't* have children
contracted, as though trying to shut out the sight. The research
concluded that women are innately primed for maternal behaviour,
while men need to have their paternal instincts roused by the
arrival of a child of their own.

In other words, take heart – whether you feel ready now or not,
you're likely to turn out far more paternal than you know.

'What's my boss going to say?'
You may now want to reassess your role at work, to cut down
on the long trips away or the long hours. But it needn't all impact

negatively on your employer – looming fatherhood can push you to provide, to work harder and accomplish more. Chapter 11 covers the potential impact on your job in more detail, but it's worth discussing with your partner early on who's going back to work afterwards, even if you later change your minds.

'Is it going to be okay this time?'
If your partner has suffered a previous miscarriage, or several, or undergone any form of fertility treatment to get pregnant, it's totally understandable if, having got this far, you still want to keep the champagne on ice. Often the higher level of monitoring and your greater awareness of what's involved can agonize as much as reassure and, whatever happens, it'll feel a long, stressful road ahead. So follow your doctor's recommendations, do all you can to support each other, and let your partner rest as much as possible.

For more on miscarriages, see Chapter 5.

For more on the support available to those undergoing fertility treatment, go to the website of the Human Fertilisation and Embryology Authority at www.hfea.gov.uk/33.html.

'Fatherhood doesn't seem much fun – it looks pretty tough.'
Parenting *is* tough, without a doubt – that's what makes it one of the most rewarding and important roles you could ever have. But because we've all felt tired, or worried about money, or impatient to get things done, it's too easy to relate to the negative aspects of having a baby, without having any real understanding of the positives. And there are positives aplenty – though for the moment you're just going to have to trust me on this one.

'I guess that means no more sex for ages.'
Unless your partner is advised against it for medical reasons, there's absolutely no need to live like a monk until after the baby arrives. If anything, it's important that you maintain your close bond. See Chapter 4 for more about sex during pregnancy.

'Hopefully that means no more sex for ages.'
However unlikely this may seem to some, it's not unknown for couples to try for a baby for so long that sex loses its appeal, becoming no more than a mechanical chore. If this is the case for you, you can at last look forward to regaining a proper love life when the mood arises, rather than face a seemingly endless series of dutiful insemination attempts.

All the above worries are perfectly natural. In fact, the really worrying thing would be if you weren't worrying at all.

Put yourself in her shoes

But whatever your concerns, consider how your partner will be feeling. Because while she may stoop to using that expression 'We're pregnant', it won't take her long to realize that *we're* not. *She* is. You may have contributed to her condition and be keen to do all you can to help, but nothing you'll experience compares to what lies ahead for her.

Alongside any fears you may have, she'll have some very specific ones of her own:

▶ *What's a baby going to do to my career?*
▶ *And what's it going to do to my figure?*
▶ *Without an income, will I lose my independence?*
▶ *Will that glass of wine I had last week harm the baby?*
▶ *How much money will I have to spend to avoid wearing nothing more glamorous than a maternity tent?*
▶ *And how is something so big going to get out of there?*

Hijacked by hormones and a growing baby, she's about to lose control of her own body. Would you be willing to go through what she's about to face? Even if it's just through a sense of gratitude, the least you can do is swallow your grumbles and support her.

She seemed to think I might resent the fact that I couldn't get pregnant. She was actually smug about the fact that her body was about to be hijacked in a process that would end in inevitable pain.

Lucas, father to Ethan and Ben

SUPPORT HER

Insight

Your partner's got to know that you're going to be there for her, doing all you can short of carrying the baby yourself. That starts with celebrating the news – buy her flowers or take her out to dinner, anything that affirms your commitment and togetherness.

Virtually every father-to-be has felt terrified about what lies ahead. But right now, how you act is more important than how you feel. If you need to, consider talking to someone *else*. Try not to burden your partner with your worries, not because you're a man and that's what men do, but because you're not the one carrying the baby.

LISTEN TO HER

Be there for her, physically and emotionally. Begin to compromise when it comes to your own expectations – get back from work a little earlier, and assume more responsibility for the shopping and the housework. Treat her with the consideration she now deserves. Read the books together and seize the experience to the full.

Listen to her fears and talk them through, no matter how ludicrous, without judging or criticizing.

I tried to make light of Eloise's worries, but she thought I was just belittling them. It got to the point that she stopped confiding in me.

Ian, father to Logan

Sharing the news

There's no right time to tell the world about the pregnancy. Many couples wait until after the 12-week scan – not only does it give you both more time to digest the news and consider the future before the inevitable barrage of advice and baby chat, but the risk of miscarriage is vastly reduced after the third month. And keeping such a momentous secret with your partner can be quite a thrill.

Then again, it might be that the very people you want to share your happiness with are those to whom you'd turn for support in a worst-case scenario.

Either way, discuss your approach with your partner and, if you opt to keep quiet, try not to let slip, however tempting it may be.

TELLING THE BOSS

The more warning you give your employer, the more flexible they can be. But don't rush into it – sound out the office culture first, review your employee manual, and be prepared for a different reaction to the one officially advertised. If you can, speak to colleagues who are fathers for advice.

I knew I was approaching a pay rise, so didn't mention the baby until afterwards. I don't feel bad about that, despite my obvious shift in priorities since – after all, it was a reward for past work as much as an expectation of my future efforts.

Aaron, father to Brooke

Go to any revelatory meeting with your boss or HR department fully prepared. Work out your finances, and how much time you'll want off. Make it clear from the start that you'll want to claim your full paternity leave entitlement (see Chapter 10), but be sensitive about pushing too hard for anything extra. There are a number of schemes to help parents at work, but give your employer time to digest the news before you grab whatever you can.

For more about the support available as a working parent, go to www.workingfamilies.org.uk or call the Working Families Helpline on 0800 013 0313.

TELLING THE GRANDPARENTS

Ideally, you'll tell your own parents in person. Try to include both sets equally – you'd be foolish to risk offending and thereby alienating a potential source of advice or support in the years ahead. This could be a particular issue for your own mum who'll miss out on a large proportion of the chat and baby-related busyness that your partner will inevitably share with her mum.

And bear in mind that your parents might not be immediately overjoyed at the prospect of becoming grandparents. They might resent any implication that they're going to play a part in the childcare, whether voiced or not. They might just not feel old enough, or worry about how you'll take to parenthood, or how it'll affect your relationship with them. Give them time to absorb the news, and they'll inevitably come round.

On the other hand, if they're overeager and threatening to take over, then you and your partner need to establish the boundaries as early as possible. Make it clear you're grateful for their help, but be confident about managing your family your way.

The role of the grandparents

While up to this point you and your partner may have lived a happy private life of two, you may find that your respective families now want to be more involved. This could be the case particularly with your partner's mother.

But before you complain (openly) about the dreaded mother-in-law, it's worth bearing in mind a few points.

Grandparents can play an enormous role in helping you raise your child, both in practical terms when it comes to childcare, and also by instilling the same values you were raised with. They are a unique source of love, experience, support and advice, and it's quite possible that you and your partner will come to rely on them more than you yet know.

What's more, a grandparent can make your child's life infinitely richer as well – studies confirm that children who feel close to their grandparents are better adjusted, and they can learn an enormous amount from the older generation through the benefit of their unique relationship.

Finally, you never know how long your own parents will be around, and should never underestimate the immense pleasure they'll get from their grandchildren.

> *Bella was only four months old when dad died. But I know he was just delighted to be a grandad.*
>
> Nathan, father to Bella

PROBLEMS WITH THE GRANDPARENTS

Involving your parents in the life of your child can be a wonderful win–win–win situation, but at times it will also lead to friction – if you expect them to care for your child and want what's best for them, you've got to expect them to have opinions about how that's best achieved.

If problems do arise, talk them through sensitively and maturely. If need be, set boundaries in your dealings with your parents that maximize on the positive interaction between them and your child, but limit opportunities to degenerate into point-scoring or comments that might later be regretted by either side. After all, if your parents want to play a part in the life of their grandchild, it's in their interests to maintain good terms with you as well.

Many expectant parents find pregnancy a time to reconsider relationships with estranged family members, aware that they're not just dismissing that person from their own lives, but denying it from their child's too. The more people your son or daughter has to love and be loved by, be they friends or family, the better their lives will be.

Ultimately, when it comes to grandparents, it will almost always pay to keep them sweet. And you may even find that your new role as a parent brings you closer, as they share their own experiences of parenthood and you gain a new appreciation of all they went through with you.

Your role during the pregnancy

MEASURING YOUR INPUT

Pregnancy is almost by definition about your partner, and her contribution to the process is easily measured by her expanding belly. For her, success is achieved, all being well, with the safe delivery of a healthy baby.

By contrast, the only way to judge your input into the process is according to how happy your partner is with it. But that's not to say you should be led only by her requests or commands, or allow yourself to be sidelined by family, friends or doctors. There's plenty of opportunity for using initiative and assuming a wide variety of roles.

BE THERE FOR HER

Insight

Your main job, of course, is to provide constant reassurance and support, doing all you can to ensure she knows she's not going through it alone. Hide your gratitude that it's not happening to you beneath an impenetrable layer of sensitivity, and adjust all expectations accordingly.

It's not enough to just start doing the things you should be doing anyway: remembering her birthday and your anniversary, picking up your socks from the bathroom floor or putting the toilet seat back down. You've got to use your initiative to take on whatever you can around the home, from cleaning and shopping to cooking and bin-emptying, so it's already done by the time she'd otherwise have to ask.

So get home from work that little bit earlier. Feign enthusiasm for the pattern on the nursery curtains, and then put them up – or at least arrange for someone else to put them up – according to instruction. Unquestioningly sacrifice your weekend to a trawl of shops in search of just the right colour of baby blanket. Run without grumbling for her phone when she mistakenly leaves it upstairs in the bedroom for the fifth time. Do all you can to demonstrate how much you value all she's enduring.

I was starting to feel like a dog, as she'd send me to fetch this and fetch that from all around the house. At least it got me fit, I suppose.

Michael, father to Amy and Tom

Listen to her worries and forgive her her moods. Whatever the complaint, meet all outbursts of fear or frustration with at least the appearance of calm control. And as she grows ever bigger, tell her she looks gorgeous and that the pregnancy has limited itself to her belly alone. Even if it's an outright lie, she'll have the rest of her life to work on her figure. In the meantime, for her sake and that of your unborn child, you have to do all you can to reduce her stress levels by making her life easier.

Insight

It's a difficult role to play – especially if your partner is the sort who runs around at all hours with a long list of tasks – and it's a role that requires judgement and sensitivity. Which makes you, as the person who knows her best, the best person for the job.

Often the only way to get her to slow down is to take on those tasks yourself, but don't be afraid to ask for help from friends and family as well. They'll likely be happy to play an active part, either by filling the freezer with a few homecooked meals or accompanying her to a check-up when you're stuck at work.

10 THINGS TO REMEMBER

1   *The best thing you can do on learning you're going to be a dad is to demonstrate your commitment to your partner in any way you can.*

2   *Worries about looming fatherhood are normal and a healthy sign that you recognize your new responsibilities.*

3   *However much you're worried, it's your partner who's going to be most directly affected by the pregnancy.*

4   *Listen to her fears without judgement.*

5   *Discuss with her when you're going to share the news, and don't be too specific with everyone when it comes to the due date.*

6   *Keep the grandparents sweet. They're a unique source of love, experience, support and advice.*

7   *You can't expect your parents to love their grandchild and not have feelings about what's best for them. So take the good with the bad.*

8   *Do your homework before sharing the news with your boss. And be sure to claim your full paternity leave entitlement.*

9   *Take the initiative around the home to limit your partner's stress as much as possible.*

10 *You are the best person to help your partner through the physical and emotional strains of pregnancy.*

4

The pregnancy: the physical stuff

In this chapter you will learn:
- *what physical changes your partner will go through*
- *how pregnancy can impact on your sex life – for good and for bad*
- *what to expect of the tests and scans available during the pregnancy.*

Insight

A pregnancy lasts for 40 weeks and is measured not – as you'd think – from the point of conception, but from the start of your partner's last menstrual period (or LMP). That's why the estimated due date (EDD) is only 38 weeks after conception, rather than 40.

The 40 weeks are divided into three trimesters, each one being a three-month period.

Physical changes

Pregnancy is an unavoidably physical condition that doesn't always bring out the best. Here are just some of the unenviable ailments your partner might suffer during the nine-month term:

- ▶ *constipation and haemorrhoids*
- ▶ *flaky and itchy skin*

- *breathlessness*
- *heartburn*
- *leg and stomach cramps*
- *headaches*
- *fatigue*
- *sciatica*
- *extreme sensitivity to smells*
- *spots*
- *vaginal discharge*
- *swollen limbs*
- *dizziness*
- *stretch marks*
- *varicose veins*
- *back pain.*

What's more, as her centre of gravity changes, she may appear clumsier. She may also suffer from what's unofficially known as 'pregnancy brain', said by some to be another consequence of changing hormones, though it's fair to say that sheer exhaustion can leave anyone forgetful and distracted.

The only consolation you can offer your partner is that all these symptoms are part of a normal, healthy pregnancy, and most will disappear relatively soon. The rest, the varicose veins and stretch marks, can only be viewed as battle scars from a glorious campaign.

___

The first trimester (up to 14 weeks)

As hormones rage, she's likely to feel sick and exhausted, and may go off her food. She'll need to pee more often, her breasts will grow tender, and her mood can swing from high to low.

For a large part of the first trimester, it might seem as though little has changed, and that life's just continuing as normal.

*For weeks the only difference to me was that I was woken
every night when she went for a pee.*

Rob, father to Bridget

But while your partner may look much the same on the outside,
inside it's all change. By the end of week six, your baby is the size
of an apple pip. Though the umbilical cord is as thin as a human
hair, the brain already has skull forming around it and the heart
has started beating on its own.

To compensate for this frantic activity, your partner's metabolic
rate will have increased by 10–25 per cent, so it should be no
surprise if she's very, very tired. Expect to notice it, and to see
her welded to the sofa or collapsed on the bed.

*My wife used to hide away in the office broom cupboard
every lunch hour just to get a bit of sleep.*

Ian, father to Logan

MORNING SICKNESS

Insight

About half of all pregnant women experience morning
sickness to some degree during the first trimester.

Despite the name, it can occur at any time of the day and last for
weeks, and hits like a bad hangover. No one really knows what
causes it, though it's thought to be related to hormonal changes.
At worst, if your partner's finding it hard to hold down sufficient
fluids, she may even need hospital treatment.

Unfortunately there's little you can do to help, other than hold her
hair out of the pan and encourage her to graze throughout the day
rather than eat fewer, larger meals. Try preparing plainer snacks,
rich in carbohydrates and proteins, and make sure she drinks
enough fluid.

FOOD AVERSION AND CRAVINGS

> **Insight**
>
> On top of the sickness, around 80 per cent of pregnant women experience some form of food aversion.

My wife went from drinking endless tea all day, to none at all. Suddenly she couldn't stand the thought of eating meat, and the smell of my coffee made her stomach turn.

Christian, father to Adrian, Kelly and Alice

Alternatively, 90 per cent develop cravings, the most popular being for ice cream. Despite the clichés, it's very rare to crave non-food items, a condition known as pica. Ultimately, as long as the aversion or craving doesn't restrict a healthy, varied diet most of the time, there's nothing to worry about.

The second trimester (up to 28 weeks)

This is the period when pregnant women are said to be 'blooming'. Despite the ever-increasing bump, things are relatively calm, and your partner may regain her appetite for food and sex.

She'll really be looking pregnant now, and putting on up to half a kilo in weight each week. Morning sickness should fade, her hair may appear thicker and skin clearer, her mood is likely to stabilize and she won't need to pee so much.

On the downside, constipation could now be a problem as hormones relax her gut muscles and, as the growing abdomen impacts on the digestive system, she may experience increasing heartburn. A dark line known as a *linea nigra* may develop on the skin, running from her pubic bone to her navel (it'll fade again after the birth). Towards the end of the second trimester, she may feel breathless and suffer backache, and stretch marks may appear on her breasts, stomach and thighs. Naturally you will deny their existence.

The third trimester (beyond 28 weeks)

As the big day draws nearer, life gets difficult again as she suffers increasing discomfort and anxiety levels rise. You may find you have to help your partner with almost everything, from putting on her shoes to rolling over in bed. The urge to pee all the time will return, and the baby's constant kicks and prods can be uncomfortable. The heartburn and breathlessness may worsen and, as everything becomes an effort, she's unlikely to be wild about any suggestions of sex.

Then there's her mental state – more on page 41.

Sympathy pains, or Couvade syndrome

A very small proportion of fathers-to-be are said to experience genuine physical aches during the pregnancy as well, as though in sympathy with their partner. The most common is stomach pain, but some also have food cravings and gain weight. It's tempting to suggest that all such symptoms are the result of stress, conscious or otherwise, but other theories point to a change in male hormones or a subconscious attempt to assume some of your partner's pain.

The aches and pains will end with the birth but, if you're worried, don't be embarrassed to see your GP for what is a recognized condition.

For more information, go to www.thebabycorner.com/page/345.

Diet and weight gain

Unfortunately for women who like their food, there's no direct correlation between weight gain and the progress of a pregnancy.

The average woman normally gains about 13 kg, though it's not uncommon to put on as much as 23 kg. Most of that extra weight will slip away again after birth, especially if she's breastfeeding, but obviously the more weight there is, the harder it will be to shift. So encourage her to keep exercising, perhaps alongside you, to maintain her fitness and strengthen those childbirth muscles.

It can be particularly upsetting for her during the first trimester, when she might put on a couple of kilos without actually looking pregnant, just fatter (a word you will *never* use). So remember to compliment her on how she looks.

Insight

Tell her you love her over and over and check the sofa's comfortable before you dare to joke about her body.

Many websites outline which foods should be avoided, from raw or undercooked meat, poultry or eggs, to paté, soft cheeses, raw seafood, and liver or liver products: see, for example, www.babycentre.co.uk/pregnancy/nutrition.

Bear in mind the self-recrimination that can follow a moment of weakness, and be supportive of a common-sense approach, with plenty of protein-rich meats and green vegetables.

SMOKING, ALCOHOL, CAFFEINE AND DRUGS

If your partner can't get by without her tea or coffee, consider a caffeine-free brand. And if she smokes, drinks alcohol, or takes recreational drugs, do all you can to encourage her to stop.

You might consider doing the same, not only for your own health but because your encouragement and support can make a positive contribution, both to your relationship and to the wellbeing of your child.

The NHS Pregnancy Smoking Helpline is open seven days a week, 12 p.m. to 9 p.m. Call 0800 169 9169, or go to http://smokefree.nhs.uk/smoking-and-pregnancy. Alternatively, try www.quit.org.uk.

Of course, when it comes to all these restrictions that the pregnancy will impose upon your partner, you may prefer to reinforce your independence and determination to maintain a normal life by changing nothing. If so, just consider the impact of your decision on her and your unborn child, and judge according to your conscience.

Mood

Even if your partner's delighted to be pregnant, if she suffers from any of the typical side effects, her mood will inevitably be affected as well.

> *Cat giggled like an excited schoolgirl the first time she discovered she couldn't do up her trousers. By that evening, though, she said she was dreading turning into what she called a 'big, fleshy balloon'.*
>
> Lindsey, father to Eva

As her mood swings from high to low, her changing emotions may upset her just as much as her changing body. And as the big day approaches, she may thrill with anticipation or grumble constantly. She may not feel ready, and still be desperately nesting, or impatient to get it over with. She may delight in the attention as people start patting the bump like it's public property, or may hide in shame at her appearance, devastated to have lost the body she was once so proud of. Or she may be an ever-changing mixture of all of the above.

All this she may take out on you. Do your best not to argue, but to listen and be sensitive. Reminding yourself that it's not you who has to squeeze out a baby can provide the strength to endure a lot of abuse.

Take any worries seriously

Jen was 17 weeks pregnant when she found a small area of thicker tissue on one breast. When she was scanned it turned out to be just one of those normal pregnancy changes and she felt foolish for wasting the doctor's time, but they were really good about it. They said it was exactly what they were there for, and that they'd rather be telling us it's nothing to worry about than anything more sinister.

Alastair, father to Iain

Breasts

One physical consequence of the pregnancy that you won't take long to notice is that your partner's breasts will begin to grow, and the areolas – the skin around each nipple – will begin to darken, supposedly to guide the baby in for feeding.

The only problem is that, along with the growth, they also become incredibly tender.

My wife called me up from the store when they measured her for a maternity bra. 36DD! She was ecstatic. I was pretty happy about it myself. Until I realized that she wouldn't let me touch them.

Callum, father to Jack and Sam

Frustrating though this stage undoubtedly is, be patient. Your turn will come...

_____

Sex in pregnancy

Pregnancy can be a great time for your sex life. Her growing belly can add a whole new dimension to the intimacy as, freed from the constraints of contraception and faced with tangible evidence of your love, you and your partner can reaffirm and celebrate your relationship and all that lies ahead.

However, when it comes to you actually getting any, it's a good idea to be led by an awareness of what stage of the pregnancy your partner has reached, and how that's affecting her emotions. And then exploit that information with all the sly sensitivity normally employed by men wanting sex.

The first trimester is, generally speaking, a time of sickness and fatigue, so loss of libido is an understandable consequence. However much you might be aching to get your hands on those upgraded breasts, they'll be sensitive and tender, so you have to be the same. Be led by her.

The second trimester is perhaps a good time to get reacquainted. The morning sickness should have passed, but she's not yet too ungainly or uncomfortable. She may also find she has renewed energy, and the increased blood flow around her vagina and clitoris can heighten their sensitivity.

By the third trimester, she'll be increasingly uncomfortable and, with swollen feet, a protruding bellybutton and an inability to move without huffing and puffing, may not feel her sexiest.

Insight

But as long as you're both up for it and logistics allow, there's no reason why you can't continue to have sex well into the ninth month.

MAKING IT WORK

The main aim is to support her growing belly and protect it from your weight, so make use of pillows and cushions, and be prepared to hand over some of the control so that she can limit the depth and angle of penetration. The usual pregnancy favourites are the missionary position, doggy style, spooning, or with her on top.

However, be aware that her changing hormones can affect the vagina's natural lubrication, making penetration painful. If so, invest in some lubricating gel.

YOUR OWN FEELINGS ABOUT SEX IN PREGNANCY

I loved every bit of Lisa's changing body, from the bigger breasts to the enormous belly. I just found the idea of her as a mother incredibly sexy.

Mike, father to Aileen

Of course, while some men find their pregnant partners a turn-on, others are put off sex entirely.

I began to think of Alana more as an incubator than anything else – a functional feeding machine for our offspring. It definitely affected our love life.

Rafael, father to Paula

If you've gone off sex, try not to let her feel you're being critical or distant. Talk about your feelings. Or, if you're unwilling to be too frank, try to find a suitable excuse – one that *doesn't* include you telling her she's just not sexy any more.

THE RISKS

One common concern is that sex will somehow be physically damaging to your baby. You may be afraid of causing hurt or trauma, or even inducing a miscarriage, but you won't.

And even if your partner's at increased risk of miscarriage and a doctor has recommended limitations for the first three months, you can still have a go at the many alternatives to penetrative sex.

Towards the end of the third trimester – and especially during sex – her breasts may leak a little milk known as colostrum, a newborn-friendly substance full of proteins, antibodies and carbohydrates. This leakage is totally normal, and nothing to worry about. When the time comes, your partner's hormones will ensure there's still plenty for your baby.

Scans, tests and check-ups

When it comes to antenatal care, there still exists something of a postcode lottery in the UK. But according to Government guidelines, your partner's entitled to ten appointments and two scans during her first pregnancy.

As with the classes (see Chapter 5), it may not be necessary for you to be there at every appointment – but show willing, even if it's just to hold her hand. And you won't want to miss the ultrasound scans.

THE PROBLEM WITH ANTENATAL TESTING

The chances are that your baby's scans will be amongst the most thrilling experiences of your life so far. And even if they reveal a problem, many issues resolve themselves over the course of the pregnancy, or need only a little extra monitoring.

But because the standard antenatal tests generally deal in probabilities, every now and then they can reveal the *possibility* of a more serious problem, causing an immense amount of – often unnecessary – stress and anxiety. And the further, more specific tests required to confirm or allay suspicions can put your baby at risk.

For that reason, some expectant parents would rather consider exactly how they'd deal with bad news before they go ahead with the tests, while others would rather ignore the 'what ifs' in the hope they'll never have to think about them. And others – as is well within their right – decide not to have the tests at all, or to have only some of them.

> ## Insight
> If at any stage a test suggests there might be a problem, there's no way of turning the clock back, and there's certainly no way of forgetting it. The only options remaining are to push on with more, higher-risk tests, or to have the issue hanging over you until the birth either confirms or dispels your fears.

INITIAL TESTS

In the first few weeks, your partner's blood will be tested for, amongst other things, two inherited blood disorders – sickle cell disease and thalassaemia major. She should also be checked for hepatitis B, HIV, rubella and syphilis – all infections that can have a serious effect on your baby. At the same time, a healthcare professional should advise her on diet, antenatal care and the medical benefits available to her, like free prescriptions and the various grants on offer (see Chapter 10).

For more on the pregnancy blood tests, go to www.babyworld.co.uk/information/pregnancy/antenatal_testing/blood_tests.asp.

THE DATING SCAN

At some point between the ninth and fourteenth weeks, you'll be offered an ultrasound scan to check for multiple births, look for possible abnormalities, and confirm your baby's due date (more accurate than the LMP calculation).

Your partner may be asked to arrive with a full bladder – it helps to raise the baby closer. A small amount of lubricant is then smeared on her belly so a handheld paddle can be run across the skin and transfer the readings to a nearby monitor as black and white – and often very grainy – images. In some hospitals, you might even be able to see your baby in 3D. The procedure is quite safe and, apart from a squirt of cold gel and some mild pressure, she won't feel a thing.

Unless a previous scan has already been carried out, either to confirm the pregnancy or to check for possible problems, this is likely to be the first sight you'll have of your child – an incredible moment. There's nothing like it for focusing the mind on the reality of what's ahead.

> *Suddenly, there was our baby, twitching on the screen. And with the sound of its heartbeat as well, the whole thing was instantly far less abstract.*
>
> Conor, dad-to-be

It'll be too early to tell the sex at this stage, but you should be able to make out hands and arms, legs, feet, the heart and the head. If possible, make sure you ask for a photo or two – you may have to pay a small fee.

Don't get worried if the ultrasound operator has a good, long look before offering reassurance – it's not always easy to catch the baby at the right angle, or perhaps the initial due date was overly optimistic and the baby's still too small for accurate measurements. In these cases, it's not unusual to have to reschedule to come back another time.

If any problems are identified, they may simply require monitoring as they naturally remedy themselves. And remember that these scans aren't foolproof – occasionally the sonographer will fail to pick something up, or may feel it's necessary to advise you that something *could* be wrong, when in fact everything turns out to be fine.

Multiple births
While carrying more than one baby is more complicated and technically puts your partner into a 'high risk' category, most result in the safe delivery of healthy children. Inevitably, your responsibilities will increase with the news as she'll need that much more help and support. She'll need to be monitored more frequently, and may want to stop work earlier. You should also prepare yourselves for an earlier birth.

For more on multiple births, go to www.babycentre.co.uk/pregnancy/twins.

THE NUCHAL TRANSLUCENCY SCAN AND DOWN'S SYNDROME

Every pregnant woman is offered the chance to test their baby for chromosomal abnormalities such as Down's syndrome. In some places, that may initially be just a blood test, while others offer what's called a nuchal scan at the same time as the dating scan, at some point between 11 and 13 weeks. It's also possible you'll be offered both the blood test and the scan, thereby increasing the accuracy.

By using the images from the ultrasound to measure the level of fluid at the back of your baby's neck, the doctor can work out the risk of Down's syndrome. Results are expressed as a probability or percentage. For example, they may indicate that your baby has a 1 in 400 risk of Down's syndrome. Usually, it's a sufficiently remote possibility to allow you to forget about it.

The effects of Down's syndrome can vary enormously. Sufferers are prone to a number of health problems as well as learning difficulties, but many are able to live good, healthy and reasonably independent lives. It doesn't run in families and, though the risk increases with the mother's age, any woman can give birth to a baby with Down's syndrome.

Again, it's important to consider whether you want your baby to be tested – it may make no difference to you, or it may make all the difference. And remember that screening tests can lead to false positives – they can wrongly indicate a potential problem. As a guide, about 3 per cent of women are offered the more conclusive diagnostic tests and, of those, most don't go on to have a Down's syndrome baby.

Insight

Remember that those not offered a diagnostic test are at 'low risk', not at 'no risk'. These screening tests can miss genuine problems altogether – of all babies born with Down's syndrome, about a quarter aren't detected. So ask about the detection and false positive rates at your local hospital.

For more information, contact the Down's Syndrome Association on 0845 230 0372 or go to their website at www.downs-syndrome.org.uk.

And for more information on the nuchal scan, go to www.babycentre.co.uk/pregnancy/antenatalhealth/scans/nuchalscan.

DIAGNOSTIC TESTS

If the initial screening tests like the nuchal scan indicate a potential problem, your partner will be offered a diagnostic test. These check for a host of chromosomal abnormalities including Down's syndrome and many forms of cystic fibrosis. They provide 99.9 per cent certainty, but they're also more invasive, and carry a risk of miscarriage.

There are two diagnostic tests available. Neither should be painful, though they can be uncomfortable – always check they're being carried out by a skilled practitioner who does the procedure at least once a week. In some cases you can have the results within 24 hours, though it can take up to 18 days.

You should be able to decide if you want to hear the results at home, in the clinic, by letter or over the phone. The waiting can be tough, so get support if you need it, and take your time over any decisions.

For support and advice, call Antenatal Results and Choices (ARC) on 020 7631 0285.

Your choice of diagnostic test will be between an amniocentesis and chorionic villus sampling (CVS).

Amniocentesis
An amniocentesis will be carried out around the 16-week mark, and takes about ten minutes under local anaesthetic. Using an ultrasound to confirm your baby's position, a thin needle will be passed through your partner's abdomen and into the womb to remove a sample of amniotic fluid.

Because this fluid includes some of your baby's cells, the chromosomes can then be counted. The results of around 1 in 100 samples aren't sufficiently clear, in which case your partner will be offered a second attempt. The test should also be able to tell you your baby's gender.

As a general guide, 1 in 100 women who has an amniocentesis will miscarry.

Chorionic villus sampling
Chorionic villus sampling (CVS) is carried out between 11 and 14 weeks. Guided by ultrasound, a needle is passed through the vagina or abdomen to take a tissue sample from the placenta. Around 2 in 100 fail to produce a result.

One benefit of CVS is that, should you decide to terminate the pregnancy, you can do so earlier, which in turn is safer for your partner. However, unlike an amniocentesis, CVS doesn't test for spina bifida.

Again, as a general guide only, between 1 and 2 of 100 women will miscarry.

THE ANOMALY SCAN

This is the second of the routine ultrasound scans, offered between 18 and 21 weeks, and another chance for the sonographer to have a thorough look at your baby and confirm their development. By this stage, if further diagnostic tests are required, an amniocentesis is the only option available.

If all goes well, this should be the last of the major antenatal tests, and should leave you with another close-up snap of your imminent arrival.

For more on the anomaly scan, go to www.babycentre.co.uk/pregnancy/antenatalhealth/scans/secondtrimesterscans.

Placenta praevia
If at this stage your partner's placenta is low and blocking – or partially blocking – the opening of the womb, it's known as placenta praevia. This affects about 1 in 200 pregnant women to some degree – my wife included. Fortunately, as is often the way, there was still plenty of time for the placenta to move as her uterus continued to grow. Those cases that don't resolve themselves will need to be born by caesarean section.

For more information, go to www.babycentre.co.uk/pregnancy/complications/placentapraevia.

Finding out your baby's gender
While the main point of the anomaly scan is to check your baby's development, that's often overshadowed by the chance to discover whether you're going to have a boy or a girl. Not all hospitals offer

this revelation, and it's a hugely personal choice for you and your partner to make.

Some say finding out the baby's sex helps bonding, especially for the father who may thus far be feeling a little left out and impatient for something more tangible. But while you may be keen to prepare when it comes to clothes shopping and painting the nursery, 1 in 15 announcements is wrong anyway – though they're more likely to miss that crucial something than misidentify it.

> *Sarah reckoned finding out would help us settle on a name, as though we weren't still left with thousands to argue over.*
>
> James, father to Adam

It's also said that discovery spoils the surprise, though I say it just relocates it. And when the big day comes, suddenly having a real, live baby on your hands might be surprise enough. It's also feasible that you'll be disappointed with the news and, without the reality of a baby to win you round, your disappointment could colour the rest of the pregnancy and your feelings for your child. And there's even a recognized condition when parents-to-be actually mourn the baby they've 'lost'.

Ultimately, it may just come down to an irrational, gut feeling, often born of excitement or a sense of the traditional. We decided not to find out first time round, and then wasted a lot of time guessing – wrongly. And my wife had developed such a fondness for pottering in the nursery by the time number two came along, that she wanted to be as prepared as possible.

Insight

Whatever you decide, make sure you tell the sonographer as soon as you walk in the room. If you choose to remain ignorant, don't read too much into their choice of pronouns and, if you go for it, remember there's no wrong answer they can give – your love will only grow with your child, whether a boy or a girl.

Breech birth

At 36 weeks, if it looks like the baby's going to come out feet or bum first – a breech birth – there may be an offer to try to turn the baby by manipulation of your partner's abdomen.

For more on this procedure, go to www.babycentre.co.uk/pregnancy/ labourandbirth/labourcomplications/turnbreechbabyexpert.

You can even watch it being done here: www.youtube.com/watch?v=6AM6wDwTjmc.

Overdue

If your baby has not yet arrived after 41 weeks, your partner may be offered a 'membrane sweep', a simple procedure in which a midwife or doctor will run a finger around the cervix, thereby releasing hormones that can help kickstart the labour.

If you and your partner don't want labour induced, you should be offered twice-weekly checks of the baby's heart rate, with accompanying ultrasound scans to ensure there's enough amniotic fluid.

For more on stimulating the birth, see Chapter 6.

IMPORTANT POINTS ABOUT THE ANTENATAL TESTS

▶ *You and your partner are entitled to refuse all or any of the tests.*
▶ *Always ask a health professional if there's anything you're unclear about.*
▶ *Your partner is legally entitled to paid time off for the tests.*
▶ *Consider writing down any questions beforehand.*
▶ *Remember that the medical professional's aim is the same as yours – the health and safety of your partner and baby.*
▶ *Don't allow them to exclude you – make eye contact, and ask any questions you want.*
▶ *Don't feel awkward asking for a second opinion if you want one.*

- ▸ *Remember, you're there to support as well as get excited, so keep focused on your partner.*
- ▸ *Listen to the experts, but also to your feelings and each other.*
- ▸ *If you'd like to have a scan that isn't offered in your area, or change your mind afterwards about finding out the gender, you can pay to have it done privately. Look for accreditation by the Fetal Medicine Foundation – their website provides useful information on the various scans and tests: www.fetalmedicine.com.*

For the full run-down on antenatal tests, have a look at the Antenatal Results and Choices website: www.arc-uk.org/tests-explained, or call them on 020 7631 0285.

And there's more information here: www.nhs.uk/Livewell/pregnancy/Pages/Antenataltestsandscreening. aspx.

10 THINGS TO REMEMBER

1   Try to encourage your partner to view the pregnancy's side effects as reassuring signs that everything's progressing as it should.

2   Even if at first she seems to be barely changing, don't underestimate all that's going on inside. Prepare for her to be very, very tired and possibly sick.

3   Don't be embarrassed about talking to a doctor if you experience sympathy pains.

4   Be sensitive to her changing weight, and encourage a healthy diet.

5   If she smokes or takes drugs, do all you can to get her to give up, and to restrict alcohol and caffeine intake as much as possible.

6   Be prepared for mood swings and, if she takes them out on you, don't take it personally.

7   If you or your partner are worried about anything, always insist on getting it checked out by a professional.

8   When it comes to sex, be sensitive to her physical condition – if she's up for it and you haven't been told otherwise, there's no reason why you can't continue to have sex throughout the pregnancy.

9   Make sure you understand the implications of the antenatal tests, and discuss with your partner how far you want to go with them.

10   Without her undergoing a riskier, more invasive diagnostic test, chromosomal abnormalities such as Down's syndrome can never be conclusively ruled out.

5

The pregnancy: ... and the rest

In this chapter you will learn:
- *how to prepare for the birth*
- *what to buy for the baby*
- *how to deal with the common pregnancy scares*
- *how to spot the onset of labour.*

The role of father-to-be

Your partner's role during the pregnancy is to care for the baby growing inside her by caring for herself, and there are a number of ways you can contribute directly to that. At the same time, you can play a crucial role in preparing yourself and your home for the new arrival.

NESTING

Although 'nesting' is a recognized instinct in pregnant women, many men report a similar urge. Either way, the preparation of the home is often looked on as the job of the father, and many expectant dads are glad of the opportunity to do something practical.

In truth, however, you're likely to be little more than a dogsbody to your partner, who may well have been picturing for years how her child's nursery is to look. As far as you can stand to, let her make the decisions about décor. The only really important things are to ensure that the room's safe and at a temperature of around 16–20°C, and that you've finished any painting in time for it to dry and air long before the baby arrives.

Chapter 9 looks at the various ways of childproofing your home.

BE REALISTIC

Nesting serves a useful function in getting you to prepare your home. But it can also put you under pressure to meet the financial challenge of a new house or renovation, so don't let a natural desire to provide the best possible environment for your child introduce unrealistic aspirations. You're doing nothing for your baby if you saddle yourself with unserviceable debt in order to rent a larger flat or convert the loft.

A BABYMOON

The second trimester is a good time to plan a last romantic trip away as a couple before she's too uncomfortable and unwilling to stray far from home. The aim is to give you both some time to relax and enjoy each other's company in peace and quiet before the drama of parenthood really begins.

But before you book anything too exotic, consider the practicalities.

▶ *If flying somewhere, what restrictions does the airline place on pregnant women?*
▶ *Is your partner likely to want to be strapped into a small seat in a pressurized cabin for several hours?*
▶ *Will she thank you for a week in the hot sun?*
▶ *Will she even want to wear a bikini?*

I was seconds away from booking us a holiday to Egypt when I realized that, if the food upset Ella's stomach, she wouldn't be able to take the normal medicines.

Conor, dad-to-be

A number of travel companies specialize in holidays for expectant parents (www.baby-moon.eu and www.babymoonguide.com), but it's not necessary to spend a fortune. Telling people you're going away for the weekend, locking your front door and turning off your phones can allow you to take it easy and focus on each other.

Bonding with the bump

One benefit for your partner of carrying a pregnancy around all day will be her ability to bond with the growing baby. You, meanwhile, lacking the 24-hour immediacy, may find it difficult to identify with something that's already causing so much disruption to your life.

> *I did look at the books and read up on our baby's development, and it was interesting. But it was pretty hard to relate to it.*
>
> Iain, father to Logan

However, there are ways to make your unborn baby seem more a part of your life:

▶ *From around 18 weeks, your baby will be able to hear and, by the time they're born, recognize your voice. So talk or sing to it, play music or read a book. An obvious condition of this is that your partner's got to be around as well, so choose something she's willing to listen to.*
▶ *Since the baby can pick up on your partner's emotions, if you feel foolish serenading her belly or she can't stand your choice of music, you could try tickling her instead, sharing a bar of chocolate, or even suggesting sex.*
▶ *At around 20–24 weeks, you should be able to feel the baby moving. Your partner will guide your hand to where she's feeling it and, as time goes by, you may even be able to identify a hand or foot. It's not unusual for the baby to respond to touch, so experiment with gentle pushes and you*

may find yourself communicating with your child for the first time.

It was when I felt Ben moving for the first time that I really began to think of him as an independent entity and not just an extension of Harriet.

Mark, father to Ben

▶ *From about week 30, you can press your ear against your partner's belly and hear your baby's heartbeat.*
▶ *If you're really desperate to picture your baby, you can pay for a private 4D scan: www.babybond.com/4d-scan.php.*

Sleep

I'm betting that *someone*, on hearing the news that your partner's pregnant, has advised you to sleep as much as possible while you can, as though it's possible to store it up and approach the birth in credit. While that might be wishful thinking, it is worth wallowing all you can, if only to contribute to the nostalgia you'll feel on remembering those happy days when lie-ins were still possible.

But if your partner doesn't sleep well, you're unlikely to do so – and the chances are that she won't. Her nose may block as hormone levels increase and, as her belly grows with her nerves, it's just not a restful time.

I was constantly woken by our baby's kicks, even while my partner slept happily through it.

Nick, father to Katriona

But however much she disturbs you as she flounders and shifts, rolls and snores, be sensitive to her discomfort. At the moment, life is infinitely more difficult for her. And if you do manage to sleep, don't wake with a broad smile to tell her how refreshed you're feeling.

But then nor should you feel guilty about sleeping when you can. Sleep will soon become your most valuable commodity, so don't waste it.

So if the snorting and grunting stops you dropping off, sleep in the spare room or get hold of some earplugs. My wife felt so guilty keeping me awake that she bought me a set, then was unable to rouse me with her shouts from the bathroom when her waters broke.

By the last month of the pregnancy I was so exhausted that I was already looking forward to that first night home alone after the birth – a whole bed to myself, and utter silence.

Johnny, father to Rachel

Shopping for the baby

Now that you're on the road to fatherhood, you've entered a whole new demographic. As you read this, clever people in smart offices are writing slogans and developing adverts, the principal aim of which is to persuade you to part with your cash in the name of giving your child the best that you can.

And at a very shallow level, it's easy to equate being able to provide for your child (usually by spending money) with success as a parent. But unless you're always going to be able to provide them with the best, with no concern for your finances or their character, I'd recommend approaching all opportunities to open your wallet with caution and common sense.

Don't let your natural and entirely understandable insecurities
be exploited.

*The most useless product we bought for Joel was a baby
wipe warmer, meant to save him from the shock of cold
wipes. We'd used less than half a pack before it dried
into a brick.*

Winston, father to Joel and Anita

And don't be fooled into spending more on everyday items simply
because they're repackaged for parents. A baby mat is, at its
simplest, a blanket. A changing station is any large, flat surface – we
found the floor to be safest – and a standard nappy bin is a normal
bin with a tight-fitting lid.

That's not to say that some of the many extras won't make your
life easier, just that you needn't feel pressure to run off and buy
them immediately.

*Most surprisingly useful piece of seemingly extraneous kit?
A machine that simulates the sound of waves. We were given
it as a present and it turned out to be the best way of getting
Grace to settle.*

Matt, father to Grace

THE IMMEDIATE ESSENTIALS

*I instinctively thought we'd have to upgrade the car when
Naz got pregnant, but we managed just fine with our little
Fiesta until after our second baby was born.*

Shal, father to Alim and Mazhar

When the baby finally arrives, it's difficult to believe how much
stuff such a little scrap of flesh seems to need. But the unsurprising
truth is that they don't need half the stuff you're told they need by
the people who make that stuff.

The immediate essentials are:

- *nappies – see page 65 for an outline of the options*
- *baby wipes – wherever the baby goes, they'll go*
- *a changing bag – aim for a neutral colour because at some stage you'll have to carry it around as well and might not fancy one that's covered in roses*
- *three or four bodysuits – the all-in-one clothing that passes between the legs to seal with poppers*
- *a Moses basket or cot*
- *a couple of cellular blankets*
- *depending on the season, a warm hat and mittens, or a sunhat*
- *a sleeping bag*
- *some zinc cream or equivalent to guard against nappy rash*
- *half a dozen muslins – like kitchen towels for catching and wiping up yack*
- *a baby bath – a moulded washing-up tub that supports your baby in all the right places and saves you filling the entire bath*
- *depending on the season, a couple of cardigans or other tops*
- *if planning to go out in the car, a rear-facing carseat – you may get this in a pack with the pram, and a good store should let you trial it and help you fit it*
- *a pram or pushchair with a lie-flat position*
- *nursing bras and breastpads if your partner plans to breastfeed*
- *bottles, teats, a bottle brush and sterilizer or microwave sterilizer*
- *a decent digital thermometer – usually used more for reassurance than because there's really anything wrong*
- *a digital camera and/or video camera*
- *a baby sling – far less cumbersome and far more intimate than a pram.*

If you haven't got one already, I'd recommend investing in a basic microwave for all the sterilizing of bottles, warming of milk and heating (and all too often reheating) of food that's going to come – ours seems to run 24 hours a day. Beware 'hot spots', though, especially in milk – always give the food or drink a quick stir before feeding your baby.

We were showered with an incredible number of gifts when George was born, almost all of them clothes or toys. I wish now we'd waited before buying more than was immediately necessary – that way we'd have saved ourselves the annoyance of discovering yet another unused outfit at the back of his drawer that's now far too small.

Lee, father to George

THE CARSEAT

Such is the importance of carseats that some hospitals won't let you drive your newborn away unless they can see you've got an appropriate seat that's correctly installed.

Studies suggest that as many as nine out of ten carseats aren't properly fitted, so take time to ensure yours isn't one of them. Have a go at installing it long before you'll need it – they can be surprisingly complicated if you're not used to them – and never improvise. If it needs extra fittings, appears to be broken, or gives you any cause for concern, always err on the side of caution.

The safest position for the seat is behind the driver, but then you can't easily see your child or be seen. And only fit rear-facing seats in the front if you can turn off the airbag.

You might be able to get help fitting the seat at your local police or fire station. Alternatively, go to www.childcarseats.org.uk.

THE PRAM

At between £200 and £500, a pram is likely to be your largest expense at this stage. As a rule, the more you spend, the more flexible it'll be, so consider what you'll want from it before you set off for the shops.

▶ *Will you only ever be pushing it on the pavement, or will you be strolling along country tracks?*
▶ *Do you plan to go jogging behind the pram?*

▶ *If they're asleep, will you want to be able to detach the bed from the chassis to carry it inside?*

▶ *Will the whole thing fit in the boot of your car?*

Some dads seem to view their choice of wheels as a mark of status – apparently 'pram envy' is a recognized syndrome these days. But even if you find the whole topic indescribably dull, it's worth doing your homework, because your baby's pram is going to be a major part of your kit for a while.

Get recommendations from friends and, once you've made your choice, practise folding and unfolding it in the privacy of your home, without the added pressure of a screaming baby or amused passers-by. And beware the temptation to use it as a shopping trolley.

> *I lost count of the number of times I overloaded our pram with bags hanging from the handles, causing our kids to flip backwards, staring in shock at the ceiling.*
>
> Giles, father to Edward and Lara

THE COT

Though a Moses basket is easier to set up and move around the home, some parents put their babies into cots from the start. More than just somewhere for your baby to sleep, cots are designed to minimize risk, so be aware if using a homemade or antique hand-me-down – they're unlikely to conform to today's safety standards.

Ideally your baby's cot should have:

▶ *bars no more than 6–7.5 cm apart – to avoid trapping head or limbs*

▶ *corner posts protruding no more than 15 mm high – a jumping baby could catch clothing, risking strangulation*

▶ *a firm, snug-fitting mattress with no space around the edge*

▶ *non-toxic paint*

▶ *no soft bedding that risks suffocation*

- *lockable castors – an active baby can shift the cot across the room*
- *no heaters, lamps, wall decorations, climbable furniture or cords nearby*
- *no reachable smothering hazards, from loose cot bumpers to toys.*

For more advice, go to www.babycentre.co.uk/baby/buyingforbaby/cotscribsbedding/bedroomsafety.

BAG A BARGAIN

Your baby will grow out of both clothes and toys at a frightening rate. So why spend a fortune on something they may never even touch when you can swap with friends or family, or pick stuff up for free or at a fraction of the real cost?

Join your local Freecycle network (www.freecycle.org) or support the National Childbirth Trust (www.nct.org.uk/in-your-area/nearly-new-sales). Obviously check that whatever you get is safe to use – if it's a pram, be sure the wheel lock works. If it's a Moses basket, be sure the handles are sturdy, etc.

Your baby really won't care if something's not brand spanking new. They will care, however, if you're spending all your time at work because you're struggling to pay the bills.

That said, there are a few items, like carseats and mattresses, that you should always buy new. For mattresses, try www.babymattressesonline.co.uk.

The great nappy debate: disposables vs. washables

As an initiate to the nappy world, I had no idea how emotive and divisive this issue can be. The main debate revolves around their relative health and environmental impacts, but there are other factors to consider as well.

DISPOSABLE NAPPIES

Thanks to their convenience, the vast majority of parents use disposable nappies. They're readily available, quick to change, and can be thrown out with your normal household rubbish. And if you're worried about a smelly nappy bin, you can buy small, fragranced plastic sacks to wrap them in, or even machines that will hermetically seal them.

Cost
The average baby gets through up to 4,000 nappies, so disposables are likely to cost you somewhere between £800 and £1,000. One benefit over washables is that the expense is spread out over, on average, two-and-a-half years, rather than being a single, up-front payment.

> ### Insight
> Experiment with the supermarkets' own brands. They're just as good and work out far cheaper than the big-name brands.

Health
There have been numerous claims linking disposable nappies to the rise in eczema, allergies and even cancer. Some also suggest that disposables contribute to male infertility by raising the temperature around the testes during the time when a baby boy's reproductive system is developing.

Many of these claims require further research, but there's no denying that the process allowing a disposable nappy to absorb your baby's urine is a chemical reaction involving synthetic gels, and that those chemicals come into lingering and direct contact with a baby's thin and delicate skin before usually being dumped in the ground.

Waste concerns

The disposable industry has worked hard to reduce the weight and packaging of their products, but disposables still make up around 2–4 per cent of household waste, most of which goes to landfill. There, according to best estimates, they then take anything between 200 and 500 years to fully decompose.

> *At least a part of every disposable nappy ever sent to landfill is still sitting out there in a hole in the ground.*
>
> Aaron, father to Brooke

Biodegradable nappies

While a proportion of a disposable nappy is biodegradable, some companies offer fully biodegradable alternatives. The problem is that, unless you're going to compost them yourself, regularly turning and aerating them, a modern landfill site just doesn't allow its contents the oxygen to biodegrade. What's more, current EU directives would have us *reduce* the biodegradable element of our landfill waste, thereby reducing methane emissions.

In other words, given that users of biodegradable nappies are motivated by environmental concern, as an everyday alternative to disposables they could be viewed as something of a red herring.

WASHABLE NAPPIES

Since our parents' generation struggled with safety pins and intricate folding, washable nappies have progressed unrecognizably. They now come in a vast range of different brands, shapes and sizes, and offer parents the reassurance of a means of nappying that's worked for centuries, but has never been simpler or more effective.

Cost

As a rough guide, a new set of cloth nappies costs around £400, though a second-hand set would be far less. And if you use them again on subsequent babies and/or sell them on afterwards, the savings over disposables can be enormous. However, there are then the additional costs of washing them, costs that potentially increase significantly if using a commercial laundering service. Check with your local council for schemes to help with the cost of washable nappies.

Health

Since you're not simply bagging up the poo with the used nappy, there's undeniably more risk of direct shit contact. And while advocates of both types claim less nappy rash, that's really more to do with the frequency of changing – you can get away with a wet disposable nappy for longer, perhaps, but then you're leaving your baby sitting in it for that much longer.

Usage

Undeniably, washables take more effort, in both changing and washing, but it's effort that's soon integrated into your daily routine – although not all nurseries or grandparents will be up for it. Washables also tend to be quite a bit bulkier – you might have to buy bigger trousers and roll up the legs.

When we were considering washables, the best thing we did was arrange a chat with a Lollipop Advisor, who talked us through the options and offered us a trial, plus discounts on purchases. Find an advisor near you here: www.teamlollipop.co.uk/advisornearyou.html.

For an outline of the different types and more information, see the Cornish Real Nappy Project: www.crnp.org.uk.

The environmental question

The green credentials of washables depend largely on how they're used but, if you follow a few basic recommendations, they're the undisputed environmental champions, by a long way.

► *Wash your nappies in fuller loads.*
► *Hang them up to dry rather than tumble dry.*
► *Reuse them on subsequent children or sell them on.*
► *Wash them at a lower temperature – 60°C rather than 90°C.*

Better yet, buy them second hand: www.usednappies.co.uk, use an eco-friendly detergent and, when the time comes to upgrade your washing machine, choose an energy efficient, A+ rated model. And sign up for a green energy tariff: go to www.uswitch.com/gas-electricity or call 0800 404 7961 to find the best rates in your area.

IN CONCLUSION...

Some people – those who've been sucked into the intricacies of the washable/disposable debate – assume that your choice of nappy is a flag for your beliefs. In truth, of course, many parents unthinkingly adopt whatever seems to be the norm, because it takes valuable time and energy to consider doing otherwise.

If you can, I'd urge you to give washable nappies a go. If you find that they work for you and your baby, then you've undoubtedly got the chance to claim the green highground. If they don't, then use disposables without guilt and look to the many other ways that you can make this world a better place.

Insight

Don't think that the two nappy types have to be mutually exclusive. Washable nappies are better for the environment, but disposables are infinitely easier when out and about.

We felt better about placing washables against our children's skin all day long, but found that disposables worked better keeping them dry through the night.

The choice is yours.

Antenatal classes

Childbirth today is safer than ever, but medical progress means increased complexity, and therefore greater choice. So it's worth being as informed as possible, especially when you may find yourself forced to make a quick decision on your partner's behalf.

The main aim of antenatal classes is to prepare you both for the experience of birth, and give you an opportunity to ask any questions or discuss any worries. They start around the beginning of the last trimester and usually take place in the evenings over a number of weeks, but more intensive weekend classes are often available as well. Reserve your place as early as possible as they get booked up quickly.

You'll learn about the various stages of labour, pain relief options, possible medical interventions during the delivery, breathing techniques for her and support techniques for you, and the basics of caring for a baby.

But antenatal classes offer far more than information. They provide you and your partner with the chance to meet others in a similar situation, and benefit from their questions. And if you're lucky, they'll continue to be an invaluable source of support through the years ahead.

> *There's no doubt that the classes were useful for us both.*
> *I discovered how best to support Clare through the birth, and*
> *she found a like-minded group willing to meet up every day*
> *of their maternity leave and beyond to talk all things baby.*
>
> Kevin, father to Natasha

The classes can be a frightening reminder of the stomach-churning physicality of childbirth and our own relative helplessness, but they're also an opportunity to reduce those fears by talking them through. So while there's no pressure to discuss your feelings, don't be afraid to ask questions, no matter how foolish or ignorant they sound. Better a calm discussion now with coffee and biscuits than a forced decision at three in the morning after 20 hours of labour.

And nothing prompts you to face reality more than walking out of your last class and realizing you should now know it all.

NHS ANTENATAL CLASSES

The availability of NHS antenatal classes will depend on your local health authority. They take place at your local health centre or hospital, and are run by midwives. Classes range in size from between six and fifteen couples.

They're free and run by the experts, but the class size may limit your opportunity to get to know others and discuss specific concerns in depth.

THE NATIONAL CHILDBIRTH TRUST (NCT) CLASSES

The NCT offers a popular and nationwide alternative to NHS classes. Groups rarely contain more than six couples and take place in the home of the teacher, so there's more intimacy and a greater emphasis on the social side, with the aim of providing a self-supporting network once the babies arrive. While you'll cover the same issues as in the NHS classes, the agenda is to a greater extent set by the parents.

Costs vary considerably, but as a general rule expect to pay around £200. You'll find full details on their website at www.nct.org.uk/in-your-area/course-finder/course-prices.

OTHER OPTIONS

There are also a few specialist antenatal groups you might want to look at:

▶ *Lamaze International aims to minimize intervention through trusting the natural instincts of the body: www.lamaze.org.*
▶ *The Bradley Method puts special emphasis on your partner's health: www.bradleybirth.com.*
▶ *Active Birth is a technique that focuses on yoga and relaxation: www.activebirthcentre.com.*

For more information on classes from the father's point of view, go to www.dad.info/expecting/getting-ready/what-goes-on-at-an-antenatal-class.

The home straight

THE HEAD ENGAGES

At about 36 weeks, the baby's head should engage, or drop down
into the pelvis in preparation for labour. Hopefully this will make
your partner a little more comfortable, but it can also further reduce
mobility. Some women are even reduced to crutches, so be prepared to
take extra time off work if she needs help just getting through the day.

Insight
Don't drink so much at any stage that you couldn't either
jump in a car or help her to the hospital if need be.

BRAXTON HICKS CONTRACTIONS

Towards the last month, your partner may begin to feel practice
contractions, known as Braxton Hicks contractions, during which
her uterus contracts and her belly hardens in preparation for the
real thing. Each one lasts for about 20–30 seconds and, although
not painful, they'll grow stronger and more frequent as you draw
closer to the birth.

These contractions can cause some confusion – if you've not
experienced 'real' contractions before, how can you identify the
'practice' ones? Generally speaking, if they're irregular and don't
intensify over time, and if they're relieved by shifting position and
aren't accompanied by any other changes, then it's not true labour.
If in doubt, call your midwife or maternity ward.

For more information, go to www.babycentre.co.uk/pregnancy/
antenatalhealth/physicalhealth/braxtonhicks/?_requestid=5851069.

*The Braxton Hicks contractions were a useful wake-up call
to make sure everything was ready.*

Alan, father to Chloe and Jo

Pregnancy scares

I turned into a nervous wreck. Every shout brought me running, heart thumping, terrified she'd fallen over or bumped the bump.

Lee, father to George

With so much at stake, it's normal for even the least anxious of people to worry that something could go wrong.

MISCARRIAGE

The risk of miscarriage is greatest within the first trimester, though it can occur later and can happen to anyone. More than one in five pregnancies end this way, with some studies suggesting a figure as high as one in three – though many of those women will have been unaware they were ever pregnant, and just experienced an unusually heavy period.

Insight

Any vaginal bleeding during pregnancy should be checked out. And if your partner feels any severe abdominal pain, especially if accompanied by bleeding, she should seek medical help immediately.

Many women report an instinctive feeling that something's wrong, but it's also easy to misread the symptoms of relatively common conditions – cystitis (an infection of the urinary tract) can cause pain and some bleeding, and even constipation can be mistaken for the onset of miscarriage. If in doubt, ask for a scan.

Throughout the pregnancy your partner will have to live with the constant threat of accidentally harming the baby. If a miscarriage does occur, the guilt – however unfounded – can be difficult to bear. Others may feel relief, sensing that nature took its course and had its reasons.

You may never find out what caused it. The only positive fact to realize is that nine out of ten women who have miscarried go on to have a healthy pregnancy the next time.

There's currently no conclusive evidence that you need wait a particular period before trying again. But regardless of when you both feel ready, recognize that you will be grieving, and respect that. Take time to talk about it together. You may also find it helpful to talk to others who have suffered in the same way.

For more on miscarriage, contact The Miscarriage Association on 01924 200 799 or visit their website at www.miscarriageassociation .org.uk.

ECTOPIC PREGNANCY

An ectopic pregnancy is when the fertilized egg develops outside the uterus, usually within the fallopian tubes, and presents with symptoms similar to a miscarriage. Any pain in early pregnancy should be checked out, and an ultrasound and blood tests may be required. Treatment is usually by keyhole surgery to remove the foetus, though a non-invasive drug treatment is increasingly available.

For more information on ectopic pregnancy, go to www.ectopic.org.uk.

GESTATIONAL DIABETES

Sometimes the mother's body fails to make sufficient insulin to cope with the increased blood sugar levels. Symptoms include thirst and increased urination as well as fatigue and irritability, and it should be picked up through routine blood tests.

The main complication is that the baby can become very large, though there can be other consequences for both the baby and the mother; see www.babycentre.co.uk/pregnancy/complications/ diabetes.

PRE-ECLAMPSIA

Affecting 8–10 per cent of pregnancies (the majority of which are first-timers), this condition is characterized by high blood pressure, so should be picked up in the course of routine antenatal check-ups.

Symptoms include sudden swelling of the lower legs or weight gain, persistent headaches, blurred vision or flashing lights before the eyes, and upper right abdominal pain, just below the ribcage.

With little known about the causes of pre-eclampsia, the only real cure is birth. However, a sensible diet and avoidance of stress can help limit its severity.

For more, go to www.preeclampsia.org.

Packing a hospital bag

Hopefully your partner will have a hospital bag packed with plenty of time to spare, full of all the things she and your baby are likely to need (and many they won't). But since you're likely to be there for at least 12 hours, I'd recommend packing a bag of your own as well.

You'll want:

- ▶ *change for the notoriously extortionate car park (though discounts may be available from the maternity ward)*
- ▶ *a fully charged mobile phone for outside the hospital*
- ▶ *change for the payphone inside*
- ▶ *change for the vending machines or canteen*
- ▶ *a music player – since it's more for her benefit than yours, try to include at least a few of her albums*
- ▶ *a list of the people to call with the good news*

- *some fruit and other snacks, especially bananas, which release energy slowly – don't rely on the vending machines, and the canteen will be shut outside normal hours*
- *a good book*
- *perhaps a flask with some ice cubes – those wards are hot and stuffy, and your partner may find sucking an ice cube helps keep her cool*
- *a few bottles of iced water*
- *a spare top – standing outside on the phone can be freezing after the heat of the hospital*
- *a copy of the birthplan*
- *a camera – but make sure you're included in the photos as well.*

Don't take too many valuables – you may have to leave them unattended if for any reason your partner's rushed to theatre.

The hospital tour

If your antenatal classes didn't include a look round your local hospital, contact the maternity wing and arrange a time to visit. It can be very reassuring to see the relative normality of a delivery room, or the proximity of the neonatal intensive care unit if needed. You can also see if they've any birthing pools, and do a recon of the other facilities. For example, is there somewhere you can get tea or coffee or ice cubes? Where's the canteen? Are there snack machines? Are they working?

The tour is also a good time to work out your possible route to hospital, and a few alternatives in case the road's blocked. Bear in mind you might be called at work to meet your partner there.

If you're driving, find out where you should park, especially if you'll be required to drop your partner by the door then park up much further away.

Despite all my homework, I ended up panicking and parked on the street outside the hospital grounds. By the time I emerged 16 hours later, I'd been ticketed.

Blair, father to Lauren

Obviously, the last few weeks are not a good time to lend your car to a friend, or to be worrying about a dodgy rear tyre. Make sure it's full of fuel, and reliable. If in doubt, look into local ambulance response times, get a list of local cab companies, or enrol a friend or family member with wheels of their own.

A birthplan

A birthplan is a one- or two-page written statement outlining your preferences for the labour. You and your partner put it together, sometimes with the input of your midwife, and hand it to the hospital staff on arrival. The idea is that it then acts as a guide to them during the labour.

Some people take a lot of time over their birthplan and produce a very detailed and specific document. Others don't bother with it at all. It's certainly not necessary – either way, you'll end up with a baby. But it can be useful, if only as a tool to get you both talking about the 'what if' scenarios.

On top of the issues you'd expect about birthing positions and pain relief, there are a host of other things you might want to agree on:

▸ *Do you want to cut the cord (though 'hack' is more appropriate)?*
▸ *Do you want the placenta to be delivered naturally, or induced?*
▸ *Would you rather find out the sex of your baby for yourselves?*
▸ *Do you have any religious or cultural needs?*
▸ *Are you willing to have a student midwife?*
▸ *Would your partner like to be encouraged to stay mobile throughout?*

- *Do you want your baby to go straight to the breast?*
- *Would your partner prefer to be cared for by women, where possible?*
- *If a caesarean becomes necessary and your partner's asleep under anaesthetic, would you like a photo taken as the baby's lifted out?*
- *Do you want foetal heart monitoring throughout with a belt, or intermittently with a handheld device?*
- *If an assisted delivery is required, do you have any preferences?*
- *If possible, would you like the first voice your baby hears to be yours or your partner's?*

Your choices may cause friction with the medical staff, but it's your birth and you and your partner have a right to do it your way. That said, you'd be foolish to ignore the recommendations of the experts.

The main thing is to be prepared to roll with it, because you can't know what to expect. My wife was all set for a 'natural' birth with the minimum pain relief, but was screaming for an epidural before we even left the house. So keep an open mind and don't be disappointed if the reality turns out to be vastly different from the serene, nurturing process outlined in your birthplan.

Insight

Knowing what your partner wants empowers you to be her main cheerleader and, if required, to make decisions that support her choices. So get involved – talk about her hopes and fears for the birth. And remember to keep some perspective. After the health and safety of your partner and your baby, everything else is just detail.

A doula or birth attendant

If you feel you could do with someone at your side throughout the labour and birth who understands exactly what's happening, can explain your options at each stage, and whose specific job is to support you and your partner towards the most stress-free birth possible, you might want to consider employing a doula.

Because of the personal nature of their role, any doula would be just as keen as you to meet at least once beforehand to ensure you're a suitable match, then they'll tailor their support to your requirements.

Though not medically trained, their great experience can be invaluable, especially when it comes to translating the issues of a more difficult birth.

> *When we overheard the doctor saying that forceps wouldn't bring about a 'successful delivery', we were terrified and naturally fearing the worst. It was our doula who was able to reassure us that it wasn't such a disaster, and that other options were available.*
>
> Matt, father to Grace

The doula acts as an informed ally, supporting and encouraging you both, whether by helping your partner with breathing, relaxation and movement, giving you the time to nip out for a break, or interceding on your behalf with the medics to stall possible interventions. They'll be sensitive to intrusion and, because it's a personal service, can take the time to share titbits of experience that the doctors might not mention.

> *When the doctors recommended a general anaesthetic, our doula suggested I put on the shirt Clare had been wearing through the labour, so even if Clare couldn't hold her, Heather would still smell her from the start.*
>
> Daniel, father to Heather

Because they have to ensure they're free to attend your baby's birth whenever that may be, doulas are expensive, with exact costs varying according to location and experience. Trainees charge significantly less, and a hardship fund is available.

For more information, check out the UK Doula Association: www.doula.org.uk.

Choosing a name

Deciding on your baby's name can be the simplest or the most daunting of jobs. You and your partner might agree straightaway, or find yourselves asking the midwife for ideas at the last minute and then still taking home an unnamed child.

Like it or not, your choice can say a lot about you and influence how others perceive your child in the future, so be sensible and sensitive. Start sifting through the possibilities as early as possible. Talk to your partner and, if you can't agree, aim for a compromise on both sides.

There are a few obvious points to consider (e.g. do you want your child to be forever forced to spell their name, or correct others' pronunciation?), but don't let the endless choice cripple you. After all, most babies inevitably grow into their names until you couldn't imagine them being called anything else. And plenty are known by something other than their first name.

The Office of National Statistics keeps an eye on the most popular names in the UK: www.statistics.gov.uk. Or you can take a look at one of the many websites offering suggestions and the meanings behind each one: www.babynames.co.uk.

> *Lucy and I took ages to agree on a name, and I wish we'd kept it to ourselves – the minute I told my mum, I could see she wasn't happy with it.*
>
> Simon, father to Alex and Emily

Worse still, you might find someone else steals the name for their own child.

One option is to wait and see what your baby looks like before choosing a name. The legal deadline is the point by which you should have registered the birth, so in Scotland you have three weeks, in England, Wales and Northern Ireland you have six weeks, and in the Republic of Ireland you have three months to make up your mind.

But even if you have a bout of remorse thereafter, it's still remarkably easy to change the name in the first 12 months by filling out a form from the register office. And it's only a little more complicated if they're already christened or over the age of one.

10 THINGS TO REMEMBER

1 *You can make an enormous contribution to the pregnancy by caring for your partner and preparing your home.*

2 *You needn't wait until your baby's out the womb before you start building a relationship.*

3 *Accept that you will be tired when the baby arrives, but that you'll cope.*

4 *When it comes to buying things for your baby, don't be bankrupted by your natural desire to give them the best.*

5 *Prams vary enormously in function and price, so think carefully about what you'll need from yours, and gather advice and recommendations.*

6 *There are benefits and disadvantages to all types of nappy – keep an open mind and settle on whatever works best for you and your family.*

7 *Use antenatal classes to gain practical information and advice about what to expect, and to ask any questions you can think of – there's no obligation to discuss your feelings.*

8 *If in doubt about the right time to take your partner to hospital, call the ward.*

9 *Though most first births are late rather than early, make sure you're ready for the trip to hospital and as prepared as you can be with plenty of time to spare.*

10 *Once you've both settled on a name, consider keeping it to yourselves until the baby arrives – you don't need others' approval, and you won't want their disapproval.*

6

Labour and the birth

In this chapter you will learn:
- *what options are available to you and your partner during labour*
- *how to recognize each stage of labour and what you can do to help*
- *what to expect when your baby is born*
- *how to cope in the first few weeks.*

The greatest thing you can do for your partner during the birth is whatever it takes to help her relax, because the more anxious she is, the longer the labour may last, with the greater likelihood of intervention.

Birthing options

HOMEBIRTH

Given the importance of a relaxed and calming atmosphere and the fact that hospitals can be intimidating places associated with pain and disease, it's easy to understand the appeal of a homebirth. And there's no hanging around amongst the infections of a hospital once the baby arrives either.

The problem is, of course, that however familiar and comfortable your home, it lacks a hospital's level of medical care. For that reason, health authorities recommend a hospital birth for first-time mothers, and fewer than 3 per cent choose to give birth at home. But ask around. Speak to others with experience of both, and make your own decision.

Insight

If you're not so far from a hospital in case of complications and comfortable with your community midwife – or want to consider hiring an independent midwife (www. independentmidwives.org.uk) – then a homebirth might be for you.

By the time the hospital was finally willing to admit her, the last thing Daisy wanted to do was leave our home for the hospital.

Ollie, father to Laura and Denise

For more information about homebirths, check out www.homebirth.org.uk or www.birthchoiceuk.com.

WATER BIRTH

Some hospitals offer pools for water births, or you can hire one to use at home: www.birthpoolinabox.co.uk. The water supports your partner and the warmth helps her relax, minimizing the need for pain relief or intervention. You can get involved by climbing in alongside your partner, and the baby is lifted from the water immediately, so there's no risk of drowning.

For information on water births, go to www.thegoodbirth.co.uk or www.waterbirth.org.

CAESAREAN OR C-SECTION

This is an operation in which the woman is anaesthetized – most often by epidural – before the abdomen is opened horizontally at the bikini line. The uterus is then cut and, when the amniotic fluid's been suctioned out, the baby is lifted through.

A caesarean might be recommended for your partner if:

▶ *your baby's head is too large for her pelvic opening*
▶ *your baby's in a breech position*
▶ *the placenta's too close to the opening of the womb (placenta praevia)*
▶ *she's diabetic.*

You'll usually be dressed in theatre blues and allowed alongside, though kept from a view of the details by a screen of material.

Once the placenta has been removed, your partner will be stitched up and, although she'll be encouraged to start moving around within 12 hours, she'll have to stay in hospital for three to four days, then rest up at home. The cut will take about six weeks to heal fully, and can end up amazingly discreet.

Although there's no official limit on how long your partner will be unable to drive following a caesarean, she should check with her insurers – they're likely to insist on at least four to six weeks.

Like any major surgery, there can be complications, ranging from infection to haemorrhaging, blood clots to bowel or bladder damage. And if your partner hasn't laboured, your baby may need more help keeping warm and getting enough air, so may be incubated for a while. A drip may also be required to give them fluid – distressing to see, but quite normal.

Given the risks, a caesarean is only recommended if deemed necessary. That said, the procedure can sometimes be negotiated without a valid medical reason.

For more information and photos of caesarean scars, go to www.caesarean.org.uk.

Pain relief options

Perhaps that's why, in some circles, women aspire to avoid analgesics or anaesthesia altogether, as though the birth is no longer 'natural' or the experience is somehow sullied if the benefits of modern pain relief are exploited.

Given the enormity of what a woman has to endure in childbirth, that seems a shame. But since we're not the ones going through it, it's perhaps presumptuous to do anything other than point out the implications of each choice, and then fully support any decision as best we can. However, since things don't always go to plan, it's also important to emphasize the need for flexibility.

For more about pain relief, go to
www.dad.info/expecting/birth/pain-relief-at-the-birth-the-options.

The main options are:

EPIDURAL

The most popular form of pain relief in the UK, this is when a small amount of anaesthetic is injected into the lower part of the spine, giving often miraculous relief within ten minutes. It's safe and relatively easy to administer, and your partner will still be able to hold the baby after birth.

However, she may briefly feel faint and sick after the injection, or start trembling. And about 1 in 250 also experience a terrible headache and a sudden drop in blood pressure. Also, because an epidural can slow contractions and will leave your partner with limited feeling from the waist down, interventions are more common under epidural than with other forms of pain relief.

PETHIDINE

This is usually an injection into the thigh or bum – after 15–20 minutes your partner should feel relaxed and sleepy for up to three hours. It's been used safely for over 60 years and, unlike with the epidural, there's no waiting for an anaesthetist. In fact, it's even an option for homebirths.

However, pethidine can restrict movement and cause sickness, so it's often combined with an anti-nausea drug. It can also slow labour and, if given too late, can affect the baby's breathing, so they may require an injection of antidote.

TENS

Transcutaneous electrical nerve stimulation (TENS) is the application of mild electric pulses, via electrodes on the skin, to key nerve areas. The result is a tingling that can help your partner deal with the pain. It's completely non-invasive, and she can remain in control of it, though its effectiveness can vary.

> *My advice if you're helping to move the electrodes into the right place – don't touch both pads at once while it's turned on.*

Johnny, father to Rachel

ENTONOX (GAS AND AIR)

This mix can make your partner feel light-headed, thereby 'removing' her from the pain. Because it's inhaled through a facemask, she can control the intake, and it can be used at any stage of the labour with no adverse effects on her or your baby. Unlike some of the other forms of pain relief, she'll be able to keep moving around, and it's suitable for home or hospital births.

However, it can cause sickness or drowsiness, and it may not be effective enough as a painkiller by itself.

Since it's best to inhale just before each contraction, you can
help by placing a hand on her bump and warning her when
you feel the contractions start.

The early stages

Before my daughter was born, I'd only ever witnessed labour
and birth on TV and in films – I had to see it first-hand to really
appreciate how little I knew of the reality.

The birth of your first child is likely to be one of the most
emotional, exhausting, terrifying, exhilarating, frustrating,
awesome, memorable and altogether wonderful experiences of
your life. So forget all you've seen on the telly – the reality is
pretty difficult to squeeze into a half-hour episode.

WAITING

Insight
The average first baby is eight days overdue.

Time can pass incredibly slowly. But however frustrating it feels
just waiting for your life to turn upside down, consider what
it's like for your partner – with no work to keep her occupied,
she's stuck at home, exhausted, nervous and uncomfortable, and
probably fending off constant calls from friends and family.

So if she's had enough of wallowing, there are some things you can
do to stimulate labour:

▶ *Sex can be a good way to while away the time – semen
contains a hormone that helps soften the cervix, and orgasms
(hers, not yours) can encourage the uterus to contract. The
only problem is it might be the last thing she feels like doing.*
▶ *Alternating, gentle stimulation of the nipples to simulate
breastfeeding can also help the uterus to contract.*

▶ *Curry contains the same cervix-ripening hormone as semen.*
  But just beware the likely after-effects of a vindaloo while
  going through one of the most momentous events of your life.
▶ *Remaining upright and mobile ensures that the baby's head*
  pushes against the cervix, so take her for a wander round the
  block.

THE START

The only true sign that labour has begun is the onset of regular
contractions, though there are other things to look out for.

At some point the mucus plug acting like a stopper in the cervix will
be discharged (known as a 'show' and often accompanied by a little
blood), and the amniotic sac will rupture and break. This breaking
of waters can happen at any time, so you might want to line the bed,
sofa or her favourite armchair with a waterproof blanket.

Contractions may still not have started by this point. A show can
mean that they're imminent, though it can also happen as much
as six weeks before birth. If the waters break and the contractions
haven't yet started, they're likely to kick off within the next 24
hours. If not, you'll probably be called into hospital to have the
baby induced as, without the amniotic fluid, there's a greater risk
of infection.

Likewise, if contractions have started hours before the waters
break, the amniotic sac might be deliberately ruptured to progress
the labour.

Insight
About one in five women in the UK is induced.

EARLY LABOUR

At this stage your partner's contractions will be regular, less than
ten minutes apart, and growing stronger and longer, with each one
lasting between 30 and 45 seconds or less. They may be so mild as
to even let your partner sleep for a while.

Progress can be slow – this is usually the longest part of labour, and at times it may seem to have stalled altogether. Keep the maternity ward informed – you can always insist on going into hospital if you feel it's necessary – but on the whole you're better off at home. This is where you have to step in, to support, encourage and distract her. Time passes so much quicker when you're not just *waiting*.

So take her for a gentle walk, run a bath, give her a massage, use those techniques learnt in your antenatal classes. Do all you can to help her rest and relax, without any undue pressure. While she may flip between relief, terror, pain and excitement, it's your job to be the rock.

Insight

Let your partner lean on you, physically and emotionally. But at the same time, you have to look after yourself. The average first labour lasts about 14 hours, so rest when you can, and pace yourself.

Labour is a marathon, not a sprint.

Lee, father to George

Do what you can to get ready – call the family, pack the car, change into some comfortable clothes and shoes. And remember to eat, and fix yourselves some snacks to take with you.

Time your partner's contractions from the start of one to the start of the next. When the gap is about five minutes or less, it's time to think about hospital. Give the maternity ward a call so they can look out her chart and advise you when to come in.

When you do get underway, drive carefully. There's every chance that, with it being a first baby, you'll make it to the ward in plenty of time. So make sure your partner's got her seatbelt on, and don't let your stress or relief or excitement push you to drive dangerously.

At the hospital

There should be some wheelchairs available at the door for labouring mums, but your partner may prefer to keep upright as long as possible. Or she may already be keen to collapse. Either way, she's in charge, and you have to go with her wishes and leave your ego at the door as you accept that, though important, your role here is secondary.

On arrival, remember to hand over your birthplan. You may also have to answer some routine questions – frustrating, but necessary. After examination and a check of your baby's heartbeat, many first-timers are sent away because they're not yet suitably dilated. This is not just the midwives being mean – home is more relaxing than hospital, and tension will slow the labour. So treat it as a useful practice run and make the most of being back amongst the familiar. Do what you can to distract and encourage her, make sure she's drinking plenty of fluids, and keep her upright and moving as much as possible.

It took hours of pain and several trips to the hospital before Jess was finally admitted. And it was crushing to discover that, even then, she was only a few centimetres dilated.

Oliver, father to Nathan

Once admitted, don't expect much privacy. You may find yourselves waiting along with others, perhaps even in the corridor, as the cries of labouring women ring through the ward. When you make it to a delivery room, your partner will be asked to change and given various routine tests. She may be linked up via a couple of straps around her belly to a monitor – one will record your baby's heartbeat, the other the strength and duration of contractions. The results are printed out, giving you the chance to spot the contractions before your partner feels them.

In some cases an electrode may be clipped to the baby's scalp – this is not only more accurate, but is less likely to stop working during a large contraction, the very time you most want to know how your baby's getting on. The downside of this type of monitor is that your partner will be less mobile and less able to exploit gravity to help the baby's progress.

THE MEDICAL STAFF

There's likely to be a duty consultant or registrar on the ward, as well as an anaesthetist and other assisting medics, but it's the midwife who'll be your main point of contact, so it pays to learn her name and inform her of your movements. For example, if you nip to the canteen, let her know how long you'll be. Try to establish at least a little rapport with her, not only to ease communication issues but also because she's going to play a part in a hugely personal moment in your lives.

Unfortunately, she'll also be dealing with other labouring women, so is likely to pop in and out until the birth itself.

The labour went on so long that our midwife's shift came to an end, at which point we had to start bonding all over again with her replacement.

Nathan, father to Bella

ACTIVE LABOUR

This stage begins when your partner's around 3 cm dilated, and lasts around four to five hours. The intensity of the contractions may make your partner turn in on herself as the sheer physical effort takes its toll.

You can help her by:

▶ *keeping her walking if she can, or at least sitting up rather than lying down*
▶ *letting her lean back on you with your arms under hers to take some of the pressure off her legs*
▶ *offering her a massage, or applying counter-pressure to her lower back during contractions*

- ▶ *helping her in and out of the bath, if you have one, or jetting hot water onto her back*
- ▶ *keeping her informed of progress, and telling her how well she's doing*
- ▶ *initiating breathing and relaxation techniques.*

My wife definitely felt that the deeper we got into labour, the less effective those breathing techniques became, to the point that we largely gave up on them. But that was her choice – your partner may feel quite differently.

Insight

The more focused you are on her needs, the better the experience will be. And however much you feel like a spare part as all attention is on her, your mere presence is a comfort and support, which in turn is aiding the process.

TRANSITIONAL LABOUR

This final and most intense stage lasts between one and two hours as the cervix dilates from around 8 cm to the full 10 cm, the point at which she can begin to push.

Insight

The pain can be terrible just to watch, with barely any time between contractions for your partner to recover. Not only that but, after the relative progress of active labour, it can seem as though everything's suddenly slowing.

This is when she needs all the encouragement and support she can get. However utterly powerless you feel, she needs someone she trusts to tell her it's all worth it, so help her focus on the positive that's going to come from her efforts. The longer it lasts, the more exhausted she'll become, but the knowledge that the end is close can help pull her through the pain.

She may scream, she may blame or even attack you. Or she may withdraw so far into herself that you feel she barely notices you're there. Just remember that if there's only one voice she hears, it'll be yours, and you have to allow her to do whatever it takes to get through it (though if, as was the case with my wife, she actually tries to bite you, it's reasonable to gently withdraw the target).

PUSHING

Even this final stage can last anything from ten minutes to three hours but, after a long and exhausting labour, many women find renewed energy as they at last have the opportunity to assert themselves.

With the end in sight, it's important that your partner waits for the go-ahead from the midwife or doctor before pushing, and then times it to match the contractions. It's the final, supreme effort, so keep up the encouragement. I felt like a useless idiot repeating the old cliché, 'Keep breathing! Keep breathing!' But whatever you say is for her benefit, not yours, so just say something, anything, to show your support. Unless she screams at you to shut up.

Your role during labour

Studies claim that women in labour have five basic needs:

- *the constant presence of a supportive person*
- *pain relief*
- *physical care and comfort*
- *unconditional acceptance and reassurance*
- *information about what's happening.*

Your support in helping her meet these needs can have an enormously positive impact on the length of labour and the likelihood and risk of any intervention. As such, your role is crucial in improving the experience for your partner and your baby.

THE CONSTANT PRESENCE OF A SUPPORTIVE PERSON

Even if your partner is one of those women who'd rather not be touched during labour, you can still talk to her constantly. Stay close by throughout, tell her how well she's doing, how proud you are and how much you love her.

PAIN RELIEF

As well as the medical options already outlined, you can help relieve the pain by massaging her lower back or applying a warm or cold flannel, by encouraging her to use the relaxation techniques learnt in antenatal class, and by urging her to change position regularly, or encouraging her to get up and walk if she can.

PHYSICAL CARE AND COMFORT

Remind her to keep drinking – the heavy breathing can quickly dry out her mouth. Be aware of her need to use the toilet, especially as a full bladder can slow labour, and keep her clean and dry in the event of any potentially embarrassing leaks. Make sure she's given the chance to rest when she can, and help her maintain what privacy is possible.

UNCONDITIONAL ACCEPTANCE AND REASSURANCE

In general, it's your partner who'll make the decisions and, for some, that realization comes as a relief. You can contribute as an adviser, of course, but whatever your partner wants, it's your job to support her and ensure she gets it.

INFORMATION

Don't allow yourself to be ignored by the professionals. It's vital that you maintain a clear understanding of what's happening throughout, not just so that you can pass that information on to your partner (and at the height of labour, you may be the only person she listens to), but because you might be called upon to make informed decisions on her behalf if, for example, she's in too much pain to contribute.

The role of advocate is not always an easy one. At times, the advice of the professionals may conflict with the wishes of your partner. You can influence the medics' judgement, but ultimately any decision is theirs, so make your feelings known but be prepared to accept what they decide, and remember you all share the same aim.

You're also an advocate for your baby, and what's best for them can at times conflict directly with what seems to be best for your partner. Imagine if she's screaming for an epidural but the medics are warning against the risk of slowing the baby's progress. You might have to be prepared to deny your partner the pain relief, and support her through it.

AND A THOUGHT FOR YOU

Even when the birth goes without a hitch, supporting your partner through it can be emotionally and physically demanding, so don't be surprised if at some point you feel exhausted, or even light-headed. Remember to rest when you can, and eat and drink – you're no use to your partner if you're incapable. But be sensitive – don't stuff your face in front of her.

Possible problems at birth

Part of being prepared is being ready to make important decisions if required. So in an effort to empower rather than scare, here's an outline of the possible issues you might face.

PREMATURE BIRTH

If your baby arrives before 37 weeks, it's officially premature. If your partner goes into labour or the waters break early, phone your hospital immediately. Since the baby's better off inside, your doctor may try to stall the birth through medication and bed rest. If this is the case, you'll need to take on even more around the home, so don't be afraid to ask friends and family for help.

> *Bridget was four weeks premature. On top of all the worry, there was the financial impact of those few lost weeks at work, for Jo and for me.*
>
> Rob, father to Bridget

EMERGENCY DELIVERY

From watching films, you'd think about half of all births take place at home while waiting for the ambulance, or on the back seats of cars. In truth, with a first birth, this is hugely unlikely. So swat up on how to deliver a baby if you want (www.wikihow.com/Deliver-a-Baby), but don't waste money on a set of clean towels.

POSSIBLE BIRTH INTERVENTIONS

About one in eight births in the UK needs some form of help, and there are a number of reasons why your medical team might think yours should be one of them. (At this stage, it's probably worth noting that, with the birth of my daughter, we tried them all.)

Your baby may:

▶ *be in a difficult breech position*
▶ *have the cord wrapped around its neck, limiting its oxygen supply*
▶ *have had its first bowel movement (meconium) inside the womb*
▶ *have stopped moving so need help continuing down the birth canal*

> *be adversely affected by pain medication*
> *be in such a position that your partner is in intense pain.*

Whatever intervention is required, it's important to remember that it's not the process but the end product that matters.

Ventouse and forceps
A ventouse is a soft rubber cup that's applied to the baby's head and kept in place through suction, allowing the doctor or midwife to help by pulling gently. More intimidating are the forceps, a large pair of prongs that fit around the baby's head and allow the doctor to pull or manoeuvre the baby more forcefully. Both can leave marks or distort the shape of the head slightly, but any such abnormalities should only be temporary.

For more information, look at www.babycentre.co.uk/pregnancy/labourandbirth/labourcomplications/assisteddelivery.

Emergency caesarean
When a stray hand hovering around her ear trapped our daughter halfway down the birth canal, it was terrifying to suddenly find myself scrubbed up and rushing with my wife to theatre when, only moments before, we'd been expecting a normal vaginal delivery.

By its very nature, an emergency caesarean is stressful for everyone, but it's all the worse for those who are emotionally involved and may not know exactly what's going on.

Some believe emergency caesareans are employed too readily for slow or difficult labours, sometimes even just to free up the delivery rooms. You can inquire about the rates at your local hospital and consider having the baby elsewhere (see www.birthchoiceuk.com), but if it gets to the stage where you're told it's necessary, you have no choice but to trust the professionals. And it can be a relief after seeing your partner in so much pain to know that at last someone is taking control and bringing it to an end.

Instances when an emergency caesarean is advised could include when:

- ▶ *the baby appears to be distressed and the delivery must be speeded up*
- ▶ *the placenta becomes detached or your partner's blood pressure gets too high*
- ▶ *your baby's premature or there's risk of trauma.*

Insight

If a caesarean becomes necessary, there may not be time for an epidural – in which case a general anaesthetic will be given instead and you may not be allowed into the theatre.

Inevitably, you'll be scared for your partner and child, and perhaps in shock at what seems like a sudden loss of control. If she's had only a regional anaesthetic and you're in there with her, keep talking to her, and reassuring her. And when the baby appears, don't let the routine tests stop you having a cuddle with the new arrival. Your partner may even be able to try breastfeeding, though you'll have to hold the baby for her.

You may be briefly separated, and the baby left with you or taken to a special care unit while your partner's stitched up – she'll now be recovering not just from childbirth, but surgery as well.

Quite apart from being physically limited, she may be suffering emotionally too, resenting the fact that it didn't go to plan and her chance to bond immediately after the birth was affected. So talk to her, and remind her that all such considerations are secondary to her health and the safe arrival of your new baby.

She may also be worried for future pregnancies, but while there's a chance that the complication that led to the emergency caesarean can cause problems in the future, that's not always the case. For the moment, you have a healthy baby to focus on.

Birth

Assuming it's a standard vaginal delivery, the doctor or midwife should let you decide if you want to be at the screaming end or the messy end. If you'd rather not get too close to the blood and gunk and maybe even shit of a normal birth, feel free to decline a closer look.

Your partner may want to see, though, and there's often a mirror available to watch the baby's head appear. The aim at this stage is for a steady, controlled appearance, and it might be your job to relay instructions from the midwife down at the working end, to your partner.

EPISIOTOMY

To prevent uncontrolled tearing as the baby appears, the midwife might snip a little of the skin on the bottom side of your partner's vaginal opening. Known as an episiotomy, it will be repaired soon after birth, and is a totally standard procedure.

YOUR BABY

As opposed to the spotless, chubby little babies you've seen being born on TV, your baby will likely be streaked in blood and covered in a white, cheesy substance known as *vernix caseosa* or, literally, cheesy varnish, the aim of which is to grease your baby's passage along the birth canal.

The head may even be slightly misshapen, and the skin faintly blue – an understandable consequence of the journey down the birth canal and the inevitable lack of oxygen. This is all normal and will diminish with time.

Not all babies will cry immediately, though it helps to expand the lungs and eject the inevitable fluid inside.

STRAIGHT TO THE BREAST

Make sure your baby is passed to your partner as soon as possible for skin-to-skin contact. The midwife will almost immediately help with breastfeeding, which has multiple benefits beyond the obvious sustenance of your baby:

▶ *The contact helps start the vital process of bonding.*
▶ *If it goes well, the relief for your partner can be enormous.*
▶ *The familiar sound of your partner's heartbeat and breathing will calm your baby.*
▶ *Breastfeeding encourages the uterus to contract, which helps to eject the placenta.*

Minor contractions will follow the birth to eject the placenta, which can take anything from five to twenty-five minutes or more. Surprisingly large, it'll be examined to check it's all out.

And then you're done – you're a dad. Have a turn at holding your baby, and wonder at how lucky some people can be.

PHOTOS

However much you may want to record the birth, don't allow it to distract you from the important role of support. Once the baby's with you, you can ask the midwife to take a snap so that you're included. The result will be amongst the most memorable photos you'll ever have.

Throughout, as well as in the days to follow, be led by your partner and be sensitive. She might not feel she looks her best, especially if pale or swollen from surgery. Or she may just want as many photos as possible of her new family.

A FAMILY

Once the standard tests on your baby have been carried out, take some time to be alone. They may respectfully leave you to it, or you may have to ask. After the flurry that surrounded my daughter's birth, I remember wondering why everyone had suddenly disappeared. But of course they'd deliberately left us in peace and quiet to enjoy those first precious minutes of being just the three of us alone as a family.

Insight

The moment immediately after the birth is important for your partner and baby, but there should still be an opportunity for you to be involved as well. Cuddle your baby and talk to them, with your face no more than ten inches from theirs so they can see you. This is where your relationship with your child really begins.

Holding Max not only made me realize for the first time all that lay ahead, but also reinforced how much I loved and appreciated Helen, after all she'd gone through.

Gavin, father to Max

When it comes to holding your baby for the first time, you'll likely feel a mix of joy and terror. The more you do it, the more the terror fades, and the more they'll get used to you. Just remember to keep their head supported throughout – the neck muscles aren't fully developed until they're about six months old.

If it's the middle of the night, don't be bullied into leaving too soon. I was so punch drunk by this stage that I meekly wandered home without question, and regret cutting the moment short.

At some stage, you'll want to call the family to share the good news and perhaps reveal the grand secret of the baby's name. If you've got to head out to use the phone, check with your partner that she's happy to be left alone.

YOUR FEELINGS

There's no normal way to react to witnessing the birth of your child. You may laugh uncontrollably, or weep in buckets. You may be bursting with pride and energy, or weak and light-headed, terrified at the reality of what lies ahead, or just overwhelmed with relief, love and admiration for your partner. Or you may feel nothing.

> *I didn't cry at the time – I was too shocked. Now I just cry almost every time I think about it. Becoming a father seems to have made me more susceptible to my own emotions.*
> Patrick, father to Julia and Lea

You may feel an immediate and intense love for your baby. Or not. You may even experience negative feelings towards this little scrap who caused your partner so much pain, or be disappointed either with the gender or their appearance. If so, just give yourself time, and try to get involved. Whatever your expectations and conflicting emotions, don't let them influence your interaction with your baby, who needs – and has as much right to – a loving father now, in these early hours, as later on, when you'll inevitably come round.

CHILDREN WITH SPECIAL NEEDS

If you face the prospect of raising a child with special needs, be it dyspraxia or Down's syndrome, dyslexia or asthma, not only will all the usual hardships of parenthood be magnified, but many specific problems will arise as well.

Insight
While life with a child with special needs may be different to your expectations, the diagnosis is not the end. You will adapt, and new futures will arise as you discover new strengths to face the new challenges.

Try to connect with others in your situation
By talking to parents facing similar challenges, you'll learn that things will get better and hear that, far from simply coping, the day

will come when you're not just enjoying life but taking pride in your child for all the things they *can* do.

Trust your instincts
Medical professionals and carers are on your side but, if you find yourself bombarded by information and advice, much of it perhaps contradictory, have confidence in your own knowledge and understanding of your child. Don't be afraid to ask for a second opinion.

Don't overlook your partner
Mothers are especially prone to searching for a cause – a fall, a stressful event, a relaxed diet during pregnancy – and blaming themselves. Talking about an issue is better than trying to ignore it, so discuss your feelings together, and avoid unjustified thoughts of guilt or shame.

The health of your continuing relationship is important to your own health and the health of your child, so never take it for granted.

Take a break
Even if it means getting extra help, accept your own limitations and give yourself time off whenever possible.

Make the most of all support networks
Fathers of children with special needs too often find support geared towards the partner – meetings can be excluding, in scheduling or management. But you deserve no less support, so always ask for help if you need it, and don't be afraid to fight for it if necessary.

By knowing your rights, you're better placed to claim the support that's due, so investigate the relevant employment legislation and social security provision.

Call Contact a Family for free on 0808 808 3555 or go to their website at www.cafamily.org.uk. Alternatively, try www.makingcontact.org.

Above all, don't let the condition define your child. Whatever the challenge, they remain – above all else – a child.

In hospital after the birth

VISITORS

Family and friends may be clamouring to meet the baby, but don't feel pressured into letting them in. One of your most important jobs in the weeks ahead will be that of gatekeeper – if you'd rather no visitors until after you've all got home, that's okay. It might mean fewer hands to help, but it also means more time to bond, to let the reality sink in and to gain confidence. Whatever you and your partner want is right.

TIME IN HOSPITAL

The length of time your partner and baby stay in hospital after the birth will vary. They might try to send you all home more or less as soon as they've carried out your baby's routine tests, or they may keep your partner and baby in, depending on bed availability and the difficulty of the birth. Don't be afraid to put up a fight if you want them to stay in longer.

> *Lou had a really tough time of it during the birth, so we managed to arrange for her and Brooke to be transferred to a convalescent cottage hospital for a few extra days. It made a huge difference to us all.*
>
> Aaron, father to Brooke

HOME ALONE

It's quite possible you'll have to leave your partner and baby and return home alone for at least one night, and it'll seem incredibly calm and quiet after the drama of the hospital. Wallow in that silence while you can – it's all change from here.

There'll probably still be plenty to do – spreading the news, tidying up, perhaps some last minute shopping to fill the fridge – but don't forget to rest as well (it's a good idea to switch your phone to silent), and at least have a shower and change of clothes before heading back out (though I remember being reluctant to lose that baby smell from my hands and top).

When you're ready to return, try to liaise with your partner in case there's anything she needs you to bring, from decent food to spare clothes for her or the baby. And you might want to take her a gift for all her hard work, at the least some flowers from the hospital shop.

> *It was the proudest moment of my life, walking back into the ward to see my wife and daughter together.*
>
> Blair, father to Lauren

BEFORE YOU ALL LEAVE

Insight

Make the most of the access you have to the midwives to ask questions because, once you're home, you're largely on your own. So inquire about bathing, about nappy changing, about breastfeeding, about taking care of the cord stump – anything that might be a concern.

The first few weeks

ADAPTING

So you've carried your baby down the hospital corridors like a trophy, you've driven home more slowly and carefully than ever before, and you've finally got your new family home. What now?

> *I couldn't actually believe they'd let us take such a helpless little life home with us.*
>
> Pete, father to Joshua

Those first few days alone with your baby can induce a strange feeling of unreality. After so much planning, excitement, anguish, trauma and joy, your head might still be spinning. Add to that the lack of sleep, the realization that you're now wholly responsible for this baby's wellbeing, and the nerves that come from not knowing what lies ahead, and it's easy to see why many parents cite this as the most frightening part of the whole process.

> *I knew my life would change completely, but I had no idea how.*
>
> Mark, father to Ben

It's the uncertainty and lack of control that seems to worry new parents most. You might think that the lottery of conception would wake us up to the fact that parenthood can at best be only partly planned. But there's nothing like the arrival of a newborn baby to emphasize the need to just roll with it.

As you face those first few days as parents, here are a few things to think about:

- *A baby's a lot tougher than it looks.*
- *In the first few days it's only going to eat, sleep, poo, pee and sometimes puke – all of which you're more than capable of dealing with.*
- *Like most things, looking after a baby is a matter of confidence, gained through practice, so give yourself time.*
- *The first few weeks will probably pass in a blur of nappies, broken sleep and cooing – don't feel you have to do more than just survive.*
- *Your life will change dramatically – less time, less sex, and less sleep, for a start – but you will adapt and slowly regain a sense of normality.*

Some aspects of life will be immediately and obviously different, while other changes are slower to materialize.

Suddenly just preparing for a walk in the park would take us half an hour.

Chris, father to Rowen and Holly

However hesitant and anxious your days and nights may seem, things will improve. Soon you'll be handling your baby with confidence and achieving levels of efficiency that you'd previously only imagined. Until then:

▶ *Take whatever help you can get from friends and family.*
▶ *Get involved from the start, and be prepared to insist on some time alone with your child if your partner seems reluctant to let go.*
▶ *Don't assume she has all the answers, as though some magical maternal knowledge is instilled in all women at birth. But nor should you overrule her wants and wishes.*
▶ *Shift work is vital – once the novelty's worn off, make sure you alternate duties as much as possible to give each other some rest.*
▶ *Even if planning a routine, don't feel the need to impose it immediately.*
▶ *Don't expect to get everything right first time – just keep trying.*
▶ *Prioritize – perhaps that valuable time when your baby's asleep could be better used relaxing together than running around doing housework.*

I started making lists about everything. With my sleep-starved brain, it was the only way I could remember to get anything done.

Lindsey, father to Eva

YOUR ROLE

> **Insight**
>
> While your partner's attention will be directed inwards to the baby, yours must be more on the environment around them – you'll be the crucial satellite that ensures they're safe and comfortable and have all they need.

In those early days, it's all about mum. Your baby will need her almost constantly, leaving her exhausted, physically and emotionally. But that shouldn't make you a mere onlooker. You prove your commitment and involvement through your actions, all of which should be based around preserving her energy and limiting her stress.

▶ *Take charge of meals, laundry, shopping and cleaning – and remember that your baseline of 'tidy' may vary from hers.*
▶ *Guard against endless visitors.*
▶ *Take the baby off her when you can, not only to give her a break, but also to start the bonding process yourself.*
▶ *If going out, be clear where you're off to and how long you'll be.*
▶ *Manage expectations by being specific about the responsibilities you're going to assume, and don't expect applause when you do get things done.*
▶ *Reassure her, listen to her fears, counsel and advise but – ultimately – allow her to do things the way she wants them done.*
▶ *Remember that many fears are born of fatigue and uncertainty, so pull together as a team and reassure yourselves that endless generations have survived first-time parenthood just fine, with far less support and far smaller brains.*

THE BABY'S PHYSICAL STATE

With little or no experience, looking after a baby can be incredibly stressful. And it might seem at times like you just can't win. If they cry, you'll think something's wrong, and if they don't, you'll think something's wrong. If they eat too much or eat too little, sleep too much or sleep too little – whatever they do, it's easy to find cause for alarm if you go looking. And it can be difficult *not* to look. But try to retain some objectivity.

General guidance on what to expect:
▶ *It's hugely variable but, as a very rough guide, a breastfed baby will feed between eight and twelve times in every 24-hour period.*

- Unsurprisingly given all they go through, it's normal for a baby to lose a little weight in the days following the birth. Weigh yours regularly and, if worried, discuss the issue with your health visitor.
- Possetting – the regurgitation of milk during or after a feed – is quite normal. As long as your baby's ultimately gaining weight, it's nothing to worry about.
- A baby's body temperature should be between 36.4 and 37°C. The ideal temperature for a nursery is between 16 and 20°C.
- Expect six or more wet nappies in every 24-hour period.
- Any misshaping of the head as a result of the birth will disappear with time.
- Your baby may be totally bald, or have lots of surprisingly long hair – anything's normal. And most is lost soon after birth anyway.
- Most babies' eyes start off blue but slowly change to their permanent colour.
- It's quite normal for babies to shit after every feed, or to only squeeze one out after three or four days. As long as they're farting freely and not uncomfortable, constipated and vomiting, there's nothing to worry about.
- A tribute to the economical virtues of breastmilk, the poo of breastfed babies is mercifully minimal. It's when they're off the breast that you'll want an umbrella and waders.
- Babies are noisy. They snort and snuffle, especially during feeds and often during sleep.
- As a result of hormones received from your partner, it's not uncommon for babies' genitals and nipples to be swollen – girls may even have a whitish discharge or even small streaks of blood. All such symptoms will clear up within a week or two.
- Yellow skin – jaundice – is common in the first two weeks but, if it persists, get it checked out by your GP. Similarly, milk spots – tiny whitish yellow spots across the nose and chin – are quite normal and will disappear in time.
- The umbilical cord will dry and shrivel and finally fall off around ten to fourteen days after birth. Until then, keep the area clean and dry, and fold nappies below it.

- ▶ *Theoretically, babies can't smile for at least a month, so don't take it personally.*
- ▶ *Your baby's neck muscles aren't yet developed, so always support the head, and hold them as close to your body as possible, for their comfort and safety.*

GOING OUT

Newborns are especially portable, so try to get out the house early on, before stepping out the door becomes a big issue. Put your baby in the pram or close to your chest in a sling. It'll do you good to have a stroll in the park, and it's a chance to strut down the street feeling ten feet tall.

NAPPY CHANGING

Ignore the denigrating clichés of bumbling dads struggling to change nappies. Like anything, it just takes practice, so the quicker you have a go, the sooner you'll get the hang of it. And at this stage you needn't fear a brown avalanche – that might come later but, for now, it's not going to be much more than a green dribble.

Make sure you've got all you'll need before you start, so that you don't leave a cold baby perched precariously while you hunt for the right equipment:

- ▶ *a clean nappy*
- ▶ *a bag or bin for the dirty one*
- ▶ *cotton wool moistened with warm water or baby lotion*
- ▶ *some zinc cream to fight off nappy rash.*

Then, with the baby on their back, hold their ankles in one hand and use the cotton wool to wipe. With girls, be sure to wipe from front to back, towards the rectum – this avoids transferring bacteria into the vagina – and don't pull back the labia to clean inside. Similarly with boys, don't try to peel back the foreskin – just gently wipe the testicles and under the penis. And don't forget to dig amongst the many creases of skin.

When you're finished, pad the area dry and, if possible, let it all air for a while. Finally, apply a barrier cream to ward off the nappy rash and, for boys, you might want to protect the penis with a dab of petroleum jelly.

CRYING

Even completely healthy newborns can cry for anything between one and three hours a day. And despite coming from such a small set of lungs, the cries can be astoundingly powerful.

Insight
Crying is the best method a baby has to tell you they're hungry, hot, cold, lonely, tired, bored, need changing or in pain. So your first response should be to check each of those issues as best you can.

Try to fathom the meaning behind the cry, and respond accordingly. Listen for changes and, as you grow increasingly in tune with their normal patterns, you'll start to anticipate their needs.

If a check of all the usual causes fails to bring calm, try:

▶ *shifting their position or your hold*
▶ *increasing physical contact or, in some cases, decreasing it*
▶ *distracting them*
▶ *swaddling*
▶ *giving them a dummy or finger to suck*
▶ *tuning in the radio to 'white noise'*
▶ *giving them a bath*
▶ *going for a walk or drive*
▶ *massage*
▶ *sitting them on top of an operational washing machine – but not unattended!*
▶ *if breastfeeding, to check your partner's diet for recent changes.*

The problem comes when your baby cries inconsolably despite your best efforts to soothe. And if you don't seem able to offer comfort, it can be just as hard for you and your partner as it is for your baby.

The fact is that almost a quarter of all babies have periods of constant crying for no obvious reason. Known as colic, it usually starts around two weeks and peaks at about six. It can be hugely stressful, but it's no reflection on you or your parenting and, assuming you've checked there's nothing seriously wrong, it's no cause for alarm and will usually fade around three months.

For more on colic, see Chapter 9.

> *Jen gets really worked up by Iain's cries. And I'm sure he picks up on her mood, then responds in the only way he can – by crying some more.*
>
> Alastair, father to Iain

Insight

Don't be dictated to by your baby's cries. If you've done all you can to see to their needs, don't feel guilty laying them down while you take a break, checking intermittently. It won't traumatize them to cry alone for a few minutes.

SLEEP

Before I became a father, I never knew it was possible to feel so tired, physically and emotionally. But nor did I realize how much I could still get done on so little sleep.

Always exploit what time you have to rest, and remember how much worse things seem through tired eyes. Forgive yourselves and each other for not being on top form, and recognize that this stage doesn't last forever.

VISITORS

Visits from friends and family – however well-meaning – can be demanding. You or your partner might feel pressure to present a picture of domestic harmony as you make tea and hand the baby around, recounting the story of the birth for the 40th time.

Against a backdrop of sleeplessness and worry, not only can such visits be exhausting but they can be stressful, too – especially if you feel you're being evaluated as a new parent.

So pace out the visits, and take your cue from your partner. You may even have to veto visits for her own good, or be prepared to cut them short. Don't feel any pressure to hand your baby round, however keen your visitors may be for a cuddle. And if you're willing to let them hold your baby, consider asking them to wash their hands first.

HEALTH VISITORS

Health visitors vary enormously in the attention they offer to the father of the baby. If you possibly can, be around for their visits, and refuse to be ignored. It's important that you understand what's being said, as it's one area you really can support your exhausted partner.

PETS

Obviously the introduction of a fragile but disruptive baby smelling of milk into a territory previously patrolled by another animal requires a bit of common sense.

If you've a dog, get them familiar with the new arrival early on by letting them sniff your baby's clothes. If you've a cat, consider putting netting over the Moses basket or pram.

Always keep the nursery door shut when the baby's resting, and maintain your pet's routine. Above all, be very wary of leaving them alone in a room with your baby. Even the best-behaved animals can be unpredictable.

BONDING

The bond between your partner and your baby is hugely important, and something to be proud of. But it can also leave you feeling excluded, even jealous.

I just didn't feel I could compete with the obvious intimacy between Charlotte and Ben, or contribute to his wellbeing in such an intrinsic way.

Aiden, father to Ben

Whether you're feeling left out or even guilty that you're not enraptured by your baby's every move, it's vital that you recognize the importance of your relationship with your child, and do what you can to get involved.

- ▶ *Have as much skin-to-skin contact as possible.*
- ▶ *Let your baby fall asleep on your chest – a wonderful feeling – but beware the risk of falling asleep yourself, especially if you've been up all night.*
- ▶ *When out and about, opt for a sling rather than the pram.*
- ▶ *Take on the bedtime routine, bathing and reading a story.*
- ▶ *Have a bath together, laying the baby on your chest.*
- ▶ *Don't feel you have to only play baby music, but avoid anything too loud.*
- ▶ *Give your baby a bottle of expressed milk – feeding provides a real connection.*
- ▶ *Talk to them about everything and anything.*

I played my guitar to Grace. Even as a captive audience, she seemed pretty appreciative.

Matt, father to Grace

Insight

If you find, despite your best efforts, that you're having problems connecting with this bawling intrusion on your

(Contd)

previously comfortable life – a pretty understandable reaction –
then don't feel bad about it. Just give yourself time – it's not a
now-or-never process.

TAKING A BREAK

The first few weeks after I became a father were a relentless cycle
of feeding, winding, washing and waking to the sound of cries.
Once the string of visitors died away, the only contact my wife and
I had with the real world was the arrival of the postman and the
ringing of the phone.

Having a baby is inevitably restrictive, and that's not such a bad
thing – it gives you time to focus, gain confidence, and bond as
a family. But it's also important to rediscover the life you knew
before, and regain a little perspective now and again.

So even if you have to go out alone, be sure to take an occasional
break, perhaps just a walk in the park – anything that bursts the
baby bubble and reminds you of a world beyond the cot and
changing table. You'll feel all the better for it, and hopefully
return re-energized and ready to get stuck in once more.

REGAINING A SOCIAL LIFE

One benefit of having a newborn baby and therefore a severely
restricted social life is that you're likely – at least at first – to
actually save money.

> *We put the cash we weren't spending down the pub into
> getting cable and the odd takeaway.*
>
> Callum, father to Jack and Sam

Besides, you may just be too exhausted to consider going out, or
quite happy to realize you've now got the best possible reason for
staying in.

But even if you weren't the sort to regularly hit the town, you might still lament the loss of freedom and the occasional night out, particularly as those friends without children may be conspicuous by their absence.

Beyond accepting that you may just see less of them, explore the alternatives to pubs and bars, or take it in turns to go out. Good friends should be willing to meet closer to your home, or come round at the weekend.

> *I tend to get friends round for Sunday lunch much more now. Sometimes Karen goes to bed while the girls are asleep, but generally it causes far less disruption to our routine.*
>
> Daren, father to Emily and Catriona

BACK TO WORK

It can be a great relief to return to work and the comfort of a world you know well, but with a sense of escape can come feelings of guilt. Whatever work arrangement you and your partner come to, remember that you're a team. Providing an income is crucial, but so is your role as a father.

Insight

Studies repeatedly show that involved fathers raise children who are better adjusted socially, and less likely to use drugs or commit crime. So don't feel that work absolves you from getting involved at home, either in spending time with your child or lending a hand with the chores.

For more on balancing work and home life, see Chapter 11.

REGISTERING THE BIRTH

It's a legal requirement to register your baby's birth. In Scotland, you've got 21 days to do so, in England, Wales and Northern

Ireland you've 42 days, and in the Irish Republic you've three months.

In return for formalizing your baby's existence, you'll receive a birth certificate and the entitlement to claim child support. Registration will also trigger payment of your baby's Child Trust Fund voucher (see Chapter 10).

If you're not married but you want to be included on the birth certificate, you have to attend the registration with your partner, or have her submit confirmation of your paternity on the relevant form.

For more details and requirements, check the relevant website:

In England and Wales:
www.direct.gov.uk/en/Governmentcitizensandrights/
Registeringlifeevents/Birthandadoptionrecords/
Registeringorchangingabirthrecord/DG_175608.

In Scotland:
www.gro-scotland.gov.uk/regscot/registering-a-birth.html.

In Northern Ireland: www.groni.gov.uk/index/births.htm.

In the Republic of Ireland:
www.groireland.ie/registering_a_birth.htm.

PARENTAL RESPONSIBILITY (PR)

If you're not married to the mother of your child, now might be a good time to confirm you have parental responsibility. This is a legal term referring to the duties, obligations and rights you have regarding your child, including the right to contribute to major decisions about their life, from choosing their name, school and religion to consenting to medical treatment.

If you and your child's mother are married, you're granted automatic parental responsibility. Similarly, if you're unmarried but jointly registered the birth with your partner – assuming your child was born after a certain date – then you'll have gained it.

In England and Wales, that date is 1 December 2003, in Scotland it's 4 May 2006, and in Northern Ireland it's 15 April 2002.

If you're unmarried and didn't jointly register your child's birth, there are a number of options available in order to gain parental responsibility:

▶ *marry your child's mother*
▶ *re-register the birth*
▶ *co-sign a Parental Responsibility Agreement with the mother*
▶ *obtain a Parental Responsibility Order from the courts.*

Obviously, if you want to play a major role in the life of your child and don't have parental responsibility, you should do something about it as soon as possible.

For more on parental responsibility for fathers and how to go about getting it, check the relevant website:

In England and Wales:
www.advicenow.org.uk/living-together/children/parental-responsibility,10266,FP.html.

In Scotland: www.ukdp.co.uk/parental-responsibility-scotland.

In Northern Ireland: www.mensproject.org/resources/parentalresponsibility.pdf.

10 THINGS TO REMEMBER

1 *Your partner's anxiety can have a direct impact on the length of the labour, so do all you can to help her relax – your contribution to the process is pivotal to her experience.*

2 *Support her choice of pain relief but encourage her to remain flexible – you never know what's going to happen.*

3 *The average first baby is eight days overdue. However nerve-wracking that time is for you, think how it must feel for your partner.*

4 *The average first labour lasts about 14 hours, so rest when you can – it's a long, tiring, emotional process.*

5 *During labour, your partner may want you to touch her – or not. She may want you to talk to her – or not. Your gratitude that it's her and not you giving birth should allow you to accept any abuse, blame or indignity with good grace.*

6 *Make sure you're always aware of what's going on – you may be called upon to make a crucial decision at any time.*

7 *Whatever method is used to get your baby out, remember that it's the end product that matters.*

8 *Even if the birth takes place in the middle of the night, don't be rushed into leaving your new family too soon – it's a moment you'll want to savour forever.*

9 *Babies are tougher than they look so, as long as you're sensible, there's little that can go wrong. And the more practice you have in caring for them, the better you'll get.*

10 *Once home, your partner will be focused on the baby – it's your job to focus on what they need from the world around them. But don't let that stop you getting involved from the beginning.*

7

You and your partner

In this chapter you will learn:
- *how to maintain your relationship with your partner and support her, physically and mentally*
- *how to cope if you're feeling excluded*
- *how to deal with the lack of sleep*
- *how to reclaim a sex life.*

Your relationship

A baby can put a huge stress on your relationship, and leave you tired and strained for the little time you still have as a couple. So it's important you don't take the bond between yourself and your partner for granted, and that you continue to work to keep the relationship vibrant.

Small things – and it may be you've only the time and energy for small things – can make all the difference, from a brief cuddle when you wake each morning to surprising her with flowers, and from taking a walk together as a family to accompanying her on a trip to the shops just so you get to spend that time together.

Having just had a baby, your partner's likely to be all too aware of the changes to her body, and probably conscious of how little attention she's able to give you. At such a vulnerable time, you've got to do all you can to reassure her of your commitment.

- Look into her eyes as often as possible and say those three little words.
- Be romantic – without the expectation of sex.
- Schedule regular time to be alone together – and limit the chat about babies and work.
- Dust off the wedding video or photo album or, if you're not married, have another think about it.
- If you can find the time, take up a sport or hobby you can enjoy together.
- Remember anniversaries and other special occasions like Valentine's Day.
- Surprise her with a cooked meal, or hire a babysitter to give you a night out.
- When at last you've got some time together, let the answer machine take your calls.
- If you're apart during the day, keep communicating with emails and texts.
- Find someone you're happy to leave your child with for a night and head off for a weekend away. Even with the guilt of leaving your baby behind, you'll both feel a whole lot better for it.

Insight
Your love is now the basis for another's being, so treat it with respect.

There's nothing like losing something to start you appreciating it, so take a moment to consider how you'd be managing right now if you had to do it all alone. Parenting is hard enough with two, but imagine having to cope without your partner, without another to recognize your efforts and exhaustion, without someone on whom to test your fears, to support you, and to share the good and the bad. And now show your appreciation, in any way you can.

Changed expectations

Dynamics shift considerably when a new person arrives in a household – especially when that person requires as much help and attention as your baby – and that change can take some getting used to.

FEELING EXTRANEOUS

With your partner spending every minute focused on the baby, it's not unusual to feel a little redundant. Unchecked, the situation can spiral – as she grows increasingly confident, you're given fewer and fewer opportunities to be involved. You become little more than an observer of your own child, while she begins to resent your lack of input.

So while it's right that your focus should be on looking after her so she can look after the baby, it's crucial that you take your turn as well, and as early as possible. Sometimes the best thing she can do for everyone is to rest and leave you alone with your baby, to prove to yourself and to her that you're just as capable.

FEELING NEGLECTED

A new baby inevitably means that your partner will have less time and energy to give to your relationship – it's unrealistic to expect otherwise.

But however much you're missing the intimacy you shared before, know that it will return as life settles down again. And meanwhile you've gained a new relationship of unimaginable value, especially as your child grows older and able to give more and more.

FEELING OVERWORKED AND UNAPPRECIATED

If you think you're shouldering more than your fair share of responsibilities, be honest with yourself, and think about it carefully. Far too often, I find myself needing to consciously recognize the hundreds of little things being done around the home without my knowledge or input.

Could it be that your partner's actually doing more than you know? Parenting is difficult – there's always something to be done and never enough hours in the day – so the likelihood is you're both feeling

stretched. Are you overlooking your partner's contribution?
Or might she just need that little extra support at the moment?
In which case, aren't you glad you're able to provide it?

FEELING UNFAIRLY TREATED

Since traditionally the father is expected to be harder of heart,
you might find you're called upon to execute the more unpleasant
necessities.

> *Claire hid out of sight when Harry was given his first
> immunizations. She left it to me to hold him tight, then came
> swooping in afterwards to soothe his screams, getting all the
> credit for comforting him.*
>
> Matt, father to Harry

It can be difficult not to feel resentful of an apparent expectation
that you're entirely immune to emotions yourself, and recognition
that your baby will forget the cause of grief long before you doesn't
always console. It's all the harder when it seems your partner's
relationship with your child is getting priority over your own.

Insight

But bear in mind that, as a father, it's your job to protect
your family, and sometimes that's done by sacrificing your
own interests in favour of theirs. Is it really so bad that
you're able to shoulder that responsibility?

At such times, you have to grit your teeth, focus on the long-term,
greater good, and do what has to be done. And you should also
be proud, not only of your contribution towards your family's
ultimate wellbeing, but also of the special bond you're protecting.
There are fewer prouder sights for a father than that of his partner
and child enjoying a close and loving relationship.

FEELING THE NEED TO DO SOMETHING ABOUT IT

However much you feel hard done by, the simple fact is that your
wants and needs no longer take priority. Your child will frequently

take precedence over you and your partner. And as one half of a committed couple, there'll be times when your partner takes precedence over you. That's what fatherhood is about.

Only you can judge if your partner is asking too much or too little of you. If you feel you're suffering unreasonably from that shift in priorities, be open about it. But be sensitive – no one finds parenting easy, particularly the first time round.

Communicating

If you're feeling angry or resentful, you can't expect your partner to know why unless you tell her. And bottling up your emotions won't help anyone – especially if there's a risk you'll ultimately explode in front of your child.

So if a problem needs addressing, set aside time to talk when you're both not exhausted or hungry or distracted by the million and one other things that need doing.

Whichever one of you is raising the issue, listen to your partner's comments without interruption or judgement, and take her thoughts seriously. Try not to respond with a knee-jerk or emotional reaction, but see the problem from her point of view. That doesn't mean capitulating every time, only trying hard to understand what's pushing her to say what she's said.

When it's your turn to talk, choose your words carefully – remember, this is not a normal time for either of you. So be calm and sensitive, and careful not to use language that criticizes or attributes blame. And certainly never use your child as a pawn in your discussions.

If possible, move towards a solution – often a compromise – that, if possible, satisfies you both, or at least leaves you both feeling you've given something up, and reinforce that agreement through your actions. But don't imagine that every issue is immediately fixable. Sometimes just airing thoughts and feelings can be enough.

Remember, you're in a position to support your partner better than anyone else, and nothing bad can ever come of a sensitive effort to communicate, so don't ever give up trying.

And when it comes to getting something off your chest, don't forget your friends and family – some of whom, if they're parents themselves, will probably recognize exactly what you're feeling. Sometimes just talking about things can help, and it might save you hurting your partner's feelings through raising the issue with her.

Insight

Above all, remember that neither you nor your partner has done this before, which is what makes it such a challenging – and hugely exciting – time. So be forgiving of her and of yourself, and mindful of how a lack of sleep lowers tolerance and frays tempers. Don't let temporary emotions born of exhaustion and worry overwhelm the more lasting, truer feelings.

For professional help, contact Relate in England and Wales through www.relate.org.uk. In Scotland, go to www.relationships-scotland.org.uk. And in Northern Ireland, try www.relateni.org.

YOUR CHILD'S VIEW

The strength of your relationship with your partner is important to your child's sense of stability, so take every opportunity to reinforce your mutual commitment in front of them – tell your partner you love her and let them hear you say it, and tell them directly how much you love their mother.

Everyone argues now and again but, if you and your partner bicker in front of your children, try to let them witness you resolving the issue and moving on as well – a valuable lesson in how to deal with conflict and differences in opinion.

Sleep

THE HARSH TRUTH

Over and over again, expectant parents are told that they'll be tired. But the mere repetition of that prediction – usually accompanied by a smile of Schadenfreude – in no way does justice to the reality.

> **Insight**
> New parents can lose up to 90 minutes of sleep each night, the equivalent of a full night's sleep every week, or two whole days of solid, blissful slumber every month.

The effect of such sleeplessness can be brutal, impacting on every aspect of your day and night. I found everything suddenly required twice as much effort – thoughts flitted through my fatigue-fogged brain without ever settling, and I'd struggle to finish each sentence. It felt like my mind had turned irrevocably to mush.

Even when your baby's eventually asleep, you may be so on edge, just waiting for them to go off like an alarm clock, that you're never able to properly settle. And that's assuming they're not snorting and snuffling in the same room.

All the crueller is that the normal satisfaction that comes at night from collapsing gratefully into bed is stolen from you with the knowledge that, in just a few hours, you'll be up again to restart the relentless cycle.

> **Insight**
> The first thing is to accept that you're not going to get enough – take that as a given. Secondly, realize that you can achieve more than you knew on very little sleep. And thirdly, acknowledge that – given time – it will get better.

ALL FOR ONE...

In those early days of novelty and willingness, don't be fooled into that Blitz spirit of collective suffering by dutifully crawling out of bed to deal with the baby together. Better that at least one of you gets some sleep so as to be in a position to give the other a break later.

Shift work can be crucial in retaining your sanity. If you have a spare room or even a sofa, make use of it – either alternate nights on duty, or divide them up into shifts of four hours and take it in turns to see to the baby. Or if you're back at work, get up early to let your partner sleep a little later, and play a greater role at weekends.

But beware sleeping separately for too long – sharing a bed is an important part of being a couple.

COMPETITIVE SLEEPING

With such all-encompassing consequences, it's no surprise that sleep – or the lack of it – can be a source of tension.

Of course Sam ended up looking after Ed more at night – she'd leap out of bed at the first sound of him waking, while I preferred to wait to see if he'd settle himself.

Brayden, father to Ed

Parenting is tough enough without harbouring resentment that one or the other isn't pulling their weight. So talk with your partner about your expectations, agree a procedure, and stick to it.

We agreed that whoever got up early on Saturday would get a lie-in on Sunday. So when Thom woke on a Saturday, we'd lie there, each knowing the other was awake and each of us trying to work out if he'd sleep later the following day.

Keith, father to Thomas

A FEW TIPS

Unfortunately most of the advice on maintaining good 'sleep hygiene' is irrelevant if you're simply lacking the undisturbed hours. But if you're struggling to sleep even when you've got the chance, it's worth making sure you:

- *keep your room dark and quiet*
- *only go to bed when you're ready to sleep*
- *try to get up at the same time to get your body into a pattern*
- *try not to nap during the day*
- *avoid alcohol or heavy meals before bed*
- *don't exercise too late in the day*
- *don't go to bed on an argument.*

If the sleeplessness is stress-related, always remind yourself that this time will pass. And if you or your partner are really suffering, speak to your doctor about the help available.

To help your partner rest
- *If she's had a caesarean, you may have to bring the baby to her to feed. Even if she hasn't, you can lie the baby alongside her and return it to the cot afterwards, saving her from rousing herself from bed.*
- *Do the winding afterwards.*
- *Give the baby a nightly 'dream feed' (more on this later in the chapter).*
- *If possible, send her away to stay overnight with friends or family, to get just one good night's rest.*
- *Give her at least an hour to herself on your return from work.*
- *Encourage her to sleep whenever the baby's sleeping.*
- *If possible, meet her for lunch during the week to take the baby and give her time off.*
- *Keep a spare set of clothes in another room so you don't need to access the bedroom if she's asleep.*
- *Don't expect weekends to be your time off.*
- *Take on as much as possible of the other household duties, and encourage her to compromise in other areas of her life.*

- *If the going's really tough and you can afford it,*
  consider employing a maternity nurse: www.bestbear.co.uk/
  parents/info_maternityNurse.htm.

At work
Lack of sleep can have devastating effects on IQ and communication skills, and your employer's initial sympathy may soon wear thin. So to minimize the impact of your sleeplessness at work try the following:

- *Find a place to take a nap in your lunch hour.*
- *Carry a notebook to back up your oozing brain.*
- *Don't get too comfortable – if it's warm, keep a window open.*
- *Eat only light lunches, and drink plenty of water.*
- *Take some light exercise in your lunch hour.*
- *Get up frequently to walk around.*

Breastfeeding

This, more than anything else, was my wife's main worry, from long before our daughter was born: would she be able to breastfeed? Being a man and therefore naïve about such things, I'd assumed that the mere presence of breasts was enough to justify a resounding affirmative – until it was fairly pointed out to me that just having eyes doesn't necessarily guarantee perfect vision.

Breastfeeding is important for a number of reasons. Not only does it provide an opportunity to create a uniquely intimate bond between mother and baby, but breastmilk:

- *transfers your partner's natural immunities to your baby*
- *provides your baby with all the nutrients it needs, in the right amounts*
- *is easily digested and so less likely to cause digestion problems*
- *is cheap, at the right temperature, and consistently fresh.*

Breastfeeding also has benefits for the mother, reducing the risk of future breast cancer and encouraging the uterus to revert to its normal size, thereby helping her lose any weight gained during pregnancy.

Insight

Because of the considerable benefits, current guidelines encourage mothers to breastfeed for at least the first six months. But be realistic – from a health perspective, even one month is better than nothing.

Many women expect to be able to breastfeed without a problem, and look forward to it, viewing it as the ultimate expression of motherhood. At the very least, it's the most direct input anyone can have into keeping their baby alive.

The problem is that the undoubted benefits of breastfeeding are so trumpeted that the responsibility and prospect – or reality – of things going wrong can place enormous pressure on your partner. For those unable to make it work, or forced to give up for some other reason, the emotional fallout – a complex mix of frustration, guilt and a sense of failure – often accompanied by real physical discomfort, can be extremely hard to handle.

Unless your partner is very lucky, you may hear a range of differing concerns, from the sheer pain of breastfeeding and the threat of cracked or inverted nipples, to worries about breast size and possible infection (mastitis). So if problems do occur and she's struggling, she's going to need sensitivity and wholehearted support.

Your role can be crucial in giving your partner the time and encouragement to persevere because, despite my assumptions, breastfeeding is not an instinctive skill. Your support has a huge impact – many women admit they'd have given up, and regretted it, were it not for their partners.

Ways to help:

- *Use cushions to get her into a comfortable position – she's going to be stuck for a while.*
- *Bring her the TV remote or the telephone, and make sure she has at least a glass of water by her side to help top up the lost fluids. Take her snacks too, but make sure they can be eaten with one hand.*
- *Offer to wind the baby afterwards, an often time-consuming but necessary part of the process.*
- *Fetching the baby in the night can go a little way towards making it a team effort – but bear in mind the importance of at least one of you getting some sleep.*
- *Discuss her hopes, and encourage her to achieve them.*
- *If she's finding it tough, help her find appropriate professional advice.*
- *Defend her choices in front of healthcare professionals, family and friends.*
- *Tell her how well she's doing.*
- *Be considerate in choosing where you sit when out in public, so she can breastfeed discreetly.*
- *Field unwanted visitors around feeding times.*
- *If travelling, plan for breastfeeding stops.*

The more a mother stresses about her breastfeeding, the worse it's likely to get. And since much of it's to do with relaxation, you can impact on its success by limiting her stress in other areas around the home as well.

For more than you could ever want to know about breasts and breastfeeding, go to www.llli.org/nb.html.

'DREAM FEEDS'

One very positive way you can directly contribute to feeding is to give your baby a bottle of expressed milk. That way, they get used to taking a bottle (reassuring for you both to know you've a back-up should breastfeeding become a problem), you get to spend some intimate time with your baby, and your partner gets a break.

With a bit of preparation, I was able to do the last feed of the day without my daughter ever waking up – known as a 'dream feed'. Admittedly there's less in it for you if they're fast asleep, and it can be awkward if you need to change the nappy afterwards, but it's still an opportunity to marvel at your baby while you give your partner a rest.

MORE PROBLEMS

Unfortunately, even if your partner and baby have mastered the technique of breastfeeding, there's still plenty of opportunity to worry. Common questions include:

▶ *Should I feed on demand, or according to routine?*
▶ *When should I introduce a bottle, and will the baby then go back on the boob?*
▶ *If expressing, should I do that before or after a feed?*
▶ *Will my breasts then recover in time for the next feed, or be overstimulated?*

> *Pretty soon we spotted a pretty serious design flaw in the female of our species – the lack of a gauge on the side of the breast to indicate how much a baby's taken.*
>
> Dan, father to Tricia and Miles

The best indicator of how well your baby's feeding will be whether or not they're putting on weight. But be aware it's normal for babies to lose up to 10 per cent of their birth weight in the first few days, and only start gaining it again after the first week.

The more your partner thinks about breastfeeding, the more questions she's likely to have. Fortunately, there are some excellent resources available to advise and support. It's even possible to hire a consultant to visit you at home.

For more information, call the National Breastfeeding Helpline on 0300 100 0212, or contact The Breastfeeding Network on 0300 100 0210, or via their website at www.breastfeedingnetwork.org.uk.

Alternatively, La Leche League (www.laleche.org.uk) is a worldwide charity devoted to providing support, encouragement and information to breastfeeding mothers. Their helpline is 0845 120 2918.

The National Childbirth Trust (www.nct.org.uk) also has a helpline, open 8 a.m. to 10 p.m. every day, on 0300 330 0771.

YOUR FEELINGS ABOUT BREASTFEEDING

You might view your partner's breastfeeding with mixed feelings. While proud or perhaps in awe of what her body is capable of, you may also find her leaking, heavy breasts a turn-off, or be worried what they'll come to look like in the future.

> *I didn't dare say it, but it was a definite concern that, when Lisa stopped all that feeding, her breasts would go saggy.*
>
> Mike, father to Aileen

In fact, it's not breastfeeding that impacts on their changing shape and size, but the pregnancy itself – breastfeeding can actually encourage the accumulation of fat in the breasts. And as time goes on and those fat deposits build up, they'll regain more of their pre-pregnancy appearance.

But even if they never revert to how they were, even if you spend the rest of your life lamenting the loss of the biggest, firmest breasts you've ever had the pleasure of knowing, don't ever be anything less than supportive and grateful of what your partner has gone through to provide you with a child.

Sex

IS SHE WILLING?

If sex is about reaffirming a loving relationship, you might be lucky and find that, as soon as possible after childbirth, your partner wants to do just that. Or she might want to reclaim her body after months of pregnancy, or take a break from the mothering role, or just reassure herself that you still find her attractive. Let's face it, her motivation isn't paramount – if she's willing, you're not going to ask why.

Insight

While many health professionals advise waiting at least six weeks after the birth, the truth is there's no reason why you can't have sex again just as soon as you both feel ready.

However, it's a rare mother who's ready to drag her partner back into the bedroom immediately after giving birth. Exhausted, battered and bruised, emotionally and physically, she'll likely still be suffering, however smooth the birth. Feeling fat and frumpy and with her every waking moment focused on your baby, sex may be the last thing on her mind – especially if, like 40 per cent of mothers, she's had to have stitches.

> *I tentatively suggested we gave it a go around week seven, but Alicia was pretty clear about what had got us into this mess in the first place.*
>
> Dan, father to Tricia and Miles

Be aware of her feelings, and be patient – she might appreciate hearing how attractive she looks when she's feeling awful and looking worse, but she won't thank you if you keep pestering her to nip upstairs. It might be that there's nothing for it but to wait until she's ready and, if need be, lock yourself in the bathroom now and again.

If she's worried about the impact of sex on her body, you could encourage her to speak to her doctor for advice. And when the time finally comes, be sensitive to what she's been through, and don't expect to pick up where you left off.

Particularly if she's not the sort who's comfortable talking explicitly about what she wants from you, be attuned to her responses, and don't push her for more than she's willing to give. If hormones and nerves are playing havoc with her natural lubrication, try using lubricant – but water- rather than oil-based, to avoid infection. Ultimately, take your lead from her and – you may or may not like this bit – be prepared to consider non-penetrative options.

For more information and advice, go to www.netdoctor.co.uk/sex_relationships/facts/sexdelivery.htm.

ARE YOU WILLING?

It's not unusual for new fathers to be put off sex. The sight of your partner splayed on a bed may be a little too reminiscent of the birth, or you may just not find her new role as mother so arousing.

Apologies for painting an extreme picture but she may be a prickly and overweight bag of hormones, dribbling milk from her breasts and blood from her vagina (something that can last for up to six weeks). These physical and emotional changes may frighten you – you may even wonder if she'll ever revert to the woman you fell in love with, or end up turning into her mother.

If you recognize these feelings, don't despair. It may take time, but there's no reason why your partner's body – even the most stretched parts – can't return to much the same shape as they were before the pregnancy.

However, if you don't fancy the idea of sex with your partner, perhaps only a few feet away from your snuffling baby, you've a difficult choice. Do you turn the lights out and get on with it as best you can, or address the situation directly?

Communication is important, and all the more so at such an unsettling time in your relationship. But bear in mind that one of a woman's biggest fears after giving birth is whether or not her partner will still find her attractive, so beware hitting her while she's already vulnerable. One alternative to being so hurtful as to admit you no longer fancy her might be to stall the issue by pleading concern.

I was terrified of hurting Sophie or causing some damage,
so insisted on waiting at least two months.

Carl, father to Claude

Insight

If, for whatever reason, you find your relationship is lacking
its previous level of intimacy, remember that the loss of a sex
life is temporary, while what you've gained is permanent.

SEX AND THE FUTURE

Even as the physical impact of childbirth recedes, sex is unlikely to
be the same, primarily because you're both likely to be exhausted
and without a spare minute – or three. And it certainly won't be
anywhere near as spontaneous. Nevertheless, it will still remain an
integral part of your relationship, so be sure to make time for it,
even if that means planning a childfree weekend away.

And as your child grows older, guard against the habit of allowing
them to sleep in your bed, however many monsters are hiding
under theirs. And judge when the time has come to get a lock on
your bedroom door.

If you are caught in the act, be prepared for some understandable
confusion. Don't yell, but reassure your child that nothing's wrong
as you calmly ask them to leave the room. Above all, don't be
embarrassed or ashamed – it may be too early to talk freely about sex,
but your reaction can lay the foundation for future communication.

CONTRACEPTION

Insight

Even if your partner's still breastfeeding and her periods haven't
returned, you still need to use some form of contraception.

She can still take the pill while breastfeeding, though she'll likely
be advised to switch to the progesterone-only 'mini-Pill' to avoid
issues with her milk production. Condoms are likely to be the best

option at first – if you want to investigate alternatives, speak to your health provider.

For more information, go to www.babycentre.co.uk/baby/youafterthebirth/sexandrelationships/contraception.

Your partner's mood

Babies are demanding, especially if they're the type to insist on constant stimulation, and the routine can make each day seem tediously like the last. If your partner's the main carer, the emotional and physical impact can be immense.

> *By the end of the second month, Rachel was craving just one day off, a single day answerable to no one, to eat what and when she wanted, without being woken by cries or dictated to by routine.*
>
> Richard, father to Rick

▶ *Be realistic in your expectations, and cut back on those demands we all make of our partners, whether consciously or not.*
▶ *Encourage her to take a break when she can, and to get out the house rather than hover around. She may appear to have an endless appetite for talk about fluid ounces, nappy contents and the timings of feeds, but she'll feel better for a break.*
▶ *If you're out at work, come straight home as soon as possible to lend a hand.*
▶ *Reassure her that it's not obligatory to love every single minute of parenthood, and that it's quite normal to feel worried, pressurized and exhausted.*
▶ *Ensure she has the opportunity to connect with others in the same position by attending local playgroups.*
▶ *Make sure her friends and family are given the chance to help.*

Insight
By demonstrating that you care and are willing to do whatever you can to help, you're affirming your commitment

to her and to your family. And you're showing that, whatever trials you face, you're facing them together.

Baby blues

The 'baby blues' is the name given to a very common phenomenon that affects up to 85 per cent of new mums. It kicks in a day or two after birth and symptoms include anxiety, irritability, confusion, tearfulness, mood swings, and appetite and sleep disturbance.

It's a short-term issue, lasting anything from a day or two to a couple of weeks, and is thought to be a natural consequence of sleeplessness, and emotional and hormonal changes. Sometimes just identifying it as part of the normal process can help to reassure.

Insight

Don't try to rationalize the blues away, however frustrating it may be to see your partner in tears with no real explanation – emotions and logic don't always mix.

All you can do is be patient, listen to her and support her – bear in mind you might be the first adult she's had a chance to talk to all day – and try to let her rest as much as possible.

Soon after Archie arrived, Jackie surprised me by saying she thought she wasn't doing a good job as a mother, and that he was suffering because of it. I tried to point out how well she was managing and, above all, how happy and healthy Archie obviously was. But for all my effort, she remained resolutely unconvinced.

Gary, father to Archie and Sam

The baby blues are only temporary, so should your partner be suffering for more than two weeks, make sure she sees her GP.

Post-natal depression

Parenthood isn't an endless idyll of love and fulfilment, particularly if you're still raw to the experience. So it's perhaps not surprising, when reality clashes with the idealized version of motherhood many women imagine, that as many as one in five develop post-natal depression (PND). This usually happens within weeks of the birth, yet only one in four of those will seek help, scared to be labelled a bad mother if they don't seem to be coping.

Post-natal depression varies hugely in severity, but symptoms to look out for include:

- *exhaustion and irritability*
- *loss of interest in usual activities*
- *significant weight gain or loss*
- *loss of appetite*
- *problems sleeping*
- *tearfulness*
- *hopelessness*
- *feelings of guilt or worthlessness*
- *loss of libido*
- *excessive worry for the baby*
- *memory loss and poor concentration*
- *a lack of interest in the baby.*

If your partner is suffering from PND, there are a number of ways you can help beyond simply minimizing her stress levels. Ensure she:

- *gets as much rest as possible*
- *sees a doctor, and follows their advice*
- *eats a good diet with lots of fresh fruit and vegetables, even if she's not hungry*
- *has someone to talk to about her worries, if that's not you*
- *doesn't drink alcohol – you can help by not drinking in front of her*
- *exercises gently, even if it's just a stroll in the park with the baby*
- *knows it's just a phase, and that PND is treatable.*

For more information, help and advice about PND or the baby blues, contact The Association of Post-Natal Illness on 0207 386 0868, or go to their website at http://apni.org.

PND AND YOU

Given the list of symptoms, as well as the oft-experienced sense of being uninvolved or usurped in your own home, you might not be surprised to hear that a significant number of new fathers suffer from PND as well.

Unfortunately, many feel an obligation to be the strong one in the relationship and so, rather than dealing with their own emotions, they ignore them, dragging them around to breaking point.

Insight

If you're finding things difficult, it's important to realize you're not alone, and to see your doctor as soon as possible with an open mind.

Make sure your partner's aware of your feelings as well, without assigning blame or judgement. Exercise and eat healthily, be forgiving of yourself, mark each achievement and each passing day, hold fast to the positive moments amongst the hardship, and know that this stage won't last forever.

Taking the initiative around the home

Don't mistake a lack of interest for a lack of ability – however domestic you were before the pregnancy, you've now got to be nothing less than fully involved. You and your partner have complementary roles – while her priority in the early days is to look after your baby, yours is to manage as much of the rest as possible.

Don't expect boundless gratitude, whether for something you've always done or always left to someone else. And don't imagine that, as your child grows more self-sufficient, your contribution to domestic chores will no longer be required. You may even be grateful for the division of labour – at least a mop doesn't answer back or insist on singing the same nursery rhyme 15 times in a row.

HOUSEWORK

A healthy, clean environment for your family is important, but so is time spent together – children need a happy home more than a spotless one. So talk to your partner about your priorities and, as long as she's happy, settle for clean enough.

Insight
Compromise on cobwebs, not on time with your child.

LAUNDRY

Especially if you and your partner opt to use washable nappies, having someone to help with the laundry can save a lot of time. If you've enough money, it's possible to outsource the lot – the nappies, the clothes and the ironing. And if you've enough charm, it's possible to enlist a grandmother to lend a hand for free.

COOKING

Too often it's meals that pay the price of our being pushed for time, so ensure you're both eating healthily by cooking a bulk batch at the weekend and then freezing it in portions for the week ahead. And always maintain a plentiful supply of fruit that's easy to scoff on the go.

SHOPPING

Shopping is a lot less stressful when you're not trailing a baby around. But if you're short of time, try doing your supermarket shop online. You can set up a list of usual items, saving you considerable time in the future, and you may even be able to get away with doing it while at work.

10 THINGS TO REMEMBER

1 *Having just had a baby, your partner's liable to feel vulnerable, physically and emotionally, so take every opportunity to remind her of your commitment.*

2 *Get involved with your child right from the start, setting a pattern for the future as an equal carer.*

3 *However disruptive your baby seems to your relationship, life will settle down again, leaving you as parents with a deeper, more fulfilling bond.*

4 *If issues or disagreements need to be addressed, do so sensitively and maturely, without ascribing blame, and aim for compromise, not victory.*

5 *However tired and worried, be forgiving of each other – neither of you has done this before, and no one finds it easy.*

6 *The loss of sleep is temporary, and you'll probably manage far better than you fear.*

7 *Be prepared for the emotional aspect of breastfeeding – especially if it doesn't go well, your partner will need support and encouragement.*

8 *Get involved in the feeding and let your partner take a break by regularly giving your baby a bottle.*

9 *Look out for signs of post-natal depression – different to the baby blues – and, if your partner's suffering, make sure she gets the help she needs.*

10 *Do as much as you can around the home, from cleaning and shopping to cooking healthy, nutritious meals.*

8

···

You and your child: Part 1

In this chapter you will learn:
- *what to expect of your child at each stage of their development*
- *what you and your child can do together*
- *how to deal with the typical toddler issues, from weaning and teething to potty training and tantrums.*

Your child's development

Those charts showing exactly what children should be able to do at each stage of their development can be hugely reassuring, and the more insight you gain into how yours is viewing the world, the better hope you'll have of meeting their wants and needs.

There are numerous overviews available online: www.childdevelopmentinfo.com/development/normaldevelopment .shtml, or you can trace your child's development more closely, week-by-week: www.babycentre.co.uk/stages.

But because such guides have to be so very general, they can also generate hours of needless anxiety by prescribing developmental milestones within a timetable that many still perfectly normal children will fail to meet.

The other thing is that progress is often two steps forward and one back, with no definitive marker to confirm you've moved on a stage. And it'll be just as you're worrying that your child's lagging behind – often as a result of a minor illness – that they'll suddenly recover with a rapid surge.

Most issues lasted a couple of weeks, then the boys seemed to catch up and we moved straight on to worrying about the next thing.

Lucas, father to Ethan and Ben

OTHER CHILDREN

It can be equally pointless comparing your child to those of your friends and family – though comparisons are inevitable for even the best-intentioned parent.

Many parents trumpet their children's development, whether defensive of other weaknesses or worried how the rate of progress reflects on their parenting. All boastful claims should be treated with suspicion – resist any neurotic urge to compare. Every child is different, with their own strengths and weaknesses and, in truth, no parent has it easy.

PUSHY PARENTING

While we all want our children to do well, pushing them too early to achieve the next developmental stage – whether it's crawling or counting to ten in another language – can backfire. At some point it's necessary to acknowledge that the process by and rate at which a young child naturally develops has served our species well over millennia, so is unlikely to be improved by efforts to encourage four-year-olds to master calculus.

Too much stimulation can interfere with your child's sleep, and your stress to progress your child's development can lead to their stress. And as one area advances, something else may well give. So let your child ripen at their own pace, and align your expectations accordingly – even when doing 'nothing', babies and young children are still processing and digesting the world around them.

> ### Insight
> There are no studies linking the early achievement of learning milestones to future success – but there are studies linking pushy parents to anxious, less creative children.

The first six weeks

In these early days, there's not much to be done beyond feeding, changing and marvelling at your new arrival – and sleeping when you can.

CHARACTERISTICS

At this stage, your baby will be sleeping for as much as 16–20 hours a day – and likely wearing away any hair on the back of their head as a result. While awake, they'll be flailing their limbs – usually symmetrically – so keep their fingernails short to avoid scratches. They'll also gain greater control of grasping and unfolding their hands, and start to suck happily on a few fingers.

Very soon after birth they'll begin communicating with their voice by cooing, and learning to appreciate differences in your own modulation. Though at first they'll focus best on objects eight to twelve inches from their face, they'll increasingly follow your movements and, at some point in the second month, you might be rewarded with a first smile.

WHAT YOU CAN DO TOGETHER

All new fathers – and mothers – feel trepidation when faced with their baby for the first time. The best thing you can do to combat this is to get involved from the start. You don't need to do anything hugely special – just spend time together. Every minute lays a foundation for your future relationship.

While initially it'll be enough that you just give your partner a break, you'll soon appreciate that babies are easily impressed. Just a little time together will quickly dispel any discomfort or bafflement.

▶ *Explore their reflexes: www.baby-can-read.com/baby-reflexes.html.*
▶ *Stimulate their senses, for a few minutes at a time, with smells, noises and textures, but watch for cues to stop.*
▶ *Give them different things to suck on – but nothing that could choke them.*
▶ *Since their main stimulation will be visual, play with unbreakable mirrors, mobiles, and high contrast, black and white objects.*
▶ *Try baby massage: www.babymassage.com.*
▶ *Maximize bodily contact by holding them or carrying them in a sling, but avoid any sudden movements, always support the head, and don't throw them up in the air or shake them.*
▶ *Read aloud anything you like, and try to establish a routine so they associate your reading voice with a peaceful, secure time of the day.*
▶ *Sing softly or play music, varying the style, key and tempo.*
▶ *Respond to their signals with talk, touch, smiles, silly faces, and so on – their first lessons that their actions can impact on the world around them.*
▶ *Talk to them, and tell them you love them – but remember the aim is to expose them to English, however simplified, not*

*some icky-wicky baby language. And don't be self-conscious
about chatting to your baby in public.*

▶ *Give them regular time on their tummy to develop upper
  body strength.*
▶ *Play peek-a-boo, a game that will offer endless fun in the
  years ahead.*
▶ *Repetition offers babies a recognizable pattern – and thus
  stability – in an otherwise chaotic world, so be prepared
  to sing the same songs or nursery rhymes over and over. If
  it's threatening your sanity, vary it – within the bounds of
  familiarity – and, as your child gets older, play with those
  variations.*

WINDING

All babies swallow air while drinking that should then be burped out
of them both during and after feeds. Because this can take time, it's a
perfect chance for you to get involved and give your partner a break.

With the baby's head on your shoulder and body upright, pat
or rub their back. Alternatively, lay them face down across your
knees, or sit them up, leaning slightly forward. Whatever you do,
don't thump them, and keep the head supported. And line yourself
and surroundings with muslins in preparation for the cascades of
milk that may well erupt at the same time.

ROUTINE

Routines can breed security for you just as much as for your baby.
Knowing exactly what they should be doing at any given minute of
the day can boost your confidence, make it easier to plan your life,
and reassure you that your child's getting sufficient sleep, food and
drink. In the face of a total lack of experience or confidence in your
parental instinct, routines offer an invaluable sense of control and a
frame of reference against which to judge progress.

Unfortunately, routines can also form a straitjacket around
your days, making you quake with angst at the mere thought of

disruption. Some claim they're too dictatorial, undermining your own judgement as a parent while allowing for no individuality in your child – especially a child that's developing so fast and often according to a timetable of its own. And don't underestimate the potential for worry if yours fails to abide by that timetable, remaining insistently awake when they 'should' be sleeping, or wanting to feed when they 'shouldn't' be hungry.

If you're tempted to establish a routine, be aware what you're committing to, and don't feel under pressure to start too soon or constantly override your own instincts.

Insight

Babies are far more adaptable than often we give them credit for. So while routines can be a helpful handle, don't let them become overly restrictive. And remember that discovering your own baby's pattern is different from imposing one – and can be far more preferable to all.

For more on routines, go to www.askamum.co.uk/Baby/Search-Results/Baby-basics/Is-a-routine-right-for-your-baby.

SLEEP

▶ *Beware getting your baby accustomed to a sleeping cue that won't then be there for them when they wake in the middle of the night, whether that's a dummy, a piece of music, or you.*
▶ *A calm bedtime routine – from bath to a final story – can help your child recognize when it's time to sleep.*
▶ *Don't come rushing in from work to throw them around just before bed, however tempting that might be.*
▶ *Be mindful of the time and length of daytime naps, and don't assume that a baby who hasn't slept much during the day will always sleep better at night – sleep really can breed sleep.*
▶ *Be patient but firm – while children need to develop the ability to sleep independently, we all have nights when we just can't settle.*

▶ *From around the age of three, it can be helpful to place suitable activities within reach of their bed – some books or a story CD – to buy yourself a few more minutes of peace each morning.*

▶ *Let your baby get used to sleeping amongst normal household noises, rather than committing yourselves to tiptoeing around for the next few years.*

Sharing beds and rooms

There are three basic options when it comes to sleeping at night: sharing your bedroom with your baby in a Moses basket, sharing your bed, or putting your baby in a room of their own.

It's natural to want your baby close in the early days, and sharing a room can ease the disruption of night feeds. But it can also mean – given how loudly babies can sleep – that everyone's regularly disturbed. And while sharing a bed with your baby may be comforting, it can also be nerve-wracking, sexually inhibiting and, if you've been drinking alcohol, dangerous. Not only that, but once your child is used to sleeping alongside you, it can be a difficult habit to break.

For more on sharing a bed with your baby, go to www.babycentre.co.uk/baby/sleep/cosleepingpros&cons.

Official advice for reducing the risk of cot death (see later) is that you keep your baby in your bedroom – though not in your bed – for at least the first six months. While issues of safety are paramount, my advice thereafter would be to move your baby into their own room as soon as you feel comfortable. Ultimately, the aim is to get them used to sleeping independently, and the more they associate your presence with their ability to settle, the worse it'll be when they wake in the middle of the night without you.

BABY CLINICS

Baby clinics offer parents the opportunity to have their babies checked regularly by health professionals in a relaxed and tailored environment.

Take your baby's medical paperwork along, and exploit the chance to raise any concerns whatsoever. But beware weighing your baby too religiously – fortnightly is plenty to avoid worrying over every downward blip in an otherwise healthy upward trend.

SURE START CENTRES

These centres are intended as nationwide, one-stop shops for parents with young children, providing access to healthcare, advice, support, early education and childcare, all under one roof. Many centres also help parents back into work, or offer additional activities, from dads and kids groups to baby massage.

For more about children's centres, go to www.direct.gov.uk/en/parents/preschooldevelopmentandlearning/ nurseriesplaygroupsreceptionclasses/dg_173054.

To find a children's centre near you, go to www.dcsf.gov.uk/everychildmatters/earlyyears/surestart/ fundedsettings/childrenscentresmap.

OUT AND ABOUT

Babies are wonderfully portable in these early days, so make the most of it – go out for dinner, strap the baby to your chest and take a stroll, or go out in the car and enjoy using a parent-and-child parking space with a totally clear conscience. But be sensitive – to your baby, to those around you if your baby's crying incessantly, and to your partner if she's breastfeeding.

Gauge how to dress your baby according to how many layers you're wearing yourself, avoid scented lotions that could attract bugs, and keep them out of direct sunlight for at least the first six months.

There's definitely a general assumption that babies are cared for by women rather than men, though I am noticing more unisex changing rooms. There's often more space in the disabled toilets, even if it's on the floor.

Rafael, father to Paula

> **Insight**
> The more the world sees you as a father caring for your baby,
> the faster it will turn to catch up and provide men with equal
> facilities to those currently on offer to women.

NAPPY RASH

It's too easy – especially with disposables – to let your baby stew
in their own mess, allowing their own urine or digestive acids to
irritate their fragile skin.

So check your baby regularly, particularly after feeds – newborns
need changing up to 12 times a day. Using water and cotton wool
instead of wipes can be a good preventative but, if a rash develops,
baby or olive oil on cotton wool will be less painful than water.
And there are multiple nappy rash creams available over the
counter, though always read the label – some recommend slopping
it on thickly, while others advise using sparingly.

If the rash gets really bad, you could risk a few nappy-free hours to
let it air and, if the rash doesn't improve, do get a doctor to check
it out.

Six to twelve weeks

CHARACTERISTICS

By the three-month mark, your baby will probably be able to stand
if held – but don't do this for more than a few seconds as their
hips aren't yet strong enough to support the weight. They can
also roll onto their side and curl up and kick, so be careful where
you leave them. Better able to focus, they'll be fascinated by their
own hands and fingers, and realizing they can interact with
objects around them. Tracking moving objects will be a favourite
pastime.

By this point you might be able to distinguish their different cries, and they'll respond increasingly to your mood, showing preference for familiar people, listening if you talk, and answering with more of a gurgle.

WHAT YOU CAN DO TOGETHER

▶ *Keep singing songs and playing music – and don't feel you have to restrict it just to nursery rhymes, or you'll be stuck listening to them for months to come.*

▶ *Offer your baby things to hold, but make sure they're soft as they're likely to bash themselves repeatedly on the head.*

▶ *Walk with them around the house giving a running commentary on all you see.*

▶ *Continue the reading routine, ideally with books full of simple drawings. Give your baby a finger to hold while you sit together, and enjoy the intimacy.*

▶ *Introduce expressed breastmilk in a bottle so you can get more involved in the feeding.*

DUMMIES

You might wonder why something with the power to stop your baby crying at the first touch could ever be divisive. But while a dummy might save your sanity – and some studies suggest it also helps reduce the risk of cot death (see page 154) – it can also bring its own set of problems.

For example, one day you're going to have to wean them off it – no easy task. And if you let your baby get used to falling asleep with a dummy, they might come to rely on it to settle, which means lots of repeated cot-side trips to retrieve it when it keeps falling out. There are also speech and language problems associated with dummy use.

If you opt to use one, never tie it to your baby in any way, and check it regularly for signs of wear. For more information, go to www.babyworld.co.uk/features/dummy.htm.

COT DEATH OR SUDDEN INFANT DEATH SYNDROME

Though most common between two and four months, sudden infant death syndrome (SIDS) can affect children up to one year old. Because the cause is unknown and it has the power to turn boundless happiness into crushing emptiness literally overnight, it has an almost unique place amongst parents' fears.

But however terrifying the prospect, bear in mind that it affects fewer than 1 in every 2,500 babies born, and there are precautions you can take to lessen the risk:

▶ *Don't smoke.*
▶ *Put your child to sleep on their back.*
▶ *Use a firm mattress.*
▶ *Don't let them overheat.*
▶ *Put them to sleep at the foot of the cot so they can't wriggle down further.*
▶ *Breastfeed your baby.*

For more information, contact the Foundation for the Study of Infant Deaths on 0808 802 6868 or go to www.sids.org.uk.

It's impossible for me to imagine the agony of losing a child to SIDS. But I can imagine how easy it must be to wrongly assume you've contributed in some way to the tragedy.

If you've suffered, always remember that help is available: www.uk-sands.org.

Three to six months

CHARACTERISTICS

During this time your baby will learn to clap, roll over, sit without support, and even raise themselves up onto hands and knees to rock in preparation for crawling – though early efforts will probably just propel them backwards across the floor. They may also try to pull themselves up, so beware overhanging objects, from mobiles to curtains.

They'll continue to happily explore, picking up everything they can for examination – a process that's often amusing to watch as they'll still be finding it easier to grasp than to let go.

Vocally, they may exchange sounds with you as though in conversation, and will happily babble a stream of vowels with a few consonants thrown in. Around six months you may even hear a 'maaa', but don't take it personally – it's easier to say than 'daaa'. Your baby may also respond to their name, and express growing emotions and preferences by crying, waving their arms to be picked up, or pushing away what's not wanted.

WHAT YOU CAN DO TOGETHER

Hopefully you'll by now be feeling far more confident, and perhaps marginally less exhausted as your baby settles into a more regular sleep routine.

▶ *Make lots of silly faces, noises and gestures and give your baby the chance to imitate you.*
▶ *Place objects just out of reach to encourage movement and muscle development – but don't torment them.*
▶ *Keep talking to them constantly, play music, and continue with the peek-a-boo, reinforcing their realization that objects continue to exist when out of sight.*
▶ *As you continue to read regularly, your baby will start to reach out, respond to your pointing, and likely try to wrestle with the book, so distract them with something else to hold. Look for stories that offer rhythm, rhyme and repetition – you'll soon learn your baby's favourites.*
▶ *Don't feel you have to give them attention all the time – it's good for them to learn how to amuse themselves and choose their own toys.*

> **Insight**
> The Department of Health recommends exclusive breastfeeding for at least the first six months, but such ideals have to be blended with your own reality.

Whenever the time comes to stop breastfeeding, it'll likely be worse for your partner than your baby – while the latter will be ready for something more sustaining, your partner's going to find it painful, emotionally and physically. And if it's enforced due to a return to work, there'll be issues of guilt as well.

If you've already been feeding your baby regularly with a bottle, they should cope with a steady introduction to formula without any problem. Instead, now that you've no excuse not to get involved, the problems will be yours: the hassle of repeatedly sterilizing bottles, the delicacy of mixing the feed (too much can cause constipation and dehydration, too little can leave your baby hungry and diarrhoeic), to say nothing of the instantly noticeable expense as you go racing through boxes of formula.

If possible, try to give your partner a positive reason to end the breastfeeding, like a romantic night away without the baby. Emphasize and exploit the greater independence that bottlefeeding should bring – for the first time since the birth, you can look after your baby alone, and her breasts can return to the life they knew before – and the size.

TRAVELLING

It's said that younger babies – especially those still breastfeeding – make easy travelling companions. What that really means is that they're not always as difficult as toddlers – hardly a lofty achievement. And even if you don't need to pack a bottle and sterilizer, you'll still be amazed by how much (your partner will tell you) your baby requires.

If you decide to give it a go:

▶ *Be sensible about your itinerary – balance your desires against your baby's needs.*
▶ *Mention your baby when booking, to ensure they've suitable facilities wherever you're staying, from cots to microwaves.*
▶ *Avoid queues – get as many tickets as possible in advance.*
▶ *Consider preparing for time differences by sliding your baby's routine earlier or later the week before you go. Alternatively, if going to the Continent, keep them on GMT and benefit from an extra hour's lie-in each morning.*
▶ *Watch what you both eat, especially if your partner's still breastfeeding, and consider bottled water for mixing formula.*
▶ *If driving, don't pressurize yourself with deadlines to arrive – leave plenty of time for breaks.*
▶ *Time any travel strapped to a seat around your baby's naps.*
▶ *Pack one emergency bag that'll never leave your side and will allow you to feed, change and clothe your baby even if your main luggage is lost.*
▶ *Take suitable distractions, from toys to food, and ration them.*
▶ *Check your family's suitably insured and, for European destinations, get European Health Insurance Cards: www.ehic.org.uk.*
▶ *Maintain as much of the familiar – and of the routine – as possible.*
▶ *For country-by-country travel advice – including vaccination requirements – check with the Foreign and Commonwealth Office: www.fco.gov.uk/en/travel-and-living-abroad.*
▶ *Always have a supply of baby wipes to hand.*

If you're particular about using the same baby food, formula, nappies or anything else, it might be worth taking a supply. And if you baulk at the ever-increasing excess baggage fees, it's even possible to have British products sent on to meet you at your destination: www.tinytotsaway.com.

But as a general rule remember – babies have very effectively colonized the majority of the planet so, wherever you go, you're likely to be able to get whatever you need.

For more advice about travelling with a baby, try www.babygoes2.com.

Most importantly, prepare to discover that holidays are very different things when children are involved.

> *When Becky was four months old, we braved a trip to Ireland. It wasn't so much a holiday as her routine relocated – without the reassurance of knowing where everything was.*
>
> Sean, father to Becky

Flying
Children under two can usually fly for free, but will be belted onto your lap for the duration. Most airlines allow you to take a travel cot, pushchair and carseat at no extra cost – but check beforehand – and you can usually take the pushchair, or even the carseat, all the way to the gate. Just give yourself plenty of time to clear security. And consider giving your baby something to suck – a dummy, finger, boob or bottle – when taking off or landing.

Doubling up
The benefits of holidaying with similarly minded friends with children the same age are obvious: while still offering the chance for time alone as a family, you get to share not only the expense, but also the shopping, cleaning and babysitting duties. And as the children grow older, they'll increasingly occupy each other, leaving you adults more time to relax.

A FAVOURITE TEDDY

Around this time your baby might develop an attachment to a particular toy or object. As soon as you can confidently identify what that is, get hold of a few spares for the inevitable day when it falls out the pram or gets broken, left behind, or becomes so filthy as to be a health hazard. Better yet, regularly exchange the replacement for the original, so they both age at a similar rate.

As your child grows, these favoured playmates can play a major role in helping them cope with their own varied and powerful emotions, by allowing them to ascribe their own feelings elsewhere. They can also provide a pretty convenient scapegoat when your child knows they've done something wrong but doesn't want to face the consequences.

So although it's okay to play along, don't let your child dodge responsibility for their behaviour, and don't underestimate your role in demonstrating reality – it may be amusing to involve Teddy as an equal in tea parties or walks to the park, but nursery staff might not be so willing to make the whole class wait while he's wrestled into a raincoat.

Six to nine months

CHARACTERISTICS

It's during this stage that your baby's first tooth will probably appear. And it's around now they'll start crawling everywhere and pulling themselves up to happily cruise (sidestep) along furniture and walls – until they find they can't sit down again.

As they become much more active, they may grow tired and irritable more quickly. But while some may sleep for ten to twelve hours at a stretch, only 38 per cent of babies are sleeping through the night by the age of one.

You may by now have heard the word 'dada' amongst the constant babbling, and they'll increasingly react to the tone of your voice, trying to mimic your intonation and elicit a smile in return. If you're lucky, you may even find they can respond to basic requests, like 'Fetch my slippers'.

WHAT YOU CAN DO TOGETHER

▶ *Sit them on your lap and read over their shoulder, using funny voices and involving them with questions about what they can see. If they're up to it, let them turn the pages.*
▶ *Play hiding and finding games, and let them imitate you. Do anything that helps develop coordination and muscle tone, from stacking, pouring and tearing to rolling and chasing. And break out the building blocks if you haven't already – experts laud them as the ultimate developmental tools.*
▶ *Keep up the varied music and direct chat. Around this stage, you might want to explore teaching your baby sign language. For more about the process and possible benefits, go to www.tinytalk.co.uk.*

CRYING DOWN

If at this age your baby's still finding it hard to settle – perhaps having grown used to falling asleep in your arms or by your side – you could try the method known as 'crying down'.

This involves gradually extending the time you take to respond to their cries, initially returning after a few minutes and, keeping your voice low and giving as little stimulation as possible, offering just a reassuring pat before retreating. The next time, leave it for a few minutes more, and then a few more.

The technique requires a certain hardness of heart. It's difficult to stand by when you know you've the means to comfort just by picking them up for a cuddle. But try to be firm, with yourself and your partner – I had to stand guard outside the nursery door to stop my wife rushing in every time, but it worked.

For more on baby-settling techniques, go to www.babycentre.co.uk/baby/sleep/crying-it-out.

TEETHING

The pain of tender gums can make your baby miserable, just as it would you – though hopefully you wouldn't drool so copiously or gnaw the kitchen table leg. Fortunately, you can help, with cooling teething rings, gels, or a mild paracetamol-based painkiller like Calpol.

For more information, go to www.nhs.uk/conditions/teething/Pages/Introduction.aspx?url=Pages%2FWhat-is-it.aspx.

When it comes to tooth care, start brushing gently twice a day with a fluoride toothpaste as soon as the first one comes through, and develop a habit of spitting rather than rinsing afterwards.

It's also worth taking your child along whenever you're visiting the dentist, even if they've not yet started teething. The more familiar and therefore relaxed they are at the dentist, the better it'll be for everyone when it's their turn to open wide.

For more on tooth care, go to www.nhs.uk/Livewell/dentalhealth/Pages/Careofkidsteeth.aspx.

STRANGER AND SEPARATION ANXIETY

It's also around this time that your baby may go through a natural phase of becoming fearful of things that previously didn't seem to matter, including the introduction of strangers and the prospect of separation from you or your partner. This can especially be the case if they've limited experience of new faces or time without one or the other parent.

You can help by maintaining the familiar as much as possible, and introducing all changes slowly and patiently. Make sure strangers speak softly and approach calmly, and hold your child close to offer maximum security. And when it comes to leaving your baby with another, be open rather than underhand about your parting, allow them time to adapt, hide your own anxieties, and work on establishing a routine as soon as possible.

CHILDPROOFING

Now that your child is more mobile, it's time to think about making your home safe. See the next chapter for more on childproofing.

WEANING

There's no need to rush into introducing solids – not only must your baby's digestive system be ready, but the earlier you start, the greater the risk of choking. And besides, it's more work for you.

> *We started Ben with a peeled peach wrapped in muslin – he soon made it pretty clear he was ready for more.*
>
> Mark, father to Ben

Remember that weaning is a gradual process often lasting months, so don't push it and avoid moments when your baby's tired or already too hungry.

- ▶ *Be realistic – your baby's never done this before and has limited coordination, so it's going to get messy.*
- ▶ *Start with single-grain cereal mixed with breastmilk or formula and, around seven months, introduce yoghurts.*
- ▶ *Watch out for constipation.*
- ▶ *A blender can help you prepare a wide range of tastes, but take it steady – introduce the new alongside the familiar.*
- ▶ *Always remember your baby's only human and some days just won't be hungry.*
- ▶ *Don't give cows' milk until they're one year old, and then go for wholemilk to keep up the fat content.*
- ▶ *Don't add any sugar, salt, flavourings or preservatives.*
- ▶ *If possible, eat at the same time – it helps model appropriate behaviour and creates a family routine that should last for years.*

- *Have fun with mealtimes – tell a story, cut the food into shapes, and reward their eating with praise and hugs.*
- *Ensure everyone involved in feeding your child is doing so in the same way.*

Insight

Given the time and effort involved – to say nothing of the fundamental importance of feeding a child – weaning can be traumatic and emotionally charged. But the more you cajole, hover, wipe, tease or thrust spoons, the more your child will pick up on your anxieties and respond accordingly.

So don't overdo it, and don't see it as a rejection of your parenting if your child refuses a meal. Just keep trying, and give it time.

For more on weaning, go to
www.eatwell.gov.uk/agesandstages/baby/weaning.

Nine months to one year

CHARACTERISTICS

By one, your baby will still need a supporting hand to walk, and their endless desire to explore and imitate may result in silent, speed-dialled phone calls to family and friends whenever they get their mitts on your mobile. They'll also be able to point to various body parts on request – my daughter used to point at her head with such enthusiasm that she'd invariably poke herself in the eye.

An occasional word should now break through the babbling, and their newfound ability to shake the head (nodding comes later) will be put to great effect. You'll be hearing 'dada' and 'mama' regularly now – try not to get competitive about it.

As their emotions develop, you'll recognize increasing signs of affection, jealousy, guilt and humour. And, being better able to understand approval and disapproval, your child may begin to test boundaries by crying, smiling or throwing their first tantrum.

WHAT YOU CAN DO TOGETHER

▶ *Keep talking all the time, and respond to your baby's noises with encouragement, expanding on their efforts and speaking in a conversational manner using vocabulary just a level above your child's.*
▶ *When reading, let them turn the pages, and find an animal book that lets them have a go at making appropriate noises.*
▶ *Maintain your routines, and enjoy your baby's increased ability to interact.*
▶ *Be specific in your instructions – for example, instead of 'No!' try, 'Please put the cup down'.*

NIGHT TERRORS

From around the 12-month mark, your baby may experience night terrors in which they moan or scream inconsolably – sometimes even sitting up or opening their eyes – but always remaining fast asleep.

Since your child will remember nothing about it the next morning, night terrors can often be worse for the parents, who find themselves powerless to help. However, though unsettling, they're normal and not indicative of any underlying problem.

Because night terrors are linked to a transitional stage of sleep, they often happen at much the same time each night. It's therefore possible to wake your child just beforehand to disturb the sleep rhythm.

For more information, go to http://kidshealth.org/parent/growth/sleep/terrors.html.

SEXUAL AROUSAL

This can be an uncomfortable topic but, for the many fathers who find themselves experiencing fleeting sexual arousal when cuddling or playing with their children, it's important to address the issue.

However disturbing it may seem, a brief and mild sexual response to your child is normal, a by-product of the natural physical pleasure a parent gains from contact with their offspring. However disquieting, it's something to ignore rather than worry about, and certainly shouldn't push you into withdrawing your love or physical affection.

Of course, should you be really concerned that your feelings are inappropriate and unmanageable, seek professional help.

COMPETITIVE PARENTING

Just as there'll always be someone determined to have the most expensive car on the street, there'll always be those who assume that the money they spend on their children reflects on their skills as a parent. And birthday parties can be an excellent opportunity to spend money.

So learn to ignore the parents who order up donkey rides or a bouncy castle when the partygoers can't yet pass a parcel. While it's great to be able to celebrate the fact that your child has survived a whole 12 months, at some point we all have to learn to be comfortable with who we are and what we do, regardless of what others think.

Besides, if your child won't remember a thing, it's a lot of money and stress for nothing.

One to two years

CHARACTERISTICS

By the end of their second year, your child will be rushing around everywhere, opening doors, climbing up and down stairs, and leaving a trail of toys as they go.

Although they'll understand most of what you say and have a vocabulary of up to 50 words, their favourite will always be 'no'. Frustration will become a common emotion as they struggle to be understood and you struggle to understand, so keep taking every opportunity to model language use, even if it's just commentating as you go through the everyday routine of dressing, feeding or washing.

With a growing sense of humour, your child will swing between butter-wouldn't-melt sweetness and stubborn tyranny, erupting into tantrums and displaying a fierce independence while clinging resolutely to rituals, whether it's an insistence on an identical bathtime routine, or a refusal to eat anything other than toast – not in itself something to worry about unless the diet remains unvaried for weeks at a stretch.

As a result of their growing imagination, things that previously caused no problem – from baths to haircuts to darkness – may now give rise to fears that, however irrational, should be taken seriously, so be prepared to give plenty of reassurance. But don't let that stop you being firm when appropriate.

WHAT YOU CAN DO TOGETHER

▶ *Try to allow your child some physical activity every day.*
▶ *Play 'pretending' games – by encouraging imagination you're helping develop empathy.*
▶ *Have a go at activities that promote manual dexterity, from building brick towers and playing with sand and playdough, to painting, drawing and preparing food.*
▶ *Use crayons and paints that build an awareness of colour, but make sure they're non-toxic and – preferably – easy to wash off walls and carpets.*
▶ *Let your child select which book to read and, if you're having trouble suppressing the yawns, change the odd word to see if they notice, or make it more interactive. And put the favourites on an accessible shelf so they can choose one to 'read' by themselves now and again.*

▶ *Keep playing music regularly, but also let them appreciate silence.*
▶ *Don't push toys or games upon them – attention span is not a reflection of intelligence.*
▶ *As they grow increasingly robust, you can be more and more physical with them – girls just as much as boys – but watch you don't strain your back.*
▶ *Given their increased ability to move around and get into awkward situations, pay particular attention to their safety.*
▶ *With their increased understanding comes an increased need to monitor your own comments and reactions.*
▶ *Encourage them to play alongside their peers – but don't expect them to play* with *them yet.*

PLAY

It's an obvious point to make, but playing with your child isn't about reading a book or watching TV while they amuse themselves alongside. And it's not always about imparting something educational, or pushing them to do something the 'right' way. It's too easy, if exhausted or stretched for time with a million and one jobs to tick off the list, to overlook the importance of seemingly purposeless play.

The benefits are many and varied – from developing coordination, communication and social skills to stretching the imagination. It's play that allows a child to understand the world, to explore different roles and identities, to build confidence and develop specific abilities. And all these benefits are achievable while you're simply engaging in fun activities, and enjoying spending quality time together.

So don't feel you have to follow rules or achieve any particular goal – just follow your child's lead, be creative, rediscover the thrill of discovery, and have fun.

TELEVISION

There's no doubt that television impacts negatively on the quality of your time as a family – every minute your child is slumped staring at a screen is a minute you could be interacting in a far more positive way.

And unless you're going to be constantly hovering with the remote, it's not just what they're missing when watching TV, it's what they might be exposed to as well, from inappropriately explicit content to blatant consumerism often parading as educational improvement. Not only does your child lack the ability to objectively evaluate what they see, but at such a young age the slightest thing can often cause enormous upset.

Add to that the greater risk of your child growing obese, and the way children's programmes – deliberately sliced into short segments – fail to stretch attention spans, and you've plenty of reason for keeping the telly turned off.

> *For at least four months, Shona insisted on only ever wearing branded clothes with her favourite TV character on it. It was a nightmare – and ludicrously expensive.*
>
> Iain, father to Shona

However, it's not all bad. Television can be a fantastic educator and entertainer, and some studies suggest that a moderate amount can, if chosen with care, result in children being less aggressive and more sociable. And if your child's bright, it might actually increase their rate of development.

And while it might be the case that children today are more exposed than ever before to the ubiquitous influence of television – to say nothing of video games, song lyrics and the internet – it's also the case that parents have never had to juggle so much.

Insight

Sometimes you've got to do whatever it takes to get through the day. So while you're living in the real world, don't beat yourself up about turning on the telly.

There are ways, though, of limiting television's negative impact:

- *Keep it to a minimum – the American Academy of Pediatrics recommends no TV for the under twos, and then no more than one to two hours of quality programming per day.*
- *Actively monitor what's watched – don't think of TV as just a passive childminder.*
- *Talk through what they're watching to engage their mind and explore the issues raised – DVDs can be good for stopping and starting, and repetition aids language learning.*
- *Don't put a TV in your child's bedroom.*
- *Don't encourage them to eat in front of the telly – they're then less likely to stop when full, and so at higher risk of obesity.*

If ever in doubt, the bottom line is that a lack of telly won't harm your child – it'll be a while before they're ostracized around the water-cooler for missing last night's show.

For more, go to
http://kidshealth.org/parent/positive/family/tv_affects_child.html.

_____

Two to three years

CHARACTERISTICS

This year is a time of immense change. While physically your child will be looking more and more like a little person, able to walk on tiptoe, dance and jump, they'll still struggle to manage their emotions, so prepare for rapid mood swings.

Although generally more cooperative, confidence continues to rise and fall, causing them to veer from insistent autonomy to baby-like clinginess – they'll demand to choose their own food or clothes one minute, then cuddle up for comfort the next. With this comes an increasing bossiness and an insistence on ritual, routine and symmetry as a means of imposing control on their world – if something's not done exactly so, you might have to go right back to the beginning and start again.

Vocally, language will become the main means of gathering information – though they're still likely to grab and explore whatever they can – and, by the third birthday, about 80 per cent of their speech will be understood by strangers. They'll probably talk, hum or sing cheerfully to themselves at all hours, and even count up to – and perhaps beyond – ten, though with limited understanding of meaning.

Around this time your child will also become increasingly aware of their place outside your relationship with your partner, and perhaps struggle with consequent feelings of jealousy. They'll also begin to identify more with the same-sex parent so, if you've a daughter, be prepared to be sidelined.

WHAT YOU CAN DO TOGETHER

▶ *Keep playing – be mindful of the larger motor skills as well as the smaller, from kicking, jumping and dancing to stringing beads, pouring and stacking. And don't be afraid to get rowdy now and again.*
▶ *Go swimming, play hide-and-seek, go for a picnic, visit the zoo – anything that allows you to spend time together.*
▶ *Cooking can be a great thing to do together, and your partner might thank you, too.*
▶ *Encourage independence through the taking of supervised risk – new skills boost confidence.*
▶ *Keep reading every day.*
▶ *Always try to bear in mind what the world looks like from your child's perspective, and manage your expectations accordingly.*
▶ *Be aware of changing circumstances beyond their comprehension that may result in mixed messages – if you're always encouraging them to put their own boots on, don't be surprised if they get upset when you're in a hurry to get out the door and try to do it yourself.*

▶ *If your child's asking endless questions, gauge their aim. If it's to gather information, be mindful of their trust in you and don't reply with an overabundance of detail. If it's to rouse you into reacting, treat it as you would all other negative behaviour (see Chapter 9).*

▶ *Be patient – however tempting it might be to jump in and finish something yourself rather than twiddle your thumbs while watching your toddler struggle, it's important to let them work things out for themselves, especially as you may not know exactly what it is they're trying to achieve. And, in the long run, the sooner they can manage themselves, the less time you'll waste.*

Denise was in tears of frustration at her inability to push her doll's buggy up the stairs. But at the same time she absolutely refused to let me help her.

Ollie, father to Laura and Denise

POTTY TRAINING

There's an understandable urge for parents to hurry their children out of nappies, but you risk only lengthening the process by starting too early.

Insight
Most children are somewhere between two and two and a half before they're physically and emotionally ready to begin potty training, but every child is different, so take your lead from them.

Build it up in slow stages, without applying pressure – let your child notice the potty on the bathroom floor, then get them to try sitting on it while clothed, then without a nappy. The first stage is to be dry during the day, then overnight – bowel control often comes some time later. In all, it's a gradual process and, while some children get the hang of using a potty in days, it can take others many months. And the chances are you'll be lending a hand one way or another for several years to come.

It's normal for boys to be a little slower than girls, partly because it's a social skill and girls have greater language ability below the age of five, but also because the principal trainer is usually the mother, whom boys are less willing to imitate – so make sure you get involved if you've a son.

- ▶ *Choose a time when disruptions are at a minimum.*
- ▶ *Model what you want them to do by letting your child watch you.*
- ▶ *Accept that there will be plenty of accidents, and downplay them when they occur. At the same time, use praise to reinforce the behaviour you want.*
- ▶ *Fit your child's bed with a plastic sheet under the normal one.*
- ▶ *Your attitude will impact on theirs enormously, so don't show disgust or anxiety over their normal bodily functions.*
- ▶ *Be positive, and make it fun, with a star chart or a game.*
- ▶ *If there's no progress after a few weeks, consider putting it off a while longer.*

I used to do a stupid little dance whenever Natasha did a pee on the loo. It worked well – until the first time I took her to a public toilet and she insisted I repeat it.

Kevin, father to Natasha

For more on potty training, go to
www.babycentre.co.uk/toddler/pottytraining.

TANTRUMS

A fifth of two-year-olds have two or more tantrums every day, varying in intensity from a relatively mild outburst of aggression to holding their breath and passing out – a trick that, however frightening for the parent, isn't actually dangerous as loss of consciousness only triggers breathing again.

Tantrums can be triggered by a number of different factors, and your response should differ accordingly, so always dig beneath the behaviour for the underlying cause. If it's prompted by fatigue, hunger, confusion or a thwarted attempt to undertake a task beyond their ability, then obviously your child needs understanding, comfort and help, not discipline.

But if it's a direct attempt to challenge your authority, you have to impose consequences, firmly and consistently. Your first response should be to use diversion to nip the tantrum in the bud. If that doesn't work and your child's in an environment where no harm can occur, then ignore them – or at least pretend to. And if the loss of audience is enough to calm the child, make up and move on – but don't overdo it or you're rewarding the bad behaviour with attention.

Time-out

If the tantrum continues regardless of your presence, return and gently lead or carry your child to their room. With committed intent, state briefly and clearly that they'll be staying there until they've calmed, and then quickly leave. And don't linger on the other side of the door – they'll know you're there and come looking for more attention.

The aim of imposing time-out is to separate two otherwise warring parties and diffuse tension. So while a dull and quiet room might be the ideal place to leave them, don't view it as defeat if your child stays on to play happily in their bedroom. The message will still be received and understood.

And as before, when they've calmed to compliance, forgive and forget, moving quickly on to leave any tension behind.

Public tantrums

Obviously if you're out and about and can't rely on sending your child to their room, you face a different problem. Typically a child waits until the most public and inescapable location – the supermarket queue is a favourite – before kicking off as loudly as possible.

This is the ultimate test for parents, and you may feel you just can't win – ignore or discipline, either way there are bound to be muttered comments. But whatever you do, don't give in, or else your child will have learnt a foolproof method of getting what they want in the future.

So prepare for stares and mutterings, and be consistent – restrain your child as best you can in a manner that won't harm them and, minimizing the attention you give, leave as soon as possible. At worst, plan the shopping around when you can do it alone.

> **Insight**
> By dealing effectively with tantrums within the home, you minimize the risk of losing control elsewhere.

Toddler violence
Some toddlers go through stages of biting, pinching or hitting everyone and everything. Don't give them the attention of an overreaction, and don't hit or bite back – it only reinforces the behaviour as acceptable and gives them the sort of reaction they're looking for. Instead, remove the target, and treat it as you would any other display of bad behaviour.

For more on disciplining your child, see the next chapter.

TALKING

Obviously children learn to speak from those around them, so talk as much as possible, both directly to them and about the world around them – the more they're exposed to language, the greater the benefit will be.

- ▶ *Don't always correct mistakes or nag – just incorporate their words into a new sentence that models the right usage.*
- ▶ *Avoid pressurizing your child into a conversation by asking too many questions.*
- ▶ *If they instigate conversation with a question, try answering with one to draw them out – for example, answer 'What's that?' with 'What do you think it is?'*

- ▶ *Give lots of praise for effort, but be specific.*
- ▶ *Keep instructions short.*
- ▶ *Take your cue for conversation topics from them.*
- ▶ *Offer a choice of two items to encourage a response.*
- ▶ *Limit interruptions and closed questions that can end a conversation.*
- ▶ *Don't leap in to fill gaps.*
- ▶ *Try to make talking fun – incorporate speech into your games.*
- ▶ *Acknowledge what your child says – use listening as a means of encouraging.*
- ▶ *Don't get too frustrated by their overuse of the word 'no' – it's an important milestone, so try to view it as a mark of progress.*
- ▶ *Use sabotage techniques to gently encourage communication – for example, hide the last piece of a puzzle, or hand over a beaker already nearly empty.*
- ▶ *Avoid answering your own questions.*
- ▶ *Keep reading – a great way to demonstrate the benefits of speech.*

Children pick up speech at hugely varying rates, so don't stress if yours seems a little behind. But if they're not making any sounds around the six-month mark, consult your doctor. Similarly, if they're still not saying anything by 15 months, or you can't understand anything that *is* being said, speak to your GP.

For more on your child's speech and how you can help, go to www.babycentre.co.uk/toddler/development/speechandlanguage/milestonetalking.

Alternatively, for information and advice, contact Afasic, the national charity for children with speech and language difficulties, on 0845 355 5577, or via their website at www.afasic.org.uk.

COMPUTERS

As an inevitable part of your child's future, it's worth introducing a computer in short bursts as soon as you think it'll survive the meeting. But keep it interactive and share the time together, prompting your child's own interest rather than forcing it. If you value your equipment, establish clear rules from the start – for example, no eating or drinking in the vicinity. And as soon as it becomes appropriate, teach your child about internet safety.

For more information, go to www.kidsandcomputers.co.uk.

FAVOURITISM

Although at some stage almost every toddler favours one parent over the other, such knowledge is pitiful consolation when it's your own child who rejects you and runs screaming for Mummy.

Approaching her third birthday, my daughter used to do just that – she'd be loving and happy when alone with me but, the moment she had the choice, she'd order me away and everything – everything! – had to be done by, or with, my wife. It got to the point that she'd see me rather than her mum waiting to collect her from nursery and burst into tears, or I'd fetch something for her and she'd insist I return it so that Mummy could retrieve it instead.

But however hurtful – and embarrassing if in public – the fact is that such behaviour is normal. It may be because, before the age of three, most children are closer to their main carer, while thereafter they tend to gravitate towards the parent of the same sex. Or it may be according to who tends to offer the most stimulation or comfort. Or it may just be because they want a reaction.

Insight
The good news is that not only is such favouritism a phase lasting a few months at worst, but it's also a sign of your child's development and of how secure they are in your love to know they can jilt you yet still be welcomed back.

By playing favourites, your child is exploring their relationships, verbalizing thoughts and feelings, making choices, and learning to influence their environment. They're also demonstrating the sensible realization that time alone with a parent equates to increased attention. And the establishment of a familial pecking order – whether based in reality or not – also helps your child make sense of their environment.

But that doesn't mean you should always retreat in deference to your child's insistence – you and your partner should present a united front, setting clear limits on what your child can and can't command.

Given the notoriously fickle nature of toddlers, don't gloat if you're the favoured one, but give them plenty of time alone with your partner. And don't take it personally if you're the one who's spurned – receive any displays of love enthusiastically, without measuring or comparing, and outlove their rejection with quality time and consistent and unconditional affection. If you play it right, you'll still get the cuddles, but your child won't let you anywhere near the nappies.

Three to five years

CHARACTERISTICS

During this time, your child's language will blossom into endless chat, questions and comments. They may also subject you to long periods of whining, a particularly attritional form of communication that will diminish as they learn more effective ways of getting attention.

The same faculty that allows them to get excited about fat men slipping down chimneys at Christmas can turn frightening pictures in favourite books or programmes into terrifying realities, so take all such fears seriously – show sympathy and offer reassurance as their grip on what's real and what's not slowly develops.

And because they're still using play to explore different identities and the world around them, don't read too much into it if the only thing that interests your daughter is a plastic tool set, or your son's intent on wearing a dress and make-up.

WHAT YOU CAN DO TOGETHER

- ▶ *As ever, keep reading – use books to explore the characters' feelings and prompt other discussions.*
- ▶ *Make sure your child has daily opportunities for physical activity, from structured play to freestyle havoc.*
- ▶ *Encourage continued development of speech using praise and modelling.*
- ▶ *When you feel your child's ready, start them on a bicycle – but be safe and mindful of your back.*
- ▶ *Be aware of your child's individual character, and remain flexible.*
- ▶ *Keep play varied, from imaginative to role-play, from arts and crafts to kicking, throwing and catching a ball.*
- ▶ *Invite other children over to encourage peer play and social skills, and to teach yours the importance of others in their life – but don't expect them all to play together (rather than simply taking turns) until nearer four years old.*
- ▶ *Use current affairs and their own activities to prompt discussion about all areas of life – talk about their drawings, and how the characters in their books or TV shows are feeling.*
- ▶ *Demonstrate the value you place on their company and, by extension, them – even if it means just taking them along while you do your chores.*
- ▶ *Keep up the music and the artwork, always with an eye open for how they use drawings or figures to express their own view of themselves and the world.*
- ▶ *Take up a hobby that the two of you can share for the rest of your lives.*
- ▶ *Involve your child in your family conversations.*
- ▶ *Continue to model social skills and the values that matter to you by example.*

- *Support their growing confidence and remember how fragile it can be.*
- *Take an active interest in your child's education.*
- *Develop a healthy awe of the world around them, in nature and in others.*

RITUALS

As soon as possible, talk to your partner and agree on a few family rituals – anything from eating certain meals together to doing the weekly shop, from visiting a particular place to following a special bedtime routine – whatever guarantees you time together.

> *My mum and dad always took us for walks on Sunday afternoons. It became part of what made us a family.*
>
> Matt, father to Grace

By establishing such rituals, you help foster a sense of identity, and therefore a bond. You also provide your child with a sense of stability and belonging, as well as creating memories that everyone will treasure. And if you've managed to incorporate a tradition that was meaningful to you as a child, you'll find something heartwarming from witnessing such continuity through the generations.

And if you're lucky, you might hit on something that your child feels it's worth coming home for in years to come.

MASTURBATION

Around the toddler stage, often as potty training increases awareness of – and access to – their own genitals, it's not unusual for children to play with themselves. Though perhaps uncomfortable for those witnessing it, it's perfectly normal and nothing to worry about – though it can be hard explaining that to the elderly woman beside you in the supermarket queue.

Your own attitude to your body and nudity will impact on your child's, so don't give the issue undue attention. Be open about the physical differences between adults and children, and calmly explain what's appropriate and what's not. The habit usually fades by school age – for the moment, at least.

Obviously, if your child's behaviour seems in any way compulsive, consider professional help. They may be expressing extreme anxiety or confusion over something they've experienced.

For more on this, go to www.babycentre.co.uk/toddler/development/socialemotional/masturbation.

10 THINGS TO REMEMBER

1 *Development charts are guides, not instructions – don't stress if your child doesn't conform exactly.*

2 *When it comes to routine, try to be led by your child, and pick and choose what works best for them.*

3 *Avoid the trap of getting your baby reliant on sleeping cues that won't always be there when they wake in the middle of the night, whether it's a dummy, music, or you.*

4 *Don't be afraid when out and about with your baby to point out any lack of father–child facilities – the more a demand is recognized, the sooner it'll be met.*

5 *Spend time reading to your baby right from the start – the benefits are enormous.*

6 *Be sympathetic to your partner when it comes to giving up breastfeeding – it can be a hugely emotional time.*

7 *If travelling with your baby, put together an emergency bag with all you'll need if separated from your main luggage. But remember, you can buy baby stuff almost anywhere you're likely to go.*

8 *Even when apparently purposeless, play can help your child develop in so many ways. Plus, it's fun.*

9 *When it comes to potty training, take your lead from your child – they have to be not only physically ready, but emotionally ready as well.*

10 *Though it's hurtful and often embarrassing if your child seems to favour your partner over you, it's a normal phase, so don't get upset, and don't withdraw your love in response.*

9

You and your child: Part 2

In this chapter you will learn:
- *how to foster your child's self-esteem and use discipline to provide security*
- *how to deal with the typical health concerns*
- *what you need to do to ensure your child's safety, both in and out of the home*
- *what issues might arise when it comes to siblings.*

Self-esteem

While we all want our children to develop a firm belief in their own worth, the traditional advice – according to which parents should never miss an opportunity to boost their child's self-esteem through praise – is now considered by many to be misguided.

While healthy self-esteem is an undoubted asset, there's a fine line between self-respect and self-centredness, and scattershot praise – often unconnected to any genuine accomplishment – risks developing only a sense of entitlement, which in turn can lead to an individual more inclined to respond negatively when expectations aren't met, and to avoid the risk of failure by veering away from a challenge.

Insight
No one will be more influential than you and your partner in building your child's sense of intrinsic value, but

self-esteem should be a by-product of your parenting, not a goal in itself. And it should be built upon firm foundations of real achievement, not propped up by empty praise.

Genuine self-esteem springs from an understanding of our own limits and responsibilities, from respect for others, a sense of belonging and engagement with the world around us, and from knowing that we're loved even when we fail. To that end:

▶ *Encourage initiative and allow your child to face risks and challenges on their own without jumping in to help – but ensure some success is achievable along the way.*
▶ *Recognize effort as well as success, and allow your child their failures – the ability to pick yourself up and have another go is a vital life skill learnt only through personal experience.*
▶ *Be constructive with all criticism, and focus disapproval on the behaviour rather than the child – 'I don't like the way you're shouting' rather than 'You're always so noisy'.*
▶ *Make it clear that your love is unconditional, and never stop showing physical affection, even if it's just an arm around the shoulder.*
▶ *Be vocal about your feelings to encourage an atmosphere where they can be vocal about theirs.*
▶ *Listen to them – really listen – without distractions, and acknowledge and respect what they say and feel.*
▶ *Be clear and consistent in the boundaries you establish – and fair in the way you enforce them.*
▶ *Demonstrate their fundamental priority in your life by being available.*
▶ *Respect your child's individuality – don't compare them negatively with others, or impose unjustified expectations.*

PRAISE

When judiciously applied, praise still remains a far more powerful tool than criticism or threats, but:

▶ *As with disapproval, restrict your praise to the behaviour rather than the individual – 'You really worked hard on that*

*picture' positively reinforces the need to try, while 'You're a
natural artist' suggests no great effort is required.*

▶ *Having praised a specific accomplishment a few times, look
for improvement before offering more.*

Discipline

Discipline isn't just about punishing bad behaviour – it's about
providing security and preparing our children for the world we
live in.

Insight

> Clear and consistent boundaries provide certainty. Still
> struggling to make sense of the world around them, children
> will naturally push against restraints, feeling for them like
> handrails in the dark. When they do, it's our job as parents to
> let them know that those boundaries can be relied upon.

We live and work and play in groups. And unless children learn
to behave within acceptable limitations, they'll never learn the
necessary skills to live within the laws of society that, at times,
require us to subjugate our own wants and needs to those of
others. By enforcing clear boundaries from an early age, you're
teaching your child to respect the rights and wants of others,
and equipping them to deal with the world around them.

Discipline shouldn't be viewed as a conflict between showing love
and imposing limits – those limits themselves are an expression of
love. That doesn't mean you shouldn't guide your child towards
being a better person – after all, they need a father, not a friend.
But the imposition of boundaries should have no impact on your
love, which is unconditional and unaffected by whatever your
child may or may not do.

So don't limit expressions of love only to when your child is
behaving. Discipline in the context of a loving relationship is

easier for everyone involved and, under clear and firm direction communicated openly and lovingly, your child will thrive.

ENCOURAGING GOOD BEHAVIOUR

▶ *Model good behaviour yourself – children learn from example, so demonstrate in all your dealings the qualities you want them to learn, especially respect for others.*

▶ *Don't leave it to others – you shouldn't rely on nursery school teachers, or even grandparents, to teach your child manners.*

▶ *Reinforce positive behaviour – praise your child for what they do right rather than only jumping on them when they do wrong, and focus on the behaviour you want. For example, try 'Please stay on the pavement' rather than 'Don't go onto the road!'*

▶ *Be clear in where the boundaries lie – if appropriate, involve your child in devising the rules.*

▶ *Be consistent – if you and your partner can't agree, discuss it away from your child, otherwise they'll get mixed messages and quickly learn to exploit the weaker parent.*

▶ *Be realistic – despite occasionally seeming unnervingly grown up, your child is still young, so don't expect adult behaviour. And be attuned to their temperament as well as the context – are they hungry, tired or overstimulated?*

▶ *Incentivize – otherwise known as bribery, some parents try sticker charts, others hand out sweeties. But beware overdoing it and making the reward the motivation rather than the good behaviour and what it can provide in itself. Better yet, try to offer more creative alternatives, like a few extra minutes at bedtime to play a special game.*

▶ *Remove temptation – keep your child interested and on the move, and place valuable objects out of reach and enticing objects out of sight.*

DEALING WITH BAD BEHAVIOUR

If, despite clear and specific instruction, your child continues to push against the boundaries, you have to decide how you're going to deal with it.

At the same time, always try to understand the underlying
motivation for their behaviour – ask yourself what it is your child's
perhaps unable to express in words.

Ignore it

While consistency is important, the word 'no' is easily undermined
through repetition, so choose your battles and avoid nagging. And
never overreact – your reactions create a model for the effectiveness of
your child's behaviour, so don't provide them with the perfect reason
to provoke again. Often, if they don't get the reaction they're after,
they'll simply give up – though such a strategy can demand patience.

> *It took Rachel about three weeks to grow bored of her
> insistence on reciting Twinkle, Twinkle Little Star several
> times over, every time we put her to bed. That took a lot
> of ignoring!*
>
> Johnny, father to Rachel

Use distraction

Identify the stimulus and then by-pass the issue with humour or by
getting creative – challenge your child to put on their coat by the
time you count to ten, or see if they can count every pea on their
fork. And don't approach recognized areas of difficulty as though
they're going to be a struggle, or your child may pick up on what
becomes a self-fulfilling prophecy.

Instruct your child to stop

Get down to speak firmly and calmly at their level, maintaining
eye contact and using positive language. And don't always feel a
need to explain or justify your instruction – yes, they may be more
compliant when rules are understood, but they're hardly likely

to be in the best frame of mind for a sensible discussion, even if they're capable of it. If questioned, turn a deaf ear or pull rank – 'Because I say so!' should be enough.

Obviously this point about not trying to democratize discipline is all the more relevant if your child's still unable to communicate feelings other than through action – before the age of about three, not only are the necessary skills undeveloped, but your child may not know the reason for their motivating feelings in the first place.

Offer a choice
This won't necessarily work for a toddler, but offering an older child a choice grants them a level of control over a situation that might otherwise incite, thereby giving them greater responsibility for their subsequent actions. But don't overdo the options on offer.

Compromise
A variant on offering a choice, a compromise can be another way of asking your child to assume responsibility for their actions – for example, by negotiating just five more minutes to finish the shopping. But make sure you stick to your agreement, or you risk undermining future negotiations.

Impose a punishment
At some point all other techniques are going to fail, and you'll be faced with the unenviable task of punishing your child. The options range from giving them additional jobs to fulfil to depriving them of privileges, from imposing some time-out to withdrawing your attention.

Time-out, as mentioned earlier, involves removing your child both from you and the stimulus for their bad behaviour, perhaps by sending them to their room, or to a 'naughty step'. But beware placing them somewhere that requires your attention in order to keep them there.

Another option is to walk away and negotiate your attention in return for improved behaviour.

Insight

Children crave attention. If they can't get the positive type, they'll take the negative – even that's preferable to being ignored.

Whatever method of punishment you choose, make sure you and your partner are both comfortable with it, and ready to see it through. Get down on your child's level, look them in the eye, and give a clear and calm statement of the consequences you're imposing and the reason why.

Finally, once the punishment's over, reinforce the link between their behaviour and the consequences before moving on in a positive manner, without lingering on it – until next time when, for consistency's sake, you've got to go through it all again.

For more on disciplining your child, go to http://kidshealth.org/parent/emotions/behavior/discipline.html.

SMACKING

The fact that the pros and cons of smacking have been hotly debated for decades suggests there's no right answer. Some, often those who've been smacked themselves as children, think it a reasonable and effective means of communicating boundaries. Others abhor the fact that smacking currently remains legal in the UK, and view its practice as outdated, if not immoral.

One problem is that smacking is not always done with clarity of intent – it's often the expression of a lost temper or outright fear (for example, when a child runs into the road). In addition, critics say that smacking is self-defeating in that it still gives the child attention, however negative.

They also point out the lesson you're teaching – that resorting to violence can be an acceptable method of communicating, even with those whom we love or those smaller than ourselves. If you smack your child rather than reason with them, the argument runs, then don't be surprised if they grow up to use the same methods.

My own feeling, reinforced by the firm but fair hand of my own father, is that a smack employed judiciously and not out of anger can be the most effective means of communicating with some children for their ultimate benefit – it's the most basic and immediate establisher of limitations. To state that smacking can never be right is to claim that all children can be made to understand those same boundaries when communicated in another form. And the fact is, as we all know, it's just not always possible to reason with a child.

And despite being smacked myself when younger – judiciously, and therefore only ever two or three times as the most extreme form of punishment – I haven't grown up to believe that might is right, or that it's okay to hit those we love. I have, though, grown up to recognize a set of circumstances in which a smack might be the best option.

That said, while I might justify the theory, I've yet to put it into practice. And I imagine if I ever did smack my children, I'd have to be prepared to deal with that sense of guilt that naturally follows the imposition of anything that upsets them. Not only that but, given the controversy surrounding the issue, I'd also be risking the censure of friends and family – to say nothing of childcare or health professionals – when they learnt what I'd done.

In short, you have to decide for yourself whether you feel it's right to smack. And your decision should be based upon a calm understanding of your own child and your own context. And should you choose to impose physical punishment, be sure you've exhausted all other options first, and be aware that, if you hit your child hard enough to leave marks or bruises, you could find yourself facing a charge of assault.

For more on the issue of smacking, go to www.kidsbehaviour.co.uk/SmackingAndChildren.html.

Your own feelings can have an enormous influence on how your child behaves and how you deal with it, each impacting on the other and, at worst, setting up a vicious circle.

If you're having a good day, share your happiness. But if you're stressed, exhausted and can sense your fuse sizzling ever shorter, do all you can to police yourself. Separate those negative feelings from your interaction with your child, otherwise you risk not only imposing boundaries that are in your best interests rather than theirs, but you're far more likely to respond to their bad behaviour by withdrawing or shouting or worse, none of which is productive.

We all get angry now and again. But if you ever feel you're close to taking it out on your child, you need to remove yourself immediately and regain perspective – a strategy that can allow your child to calm down as well. And if your child does witness your anger, be sure they also see you managing it. By demonstrating how to cope positively with your moods, you're teaching your child the vital skill of self-control.

Insight

Don't be too hard on yourself when it comes to issues of discipline – no parent can control their child's behaviour every minute of the day.

Health

Babies and young children can experience a wide range of illnesses and other problems, especially once the natural immunities inherited through breastfeeding have faded. Thereafter, life can seem like an endless stream of coughs and colds.

And that's hardly surprising given that children's immune systems are still developing, that they're hardly hygiene-conscious when it comes to what they touch or shove in their mouths, and that, with the start of nursery, they're regularly exposed to a wide variety of rampant bugs.

> *There's barely been a day in the last three months when Charlie hasn't had some sort of cough or sniffle.*
>
> Hugo, father to Charlie

Insight

If at any stage you're worried, don't hesitate to speak to your doctor or health visitor – they expect new parents to raise concerns, and it's a large part of what they're there for.

Similarly, if you feel at any stage that your doctor's not taking you seriously, trust your instincts – don't be put off taking your child to hospital if you think it's necessary. When it comes to your child's health, safe is always better than sorry.

Having to watch your child suffer is brutal and demoralizing, especially if you don't know what's causing their pain. But make sure that, by supporting each other, you and your partner deal with all such problems together.

Insight

Remember that, while it's relatively common for babies to be born with minor health problems and pretty much expected for young children to develop them, they rarely last.

INFORMATION AND ADVICE

As well as your GP, health visitor or local casualty department, you're never alone as long as you're near a phone. For anything related to health, call NHS Direct at any time on 0845 46 47 (www.nhsdirect.nhs.uk) or, if you're in Scotland, on 08454 242424 (www.nhs24.com).

Another helpful website is www.patient.co.uk, designed to offer comprehensive health information as provided by GPs and nurses during consultations.

BABIES

The first few years are an especially tough time for any parent – lacking experience, it can be near impossible to tell what's normal and what's not. And because babies have such a large surface area in comparison to their body mass, they're particularly vulnerable to fluctuations in temperature so, when things do go wrong, they tend to go wrong much faster.

It doesn't make it any easier to gauge an appropriate reaction when you learn that a lot of the everyday changes you'll see, from blotches and swellings to spots and secretions, are totally normal and will soon sort themselves out.

There are, though, a few general danger signs to look out for. You should consult a doctor if your baby is:

▶ *floppy or listless*
▶ *unresponsive, dull-eyed or distant*
▶ *crying strangely, or inconsolably*
▶ *sleeping excessively – on average a newborn will wake, hungry, every two to three hours*
▶ *turning increasingly yellow in colour, both in the skin and the whites of the eyes; while mild jaundice is common and self-resolving, treatment may be required for more serious cases*
▶ *showing a high temperature – anything above 38°C*
▶ *pallid in complexion and breaking out in a cold sweat*
▶ *dehydrated, often as a result of persistent vomiting, diarrhoea or a refusal to drink – look out for especially dark or smelly urine, sunken eyes, a dry mouth and tongue, and skin that remains puckered when gently pinched*
▶ *showing sunken or raised fontanelles – the soft spots on your child's skull between the growing bone can be indicative of dehydration if sunken, or meningitis if raised. That said, they might also just mean your baby's crying hard, so don't immediately assume the worst*

▶ *not peeing or pooing – by the end of their first week, your*
  baby should be filling at least two nappies a day, and wetting
  at least four. Bear in mind, though, that some of that will mess
  the same nappy.

IMMUNIZATIONS

Though it's possible to opt out of the national immunization
programme, by doing so you not only put your own child at risk,
but everyone else's too. Some of the diseases may sound so rare
as to make a vaccination unnecessary, but that's precisely *because*
of the jabs.

Insight
Don't gamble with your child's health – the benefits of
protecting your child far outweigh any risk, and every year
there are still severe illnesses and even deaths amongst
unvaccinated children.

Many vaccinations are now given together in the one jab – your
child's body is capable of developing immunity to more than one
disease at a time, and the immunization schedule is timed to avoid
negative interaction between the vaccines. And it's plain that
limiting the number of injections is preferable for everyone involved.

Each vaccination is given as a single injection into the thigh or
upper arm. It's quite normal for children to have a mild temperature
afterwards, or for there to be a little swelling around the needle
mark. As ever, if you've any concerns, get professional advice.

And however upsetting it may be to see your baby being assaulted
with a sharp metal spike, remember it's likely to be a far more
memorable and therefore unpleasant experience for you.

> **We actually used to look forward to the jabs. For some**
> **reason, Maddie always slept much better the following nights.**
>
> John, father to Maddie

Routine immunizations

Although you may be offered a variation on the standard depending on your context, here's the current routine schedule of vaccinations:

TWO MONTHS
▶ *The first of three, five-in-one vaccines against diphtheria, tetanus, pertussis (whooping cough), polio and* Haemophilus influenzae *type b (Hib).*
▶ *The first of three jabs against pneumococcal infection.*

THREE MONTHS
▶ *The second of the five-in-one vaccine.*
▶ *The first of three against meningitis C.*

FOUR MONTHS
▶ *The last of the five-in-one shots.*
▶ *The second meningitis C jab.*
▶ *The second against pneumococcal infection.*

AROUND 12 MONTHS
▶ *A single Hib and meningitis C booster.*

AROUND 13 MONTHS
▶ *The first of two vaccines against measles, mumps and rubella (MMR).*
▶ *The final pneumococcal booster.*

THREE YEARS AND FOUR MONTHS, OR SOON AFTER
▶ *The final shot against diphtheria, tetanus, pertussis and polio.*
▶ *The MMR booster.*

For an up-to-date schedule and explanations of all the vaccines, go to www.immunisation.nhs.uk.

The MMR vaccine

When it comes to immunizing your child against measles, mumps and rubella, it's possible to request three single vaccines rather than the much-publicized triple vaccine that, at one stage, was rumoured to be linked to autism.

However, despite extensive research, no link has ever been proven. What's more, no country in the world recommends the three single vaccines as a wise alternative – not only would your child then run the risk of catching the unvaccinated diseases while their immunity's building up between each injection, but all the tests confirming the vaccines' efficacy relate to the triple injection. In other words, if you opt for three single vaccines rather than the MMR vaccine, there's no guarantee that your child will be fully immunized.

For all you need to know about the MMR vaccine, go to www.immunisation.nhs.uk/Vaccines/MMR.

GENERAL HEALTH CONCERNS

Coughs and colds
Because a cold can be caused by any one of an infinite number of different viruses, your child's may seem to last for months when in fact they're suffering from a series of different ones. But unless it's accompanied by other symptoms, for example a high temperature, breathing problems or excessive vomiting, the chances are you've nothing to worry about.

Eventually a cold will die out of its own accord. Antibiotics don't help (see page 205) but there is a range of child-specific paracetamol medicines like Calpol that can help alleviate the symptoms.

To minimize such colds and limit their spread, teach your child as early as possible to cover their mouth when coughing or sneezing, and to wash their hands regularly.

Fever
A fever could be the result of any one of a number of ailments, from an infection of the middle ear or urinary tract to a chest infection or tonsillitis. Importantly, what your child feels like is no accurate indication of temperature, so make sure you use a

good thermometer. At the same time, be aware that the height of a temperature doesn't always relate to the seriousness of an illness.

Insight

In the first four weeks, anything above 37.5°C needs urgent medical attention. Beyond that age you can relax unless the temperature's above 38°C. In any case, if the fever lasts more than 48 hours or if your child appears really unwell, seek medical advice.

At worst, a rapid fever can induce a fit, known as a febrile convulsion. This is most common between six months and three years, and has no permanent effect. It usually lasts fewer than five minutes, during which time you should stay with your child, lie them on their side, and ensure they're out of harm's way. Once they've recovered, take your child to a doctor.

Allergies

It's quite common for parents to suspect an allergy as being behind any number of ailments, whereas in fact fewer than 5 per cent of children under three are actually allergic to any foods, a figure that drops to around 2 per cent once over five.

Perhaps such paranoia is understandable when, for a tiny minority of worst-hit sufferers, an allergic reaction can bring about anaphylactic shock, evidenced by an itchy rash, swelling of the lips, tongue or throat, lowered blood pressure and finally collapse. If suspicious, call for an ambulance immediately.

Vomiting

Babies can effortlessly regurgitate often surprising quantities of milk after feeding. Known as possetting, it's a very common consequence of the ring of muscle holding down the contents of the stomach not yet being fully developed.

By comparison, vomiting will usually be even more copious and forceful and, unlike possetting, is less likely to be connected to feed times and more likely to upset. It can accompany almost any illness, and should be discussed with a doctor. Meanwhile, try to keep your child topped up with plenty of clear fluids taken frequently in small amounts.

For more information, go to www.babycentre.co.uk/baby/health/vomiting.

Croup
Croup is usually the result of a virus that causes your child's voice box and windpipe to swell. The result is a distinctive cough that sounds like a barking seal and, as it worsens, a high-pitched crowing noise when inhaling.

It's most common in children between the ages of six months and three years, and often appears after several days of cold-like symptoms, usually worsening at night, but fading entirely after about a week.

Croup isn't usually serious, but you should see your doctor, especially if your child's having severe problems breathing. If it's just a mild case, they may decide you're better off treating it at home with humidity by holding your child upright in a steamy bathroom, or sitting them over a steaming basin. You could also try installing a humidifier in their bedroom. Because it's viral, antibiotics won't help, but make sure your child's getting plenty of fluids.

For more information, go to www.mayoclinic.com/health/croup/ds00312.

Asthma
Because the symptoms of asthma can accompany a range of childhood illnesses, it can be difficult to diagnose, especially in children younger than two. The good news is that while one in five UK households are affected by asthma, it usually only occurs in its milder form and, thanks to effective treatment in the form of an inhaler, no longer has anything like the lifestyle impact it used to.

For information or advice, call the Asthma UK Helpline on 0800 121 6244, or go to the charity's website at www.asthma.org.uk/all_about_asthma/for_parents/index.html.

Cradle cap

Though it's hardly reassuring to see enormous crusts of skin flaking off your child's scalp, it is quite normal and will sort itself out, so avoid the temptation to pick. A little olive oil rubbed into the head can help loosen the flakes, but remember to wash it out afterwards – you can buy specialist cradle cap shampoos over the counter.

For more on cradle cap, go to www.babycentre.co.uk/baby/health/cradlecap.

Sticky eye

If your baby's tear duct becomes blocked, you may notice crusting on the eyelid. If this is the case, use cotton wool soaked in cooled, boiled water or saline to remove it and, with clean hands, try to massage the duct clear. Alternatively, your doctor can recommend drops or a bathing solution.

If the crusting is accompanied by inflammation or redness of the white of the eye, it may be the result of a more serious infection known as conjunctivitis, so get your doctor's advice as soon as possible.

Baby acne

Almost half of newborn babies develop tiny yellowish white spots around the nose and face. Known as milia or milk spots, they will disappear within a few weeks.

Around three to four weeks, your baby may suffer a version of acne, when small whiteheads ringed by red skin – not unlike adult pimples – break out on the cheeks, forehead, chin, and sometimes even on the back. Their exact cause is unknown, and they're likely to appear even worse when your baby's upset. But although it can be pretty unsightly just as you're gearing up to show off your perfect little bundle to the wider world, these spots should also resolve by themselves within a couple of weeks. If it hasn't cleared up within three months, consult a doctor.

Burns

> ### Insight
> A baby's skin is far, far thinner than an adult's, so it's essential that you take care when placing them near any source of heat, and respond immediately to any contact.

Remove all clothing covering the burn as soon as possible – unless it's actually sticking to the skin – then run cool or tepid water over the affected area for at least 20 minutes before covering it in a light, non-fluffy material such as clingfilm or a clean plastic bag. Then seek medical attention.

Clingfilm is perfect because it's sterile, protective, soothing, it doesn't stick to skin, and medics can see through it to assess the burn. But apply it in layers rather than wrapping it around on itself in case the wound swells.

For more on dealing with burns, go to www.patient.co.uk/health/Burns-and-Scalds.htm.

Choking
It's easy to freeze in terror if your child starts to choke, but it's essential to act quickly. If the obstruction can't be manually removed from the mouth, bend your child over or lay them across your lap and slap them firmly between the shoulder blades. After five unsuccessful blows, move on to the Heimlich manoeuvre – stand behind with both your arms around your child's waist, and instruct them to cough as you pull sharply up beneath the ribs with interlocked hands.

For children under 12 months, use chest thrusts rather than the Heimlich manoeuvre – lay them down, face up, and, using two fingers, deliver five sharp chest compressions to the area just below the bottom of the sternum.

If the problem continues, call for urgent medical attention and, if your child becomes unconscious, begin CPR.

For more on removing choking hazards, go to www.patient.co.uk/doctor/Choking-and-Foreign-Body-Airway-Obstruction-(FBAO).htm.

Consider taking a course in infant resuscitation (see later), or at least watching one of the many instruction videos available online, for example at www.youtube.com.

Head injuries

Children often seem to go out of their way to discover exactly how hard the hardest objects in your household really feel when bounced against their heads. Fortunately, most such efforts are nothing to worry about, especially if they're still conscious and there's no deep cut or other damage.

However, if there are any signs of double vision or hearing loss, drowsiness or dizziness, a steadily worsening headache, repeated vomiting, fits or convulsions, confusion or problems understanding or speaking, unusual breathing or discharge from the nose, eyes or ears, take your child to a doctor immediately.

Of course, lots of children cry after taking a knock, then settle, and then want to sleep for a bit – nothing to worry about in itself, as long as they're breathing normally and in a regular sleeping position.

If you're worried, or the accident happens just before bedtime, you can always wake your child up after an hour or so. They may not thank you for it, but a brief moan is a small price to pay for peace of mind.

Poisoning

More than 100,000 NHS admissions every year are attributable to poisoning, with children under five being at highest risk.

Fortunately, fatalities are extremely rare – most usually result in minor side effects such as a stomach upset.

If in any doubt as to the seriousness of your child's case, call NHS Direct on 0845 4647 (or 08454 242424 in Scotland), with details of the substance swallowed. And if your child develops any breathing problems, rashes, dizziness, nausea, or swelling around the mouth and throat, call an ambulance immediately.

For more on poisoning and how to avoid it, go to www.nhs.uk/Conditions/Poisoning/Pages/Introduction.aspx.

Bedwetting
The average child is dry through the night by the time they turn three, but up to about 20 per cent of five-year-olds still wet their beds regularly, and infection or emotional trauma can cause a previously dry child to regress.

It's not an issue of laziness, so it's no good making them feel guilty about it. Instead, you can try the following:

▸ *Make sure they don't drink too much close to bedtime.*
▸ *Fit a rubber undersheet on their bed.*
▸ *Ensure your child pees before going to sleep.*
▸ *Leave beside their bed a potty, a nightlight, a change of pyjamas and some fresh sheets, so they can at least try to get back to sleep independently.*
▸ *Wake your child last thing to take them to the bathroom, then set an alarm to do it again progressively later each night.*

For more information, call 0845 370 8008 or go to www.eric.org.uk.

COLIC

Like teething, colic is a favourite fall guy for beleaguered parents unable to settle otherwise healthy babies. It usually starts around the baby's third week, often in the evenings, and presents as inconsolable crying for hours in a row, sometimes accompanied by convulsive movements.

Although the cause of colic is unknown, usual advice revolves around limiting the swallowing of air, so keep your baby upright during feeds and, if bottlefeeding, experiment with different-sized holes in the teat.

Colic isn't a disease and won't do any lasting damage, usually disappearing around five months. But that's a long time for you and your partner to suffer, to say nothing of your baby, so look after yourselves as well, and take whatever help you can get.

For more on colic, go to www.mayoclinic.com/health/colic/ DS00058. For a long list of suggested remedies, try www.babycenter.com/0_colic-how-to-cope_1369745.bc. And you can always speak to your doctor or health visitor for advice.

Rashes

Rashes are common in children and, like vomiting or a fever, can indicate any one of a number of different problems of varying seriousness. Viral infections are the most common cause, from minor respiratory and gastrointestinal infections, to chickenpox (see below), measles or rubella. Bacterial infections include impetigo or meningitis (see facing page).

Rashes can also be caused by scabies mites, by a fungal infection such as ringworm, a complicated nappy rash, an allergy, an insect bite or sting, or a chemical irritant.

The type of rash and how it spreads provide clues to the cause, although it can be difficult to diagnose a rash with complete certainty. Treatment depends on the diagnosis, so look to how it appears and spreads for clues, and see your GP if at all concerned.

Chickenpox

Anything from one to three weeks after exposure to the chickenpox virus, your child will develop a rash of itchy, raised red spots, usually on the trunk of the body. They're sometimes accompanied by a stomach ache and general malaise, perhaps even a mild fever, but you may equally find your child is otherwise fine.

The spots will spread and grow bigger, blister, and then eventually scab over, leaving most children clear of chickenpox in less than two weeks. While it lasts it can look terrible, spread easily and, being very itchy, may leave tiny scars, so many parents resort to putting gloves on their children to limit the scratching.

A cool bath can relieve the worst of the itchiness, though calamine lotion works best, and it's also worth trying antihistamine medicine to reduce the itching and help your child sleep.

Insight

Chickenpox sufferers are highly infectious from 48 hours before the rash first appears until all the spots have crusted over, usually about a week later. During that time your child should avoid pregnant ladies (in case they've not yet had chickenpox themselves), and the immuno-suppressed. They should also be kept out of nursery.

For more on chickenpox, go to www.patient.co.uk/health/Chickenpox-in-Children-Under-12.htm.

Meningitis

Because it's so easily mistaken for flu or a bad cold, meningitis is always something to be aware of. Usually caused by infection, it's an inflammation of the brain lining – classic symptoms include a headache, high fever, confusion, sleepiness, and a stiff neck.

Symptoms usually develop over one or two days and, depending on the type of meningitis, can resolve themselves, or can be fatal.

In babies and young children, the usual symptoms may not appear. Instead, look out for constant crying, excessive sleepiness, a bulge in the soft spot on the top of your baby's head (the fontanelle), poor feeding, an inability to maintain eye contact, and stiffness.

Another symptom is skin rash. Use a glass to press against the skin – if the rash remains, or if your child shows any of the symptoms of meningitis, see a doctor as soon as possible – early treatment can prevent serious complications.

For more information, go to www.meningitis-trust.org or call their 24-hour helpline on 0800 028 18 28.

Obesity

It might seem a little early to be worrying about your child's weight, but the household they grow up in has an enormous influence on their future health, and you can help them develop the right habits from the start.

In the UK, around 27 per cent of children are now obese, meaning that they're at greater risk of developing health issues as a result of being overweight. At its simplest, obesity is the result of eating too much high-sugar food and not doing enough exercise to burn off the calories consumed.

Insight

Start setting a pattern now for healthy living. And if you're worried your child is obese, don't impose a diet – introduce gradual changes that replace high-sugar foods with a more balanced intake, and ensure your child does some exercise every day.

For more information, go to www.eatwell.gov.uk/agesandstages/children.

FIRST AID

If only for your own reassurance, it's worth equipping your home with a basic medical kit. Ideally this will include a decent thermometer, a supply of antihistamines such as Piriton, a paracetamol-based medicine like Calpol and some ibuprofen, but always check the label before administering – some medicines require your child to be above a certain weight.

It's also worth familiarizing yourself with the fundamentals of first aid – there are a number of organizations running life-saving courses specific to babies and young children right across the country. To find out more, go to www.babycentre.co.uk/baby/safety/firstaiddirectory.

ANTIBIOTICS

Many parents blindly demand antibiotics as the cure to all their children's ills, but there are a number of reasons your doctor may be unwilling to agree:

- *As the name suggests, antibiotics are for treating bacterial infections – the more common viral infections are left untouched.*
- *Not all bacterial infections respond to antibiotics.*
- *There may be alternative medicines that are equally effective.*
- *Your child's own defence system may do a better job.*
- *Antibiotics can kill off the 'friendly' bacteria which help to keep your child healthy.*
- *Inappropriate use of antibiotics encourages the evolution of drug-resistant bacteria.*
- *Overuse can cause side effects like diarrhoea.*

If your child does start a course, make sure they finish it, even if the original symptoms disappear – if the infection's not been entirely killed off, it may return having become resistant.

ADMINISTERING MEDICINE

Too often, doctors and pharmacists recommend medicines without much consideration for exactly how they'll be administered. And don't expect the label on the side of the box to be much help either.

If your child has a real aversion to the taste, your doctor may be able to prescribe a more palatable alternative, or at least a more concentrated version that requires fewer doses. For babies, it's possible to get medication-dispensing dummies, but we found the best method was to use a syringe, squirting small amounts into the side of the mouth. It's still not an easy task if the taste is foul, though, and requires determination and an element of hardheartedness.

Timing is difficult, too. According to the instructions, many medicines should be taken on an empty stomach but, when your child's still feeding every few hours, that doesn't leave a particularly wide window of opportunity. The bottom line is that it's often better to just get it in than worry too much about the timing.

If at all possible, try to maintain a similar level of practicality when it comes to your child's illnesses – not always easy if they're suffering. But if it's only a mild illness, for example, ask yourself if it's really worth the struggle and the misery – there's little point forcing down medicine to stop your child being sick if they're only going to sick it straight back up.

Safety

Without an element of fatalism, your child's first breath is likely to herald a lifetime of anxiety – the more you love, the more you have to lose. Somehow you have to strike a balance between worrying for your child's wellbeing, and allowing them to live normal lives of their own.

For a website dedicated to children's safety and wellbeing, go to www.childalert.co.uk.

CHILDPROOFING

> **Insight**
> Part of achieving a balance between care and freedom is to be sure you've done all you reasonably can to limit risk, especially as accidents far exceed disease and illness as the leading cause of injury and death among children.

So preferably *before* you discover your child's able to zip across the kitchen floor in the time it takes you to open the fridge, look around your house and imagine you're an inquisitive toddler keen to pull yourself up and tug at whatever you can find, with neither a sense of danger nor an understanding of the cost of your family's most prized possessions, with the single aim in life of creating potentially hazardous situations.

- *Tie up all the wires that you can't hide beneath carpets or floorboards.*
- *Put breakable or valuable items high up out of reach.*
- *Fold away the expensive rug you'd rather wasn't splattered with sick.*
- *Allocate a trunk or basket to hold toys so they're not spread everywhere.*
- *Get into the habit of turning off appliances, shutting doors and using the back burners on the stove, with the pot handles turned to the wall.*
- *Make sure your bookshelves and television aren't likely to topple over if tugged – if necessary, attach them to walls or tables.*
- *Think about where you place furniture that might be easily climbed – especially if near a window.*
- *Ensure all alcohol, medicines, cosmetics, bleaches, pesticides and other cleaning and gardening products are locked away or well out of reach. This includes houseplants – many can be poisonous if eaten.*
- *Fit safety gates at either end of the stairs – you can move the lower one up a few steps for climbing practice.*
- *If you've a fire, get a large fireguard.*
- *Make sure all toys are age appropriate, and place all small items that could choke out of reach.*
- *Fit window locks to prevent them being pushed open wide enough for your child to fall out.*
- *Post emergency numbers by your phone – including NHS Direct on 0845 4647 or, if based in Scotland, 08454 242424.*
- *Fit thermostatic locks on baths and showers, or turn down your water heater to about 49°C (120°F).*

- *Make sure your household insurance supplies adequate cover.*
- *Keep your mobile phone charged and, if applicable, maintain plenty of credit.*

Many hardware stores, supermarkets or children's shops sell home safety starter packs with a variety of useful items, including plug socket covers for electrical outlets, attachable corners to soften the sharp edges of tables, locks for cupboards and drawers, and wedges to stop doors slamming on little fingers.

ABDUCTION AND ABUSE

Below about five years old, children are naturally curious and trusting, and unable to grasp the full consequences of potentially threatening situations. As early as possible, teach yours acceptable and specific boundaries in their interaction with strangers.

But try not to let the media skew your perception of reality. While a tale of abuse or abduction will sell papers, a story about the hundreds of children in that same day who've been safely returned to their parents by helpful strangers does not. So beware passing your anxiety on to your child, and allow them the childhood they deserve – not one under constant supervision or, worse still, 24-hour GPS tracking.

CARSEAT OR BOOSTER SEAT

Until your child is 12 years old or 135 cm in height – whichever comes first – you're legally responsible for ensuring they use an appropriate child restraint in the car. Make sure you've got the right one for their age and weight.

For more information, go to www.childcarseats.org.uk.

STREET SAFETY

Not so long ago, taking our daughter to nursery, I opened my car door to throw in a bag, then turned back to the pavement to find she'd disappeared. Quite understandably, she'd assumed we'd be going straight to her door, and so had stepped out into the road. So despite always being told to look out for oncoming cars, she was waiting patiently beside ours as another sped along towards her.

Fortunately, the driver noticed her, and slowed. But the experience terrified me, and made me re-evaluate the benefit of child reins, which I'd previously dismissed as overly restrictive. The fact is that around 500 children are killed on the streets of the UK every year, and another 24,000 are injured.

Insight

It's never too early to start demonstrating the Highway Code, even before your child can walk. Thanks to the appeal of a flashing green man and the accompanying beeps, learning about crossing the road at the right time can be fun, as well as life-saving.

FIRE

It's easy to overlook the increased difficulty of escaping a house fire with another body in the house, so take two minutes to decide an evacuation plan. Fit smoke alarms and test them regularly (changing the batteries at least once a year), consider investing in a fire extinguisher or two, and don't place heaters too close to walls, curtains or other hangings.

For more information about fire safety, go to www.direct.gov.uk/firekills.

Siblings: having another baby

Though one child may be quite enough to worry about for the moment, it won't seem long before the question of a second arises, as much for your first child's benefit as your own.

THE OPTIMUM AGE GAP

The longer you wait, the more time your partner has to recover from the gruelling experience of pregnancy and childbirth. You also give yourselves the benefit of spreading the cost that little bit more, and escape the difficulties of raising a toddler and baby at the same time. Besides, it might just be that you can't yet face going through it all again.

However, there's something to be said for getting the baby years over with while you're both still young enough to deal with it. And, in general terms, the longer you leave it, the harder it becomes to conceive, and the greater the risk to mother and baby. And don't imagine if your partner fell pregnant immediately the first time round that it'll necessarily be the same again – you're not only both older, but neither of you are likely to be at your physical peak after a year or two of parenthood.

For more on the pros and cons of differing age gaps, go to www.babycentre.co.uk/preconception/ref/siblingagegaps.

> *Leonie's biggest concern seemed to be whether or not she could love a second child as much as the first, as though her capacity for love was finite.*
>
> Lucas, father to Ethan and Ben

Another big influence on parents considering a second is the potential for sibling rivalry (see facing page). This tends to peak with a two-year age gap, by which time the eldest will have developed a sense of their own identity and so be able to recognize another usurping the love and attention they've thus far exclusively enjoyed.

Thereafter, from about three onwards, a child's better able to understand what's going on, and probably more sociable and confident with a life outside the home so as not to be so threatened by a new arrival. But of course there are no guarantees.

The truth is that the relationship between siblings is subject to infinite variables, from gender and family dynamics to their individual temperaments, and everyone's experience is different – a close gap in one family can result in a close relationship, while the same gap in another leads to endless conflict. And what may seem a benefit in the early years may not be the case later on, and vice versa.

Insight

Every age gap has its own strengths and weaknesses. So once you've considered the reasons for and against having another baby sooner or later, the real question should be whether you and your partner feel ready.

DEALING WITH SIBLING RIVALRY

While some children seem to adjust relatively easily to the arrival of a sibling, others need time and sensitivity. And even if they're able to express themselves, they may still be inwardly unsettled.

It's impossible for a young child to imagine the future benefits of a younger brother or sister – and it can be a hard thing to sell even when the baby's arrived and does nothing but sleep, cry, and steal attention.

It's not difficult to see how it must be a tough time for an older child. Remember how your life exploded with the arrival of your first, and now imagine a similar disruption but with even less understanding or control over what's happening.

> *It's like your wife turning round and saying she's bringing another man home. Of course an older sibling's going to get upset.*
>
> Dominic, father to Millie and Tamsin

Before the sibling arrives

▶ *The bigger the bump, the easier it'll be for your child to grasp what's going on, so delay the revelation until your partner's at least showing.*

- Let your child see a picture of the scan and feel the baby moving, and set up a calendar to mark off the days until the birth.
- Be aware of questions, whether expressed or not, about how the baby got in there, and how it'll get out.
- Be careful what associations you set up with the new baby – make any necessary disruptive changes around the home well in advance, downplay expectations of an immediate new playmate, and try not to link the arrival of a sibling with Mummy's increasing need to lie down rather than join in the usual games.
- Although continuing routines will provide reassurance, check that they'll still be practicable after the baby arrives and, if necessary, alter them slightly – my wife used to wake my daughter every morning, a task that became mine when we realized several months before our son arrived that she'd likely be too busy feeding him to keep it up.
- Involve your child in making decisions over preparations, for example by choosing a few toys for the baby.
- Strengthen your relationship with plenty of one-on-one time.
- Get hold of one of the many books for children dealing with the issue of new siblings, and make it a regular read.
- Be clear about what will happen on the big day, but keep it simple. If they'll be staying with relatives or friends during that time, try to arrange a dummy run.

After the birth
- Let your child visit the baby in hospital, but consider using a bedside cot so their first sight isn't of a potential competitor comfortably settled in your – or your partner's – arms.
- Take pictures of them both together, emphasizing the baby's arrival as a special coming-of-age moment for the big brother or sister.
- Arrange for your eldest to receive a present 'from the baby', and stress how much the baby likes them.

- Get your older child involved from the start, helping out with the baby and telling everyone the news – but don't force it if they seem unwilling.
- Make sure visitors fuss over the older child as well, or restrict visits until after bedtime.
- Recognize that friction, and even some aggression, is normal – you can't expect a young child to deal with jealousy in a mature manner.
- Praise good behaviour and be consistent in tackling the bad, setting clear boundaries for all physical interaction with the baby.
- Let your child know it's okay to talk about their feelings, and encourage them to express them in other ways, such as drawing.
- Show them photos of themselves as a baby, and point out how they needed extra help then, too.
- If at all possible, set aside specific time to give your older child plenty of positive attention, and allow them 'privileges' to emphasize the benefits of being the oldest.
- Get them involved in the baby's care by offering a choice of two options – for example, 'Would he like to wear the red trousers today, or the blue?'
- Be wary about leaving them alone together, and only let the older child hold the baby if sitting and supervised.
- Be prepared for your older child to regress in some way, from potty training to thumbsucking – and be patient in dealing with it.

We used to say things like, 'No, baby, it's not your turn – it's Chloe's turn now', so Chloe didn't always feel she came second.

Alan, father to Chloe and Jo

For more about sibling rivalry as your children grow older, go to www.familiesonline.co.uk/Locations/Surrey-West/Articles/How-To-Manage-Sibling-Rivalry.

No two children are the same

It's natural to expect a second child to be easier than the first – after all, you've done it all before. But even if there's no difference in gender, remember you'll still be dealing with a whole new set of ingredients, so don't assume that whatever worked last time will necessarily produce the same result.

Despite the enormity of a parent's influence, every child develops their own personality and qualities that need to be recognized and respected – while one might never go near a staircase, the other may like nothing better than to throw themselves headfirst from the top. One may be analytical and deliberate, another may be instinctive and unconventional.

Insight

It's your job to identify your child's approach to the world around them, and build on their strengths, guiding and encouraging them down paths of their own, and taking pride as they develop and stand alone as an individual.

That means avoiding overt comparisons between siblings or with other children, and being aware of the pressurizing – and even straitjacketing – power of labels. It also means not pushing your children to conform to your expectations. Rather, amend your expectations to match each one's changing individuality, and recognize the full spectrum of values, from self-confidence and competitiveness to humility and compassion.

Around the age of five I expressed a liking for what, at the time, I apparently called 'floppy bacon'. I'm now 28, and my family still feed me flaccid, half-cooked strips of pig.

Mark, father to Ben

10 THINGS TO REMEMBER

1 *Praise can be a valuable means of encouraging and guiding your child, but it must be grounded in substance – don't bolster self-esteem artificially, nor shelter them entirely from failure.*

2 *Effective disciplining is founded in love, and is about setting and enforcing clear and consistent boundaries for your child's benefit.*

3 *Take responsibility for your child's behaviour by setting a good example.*

4 *Punishment should be a last resort, to be used only when the other more positive techniques to discipline have proved unsuccessful.*

5 *We all have good days and bad days, so share the good and let your child see how to cope with the bad.*

6 *Never hesitate to get professional medical help if you think it's necessary.*

7 *It takes a thermometer to accurately gauge a child's temperature, not the palm of a hand.*

8 *Equip your home with at least a basic first aid kit, and stick up a list of emergency numbers near the phone.*

9 *You can't remove the everyday element of risk that your child will face around the home – but you can limit it.*

10 *Don't let the potential impact of a sibling on your first child overly influence your timing when it comes to having another baby – the real question is whether or not you and your partner feel ready.*

10

Finances and entitlements

In this chapter you will learn:
- *how to find out what benefits you and your partner may be entitled to*
- *what rights you have as a father to time off work*
- *how to ensure your finances are in good shape*
- *how to introduce your child to money.*

There's no getting round it – children are expensive. The latest report put the cost of caring for a child, from birth to the age of 21, at just under £200,000, and that doesn't include notoriously pricey extras like private schooling.

To rub it in, just when you could really do with a little extra income, the chances are that your partner will face a significant drop in earnings – or at least enormous childcare bills.

> *Of course finances are an issue. We went from two incomes supporting two, to one income supporting three.*
>
> Gareth, father to Mark and Carys

Be open

Inevitably, finance can be a major – and very emotional – issue, especially for fathers who, even in families where the woman's

the main breadwinner, will be aware of at least the vestige of
traditional thought, according to which it's a man's duty to
provide.

Insight

If you're worried about your finances, it's important that
you talk to your partner about it. You may both have quite
different expectations, from the type of family holiday to the
amount you'll spend on Christmas presents, or even just the
brand of food you'll feed your child.

The more you communicate now, the more hope of avoiding
unnecessary disputes further down the line.

The ins and the outs

The good news is that your contribution to society as a
parent is recognized, and help is available. Depending on your
circumstances, you could get support with anything from council
tax payments and housing to your child's nursery costs and school
meals. You just need to be aware of your full entitlements, and
that means gaining a comprehensive understanding of your current
financial situation.

As soon as you can, sit down with your partner and draw up an
honest spreadsheet of your joint income and expenditure. Gather
as much information as you can, and include all debts. You have
a financial responsibility to your child, whether you're married
or not, and time spent now can save both money and grief in the
future.

For help compiling a budget, go to
www.moneysavingexpert.com/banking/budget-planning.

For the Financial Services Authority's Parents' Guide to Money,
go to www.fsa.gov.uk/financial_capability/pgtm.

State benefits

There's a wide range of benefits available to you and your partner, both before and after your baby's born, and many of those benefits are paid regardless of income. So be sure to investigate and claim your full entitlements.

For an overview of the Government's financial help for parents, go to www.direct.gov.uk/en/Parents/Moneyandworkentitlements/YourMoney/index.htm.

To ensure you're not missing out on entitlements, go to www.entitledto.co.uk.

And for advice on money issues for unmarried couples, go to www.advicenow.org.uk/living-together/money.

Please note: Obviously legislation can and does change, so be sure to check that all the information in this section remains valid before relying on it.

Some of the benefits available include:

CHILD BENEFIT

Regardless of income or savings, you and your partner will qualify for a contribution – currently £20.30 per week – towards the maintenance of your child. Additional, smaller payments exist for subsequent children.

For more about Child Benefit, go to www.direct.gov.uk/en/MoneyTaxAndBenefits/TaxCreditsandChildBenefit/Childbenefits/index.htm.

WORKING TAX CREDIT AND CHILD TAX CREDIT

According to HM Revenue & Customs, nine out of ten families with children are entitled to tax credits. To find out if you're one of them, call the Tax Credit Helpline, open from 8 a.m. to 8 p.m.: 0845 302 1415 for new customers, 0845 300 3900 for existing customers.

Alternatively, go to the HM Revenue & Customs website at www.hmrc.gov.uk/taxcredits.

HEALTH IN PREGNANCY GRANT

This one-off payment of £190 towards the cost of preparing for parenthood will soon be stopped, but if your partner reaches the 25th week of pregnancy before 1 January 2011, she will still be entitled to claim it.

More information here: www.direct.gov.uk/en/ MoneyTaxAndBenefits/BenefitsTaxCreditsAndOtherSupport/ Expectingorbringingupchildren/HealthinPregnancyGrant/ DG_173502.

CHILD TRUST FUND

A Child Trust Fund (CTF) is a long-term savings and investment account for your child, intended to provide them with a lump sum when starting their adult life.

On registering your baby's birth, they should automatically receive a £50 voucher with which to open their account. You can choose whether to invest the voucher in a straight savings account or a share-based one with an element of risk, and can top up the savings to a maximum of £1,200 each year. However, no one but your child can withdraw the money, and only when they turn 18.

Note that the Government is proposing to end its CTF payments from January 2011.

For more information, go to the CTF website at www.childtrustfund.gov.uk or call 0845 302 1470.

And for up-to-date information on the best CTF providers, go to www.moneysavingexpert.com/childtrustfund.

It's brilliant. It's like a financial reward just for having sex!

Rich, father to Freddie

CHILDCARE VOUCHERS

Depending on your employer, you may be able to use the childcare voucher scheme to pay towards the cost of childcare. Payments are managed by third-party companies and taken from your gross earnings, meaning they're free from tax and National Insurance. It may be that you and your partner both qualify, in which case you'd be eligible for twice the amount of savings.

Some of these schemes involve sacrificing your claim to Child Tax Credit and other Tax Credit contributions, so be sure to take advice and consider the financial consequences of joining (more here: www.hmrc.gov.uk/childcare).

For a full guide on help with the costs of childcare, you can download HM Revenue & Custom's booklet, here: www.hmrc.gov.uk/leaflets/wtc5.pdf.

Or, for information from the Daycare Trust, go to www.payingforchildcare.org.uk.

My boss was initially reluctant to set up a childcare voucher scheme, so I had to really emphasize the benefits to him: fewer sick days, increased performance, improved recruitment, etc. And it worked!

Rafael, father to Paula

FREE EARLY LEARNING

If your child is three or four years old, they may be entitled to a minimum number of hours free or subsidized learning each week. This can take place in registered nurseries, playgroups or preschools, or with registered childminders.

For the latest on free early learning in England, go to www.direct.gov.uk/en/Parents/Preschooldevelopmentandlearning/NurseriesPlaygroupsReceptionClasses/DG_10016103.

For information about provisions in Northern Ireland, go to
www.nidirect.gov.uk/index/parents/preschool-development-and
-learning/nurseries-playgroups-and-reception-classes/funded
-pre-school-education.htm.

In Scotland, look at www.scottishchildcare.gov.uk.

In Wales, go to http://wales.gov.uk/topics/educationandskills/
?lang=en.

SURE START MATERNITY GRANT

Mothers on low incomes may qualify for a one-off payment of
£500 for each child. (From April 2011, this will apply to first
children only.)

For more information: www.direct.gov.uk/en/
MoneyTaxAndBenefits/BenefitsTaxCreditsAndOtherSupport/
Expectingorbringingupchildren/DG_10018854.

COMMUNITY CARE GRANT

Parents already receiving certain benefits and facing exceptional
pressure (e.g. family breakdown or long-term illness) may be
eligible for a varying one-off payment.

For more information: www.direct.gov.uk/en/
MoneyTaxAndBenefits/BenefitsTaxCreditsAndOtherSupport/
Caringforsomeone/DG_10018921.

HEALTHY START SCHEME

Depending on your income and the age of your child, you may
be entitled to free milk, fresh fruit and vegetables, infant formula
and vitamins (though at the time of writing, this scheme was
'under review').

For more information, go to the Healthy Start website at
www.healthystart.nhs.uk.

CARE TO LEARN

If you're still studying, are under 20 and living in England, you may be entitled to help with childcare costs.

For more information, call the Learner Support Helpline on 0800 121 8989 or go to www.direct.gov.uk/en/EducationAndLearning/14To19/MoneyToLearn/Caretolearn/DG_066556.

CHILDCARE GRANT AND PARENTS' LEARNING ALLOWANCE

If you're a full-time higher education student with dependent children, you may be eligible for financial support towards the cost of childcare: www.direct.gov.uk/en/Parents/Preschooldevelopmentandlearning/NurseriesPlaygroupsReceptionClasses/DG_10016103.

DISABILITY BENEFITS

Parenting a child with a disability or medical condition can be extra tough, but there is help out there.

For advice and support, call Contact a Family for free on 0808 808 355 or go to www.cafamily.org.uk.

For details about disability benefits, see the website of the Disability Alliance at www.disabilityalliance.org.

OTHER HEALTH BENEFITS

Your partner will benefit from free prescriptions and free dental care during the pregnancy, while your child will get free prescriptions, dental care, eye tests and vouchers for glasses until they're at least 16 years old.

For more information, go to www.direct.gov.uk/en/MoneyTaxAndBenefits/BenefitsTaxCreditsAndOtherSupport/Illorinjured/DG_10018978.

Paternity leave

The modern system of maternity and paternity leave just doesn't reflect the reality of modern families, in which mothers and fathers are playing an increasingly equal role. The vast majority of fathers are willing and actively want to be involved in the day-to-day care of their children, but lack the level of support offered to mothers.

Fortunately, society is recognizing the imbalance, and there's a general trend towards improving the situation. It's important, therefore, that you keep abreast of the latest changes to legislation.

For up-to-date information about paternity leave, go to www.direct.gov.uk/en/Parents/Moneyandworkentitlements/ Parentalleaveandpay/DG_10029398.

CURRENT LEGISLATION (AS OF AUGUST 2010)

Insight

As things stand, if you're employed, you have a right to either one or two weeks paternity leave after your baby's born.

To qualify, you must:

▶ *have been employed by your current employer for at least 26 weeks by the 15th week before the baby's due*
▶ *be responsible for bringing up the child*
▶ *be the biological father, or living with or married to the child's mother.*

Similar rights exist if you adopt a child: www.direct.gov.uk/en/ Parents/Moneyandworkentitlements/WorkAndFamilies/ Adoptionrightsintheworkplace/index.htm.

Points to be aware of:

▶ *You don't have to take the full two weeks but, if you choose to take only one, you can't take the second week later on.*

- *You can't take just occasional days off.*
- *You have to inform your employer (ideally in writing) at least 15 weeks before the baby's due how much leave you intend to take and when you want it to start.*
- *Unlike maternity leave, paternity leave can't start before the baby's born.*
- *You have to take the leave within 56 days of your baby's birth.*
- *You only get one allowance, regardless of multiple births.*

STATUTORY PATERNITY PAY

Currently, as long as you earn at least £97 per week, you'll get paid during your leave either 90 per cent of your average weekly pay, or £124.88 – whichever is lower. However, you may have a more favourable agreement within your own employment contract, so be sure to check it out.

If you earn less than £97 per week, you won't be entitled to Statutory Paternity Pay. You will, though, almost certainly be able to claim tax credits or income support instead.

To get advice about your entitlements, find your nearest Citizens Advice Bureau: www.citizensadvice.org.uk/index/getadvice.htm.

For a leaflet on the rights of working fathers that's updated every month, go to www.adviceguide.org.uk/e_rights_of_working_fathers.pdf.

THE IMPORTANCE OF PATERNITY LEAVE

Insight

If you possibly can, make sure you claim your full paternity leave entitlement – even if your partner's confident she'd manage without you.

Those first few weeks can be formative not just for your relationship with your child, but also for the balance of involvement between your partner and yourself. That brief period can go a long way towards defining your roles as parents.

By taking time off around the birth to get involved, you gain confidence and strengthen your bond with your baby, you relieve the pressure on your partner, and you help create a better family environment.

> *I lost my job just before Lauren was born, so had two months at home to really get to know her and gain confidence as a dad. As it worked out, it was the best thing that could have happened. Now I'd advise all new fathers to take as much paternity leave as is available.*
>
> Blair, father to Lauren

Unfortunately, taking time off is easier said than done.

Insight

Recent research revealed that almost half of working fathers don't take the two weeks statutory paternity leave to which they're entitled, mainly because they can't afford to.

Instead, many new fathers are forced to take their paternity leave as paid holiday, leaving themselves with even less family time later. The result, as mothers feel unsupported and fathers miss out on time with their children, is families under increasing strain.

Maternity leave

If your partner is employed, she has a statutory right to a minimum amount of leave (currently 52 weeks), of which a minimum amount will be paid leave. This is currently up to 39 weeks, the first six of which will be at 90 per cent of her salary, and the rest at the statutory rate of £124.88 a week. Her employer may also offer a company maternity leave scheme.

In order to plan effectively, you need to know how long your partner is planning to stay at home after the birth. But be flexible and, however dire your finances, try not to put undue pressure on her to return to work. (See Chapter 11 for more on the struggle between work and family.)

> *Jen negotiated to carry over a whole month of holiday entitlement from before Josh was born, so she had four extra weeks of maternity leave at full pay.*
>
> Lewis, father to Josh

For more on pregnancy and employment rights, go to www.direct .gov.uk/en/Parents/Moneyandworkentitlements/WorkAndFamilies/ Pregnancyandmaternityrights/index.htm.

Your partner is also entitled to paid time off work to travel to, and attend, antenatal classes during work hours, no matter how long she's been with her current employer. But be sensitive – it's always worth requesting rather than demanding time off, at least initially.

For more on her rights to antenatal care, go to www.worksmart .org.uk/rights/can_i_take_time_off_work_to.

Flexible working

Insight

While your child is under 17 (or 18 if disabled), you may have a right to ask your employer for flexible working. This could mean anything from going part-time or working from home, to working during school hours, or staggering or compressing your hours.

Flexible working is highly valued by fathers, and can be of immense benefit to family life. Unfortunately, though, while an employer must take such requests seriously, they aren't obliged to agree to them. And not every father is willing to risk jeopardizing his career by raising questions about his commitment.

I asked my employer for flexible working and was finally offered a compromise that would've stalled my career entirely.

Jeremy, father to Evie and Dan, stepfather to Pete and Trish

As a result, while flexible working in some form is available to about half of working fathers, only about 30 per cent of them take advantage of it. However, you can increase the chance of your request being accepted if you approach your employer with a plan of action that takes their own needs into account and provides a strategy for dealing with any problems that may arise for them as a result of your changing hours.

For more, go to www.direct.gov.uk/en/Employment/Employees/Flexibleworking/DG_10037051 or www.dad.info/work/your-workplace-rights/flexible-working.

Parental leave

Providing you meet certain requirements, you or your partner could be entitled to a total of 13 weeks unpaid leave over the first five years of your child's life.

For more on parental leave, look at www.direct.gov.uk/en/Parents/Moneyandworkentitlements/WorkAndFamilies/Parentalleaveandflexibleworking/DG_10029416.

Compassionate leave

You or your partner may also be entitled to time off to care for your child, for example if they fall ill and are unable to go to nursery.

For more, go to www.direct.gov.uk/en/Employment/Employees/
Timeoffandholidays/DG_10026555.

Making a will

A will is a document that allows you to specify who will inherit your
assets and who will act as your child's guardian upon your death.

Without a will, your assets can be distributed according to law
rather than your wishes. So however uncomfortable it may be to
ponder your own mortality, consider it part of your responsibility
as a parent, to help care for your child after you're gone and limit
as much as possible the impact on them of such a terrible loss.

It's possible to buy the necessary documents to create a will online:
www.clickdocs.co.uk/legal-wills.htm.

However, it's always best to seek professional advice, or at least
speak to friends and do your homework. You might want to
consider a professionally drawn-up will if you:

> - *have total assets valued above the inheritance tax threshold
>   (www.hmrc.gov.uk/rates/iht-thresholds.htm)*
> - *have children from an earlier marriage*
> - *want to make specific bequests*
> - *are responsible for someone with a disability*
> - *have complicated financial circumstances, for example assets
>   held abroad.*

For more information about making a will, go to www.direct
.gov.uk/en/Governmentcitizensandrights/Death/Preparation/

DG_10029800 or www.adviceguide.org.uk/index/family_parent/
family/wills.htm#importanttomakeawill.

Spending, saving, selling and borrowing

*I only began to relax about money when I realized that,
however much we saved, we could never guarantee having
enough to cover every eventuality.*

Rob, father to Bridget

SPENDING

Your children need you, not the gifts you can buy. However, unless
you're going to spend quality time with them while foraging bins
for food and patching together clothes from cast-off scraps, you're
also going to have to spend some money. So here are a few ways
you can limit your outgoings:

▶ *Consider the cheaper alternative – the walk in the park instead
of the cinema, making a toy together instead of rushing out to
the shops.*
▶ *Buy in bulk, then cook in bulk and fill the freezer.*
▶ *Use vouchers and coupons wherever possible (e.g. www.
moneysavingexpert.com/deals/cheap-days-out).*
▶ *Use your local library for books, CDs and DVDs.*
▶ *If you can afford to, use cashback credit cards and pay off the
balance every month.*
▶ *If you can't afford to pay them off immediately, try to ditch
the credit cards altogether, or at least negotiate on the rates.*
▶ *Avoid 'buy now, pay later' offers.*
▶ *Use any savings to pay off outstanding debts.*
▶ *Shop around, and at least try to haggle over prices.*

SAVING

If you're lucky enough to find that your income exceeds
requirements, you can save by putting money aside – regular

Direct Debit contributions to a savings pot, however small, can be a relatively painless method.

If you've cash to spare, ensure you're maximizing on your annual tax-free ISA allowance (www.moneysavingexpert.com/savings/ ISA-guide-savings-without-tax), and consider topping up your kid's Child Trust Fund.

A pension
And unless you like the idea of getting your own back when you're elderly by being utterly dependent on your child, the sooner you start thinking about a pension, the better.

For free independent advice and guidance, contact the Pensions Advisory Service on 0845 601 2923: www.pensionsadvisoryservice .org.uk.

Alternatively, look at www.direct.gov.uk/en/Pensionsandretirement planning/index.htm.

Other savings

Insight
You needn't have excess cash to save – you can make a difference by slashing your regular expenses in a way that needn't have a painful impact on your lifestyle.

For example, use comparison websites like www.mysupermarket .com to reduce your weekly food bill, www.energyhelpline.com to lower your gas and electricity bills, and www.confused.com or www.comparethemarket.com to get the best deal on car, household and health insurance. You needn't wait until renewal to switch and, even if you're happy with your current insurers, a lower quote from elsewhere could help you negotiate a better premium.

For a full Money Makeover, go to www.moneysavingexpert.com/ protect/money-help.

SELLING

Now that there's that much less space at home, this is a good time to declutter, so have a think if you've any assets that you could usefully sell, whether on eBay, in a car boot sale, or in a local paper.

BORROWING

For smaller amounts, think about asking your parents for a loan – better you owe them than a credit card company. Weigh your damaged pride against your own feelings as a father – if you were in a position to help your child, wouldn't you rather they asked you than got badly into debt?

Mortgage

Choosing a mortgage in order to buy a home is likely to be one of the biggest financial decisions you'll ever make, so beware unrealistic expectations, and consider your priorities. Yes, it might be nice to have a bigger house with a garden, but if that means commuting further and working harder, perhaps it would be better to make do with somewhere smaller and nearer to work, that allows you to see more of your child each day?

For help and information about the best mortgage deals, try www.mortgagesorter.co.uk.

Debt

If you find yourself in debt, communicate with those you owe, and get professional advice. The sooner you deal with it, the sooner you'll be free of it.

For free confidential and independent advice, contact the National Debtline on 0808 808 4000 (Monday to Friday 9 a.m. to 9 p.m., Saturday 9.30 a.m. to 1 p.m.) or go to their website at www.nationaldebtline.co.uk.

Alternatively, call the Parent Debtline on 0800 652 0775 or go to www.moneystuff.co.uk.

Investing in yourself

When it comes to allocating your family's finances, don't overlook your own importance. Investing in a course or class to redirect or further your career, improve your income potential or simply raise your self-esteem can bring enormous benefits for yourself and your family.

For advice on continuing education and courses, go to www.learndirect.co.uk.

For possible financial aid while studying, go to www.direct .gov.uk/en/Parents/Moneyandworkentitlements/YourMoney/ DG_10039513.

Getting help

Whatever your financial situation, there's someone out there willing to help.

You may want to employ an independent financial adviser (IFA) to provide a financial health check. They can advise on all aspects of your finances, from mortgages and savings to tax efficiency and insurance.

Our IFA helped me set up my life insurance cover and income protection. Now I know that, if anything happens to me, Abi and Heather won't have to sell the house or anything else to carry on living as they are.

Daniel, father to Heather

To find an independent financial adviser, mortgage adviser or solicitor, go to www.unbiased.co.uk.

To carry out a health check of your own and for help with budgeting, planning and finding the best-priced financial products, have a look at the Financial Services Authority's website: www.moneymadeclear.fsa.gov.uk/tools.

And for clear advice and up-to-date information about all things financial, go to www.moneysavingexpert.com.

Parenthood is a costly and worrying business. But hopefully your salary will rise as you climb the ladder and, even if your partner's given up work, she may want to return once your child's at school. And there's always the hope that, one day, your child will be able to rely upon their own wallet.

Pocket money

You might think a preschooler too young to understand even the basics of how money works. But as soon as a child's old enough to grasp that it can only be spent once, they're old enough to start learning about spending and saving, and pocket money can be a valuable tool in teaching your child how to manage money – a fundamental skill they may not learn anywhere else.

Insight

Even if you decide not to give pocket money at such a young age – or at all – your child will still learn from you, and every time you spend, save, withdraw or give away money, it's a chance to teach them more of the basics.

Because I often get money out from the ATM by the supermarket, Josh actually thought I received money by going shopping.

Pete, father to Joshua

Some parents give pocket money as payment for chores done around the home. Others feel that those chores should be recognized as part of their family contribution to the household, unrelated to income, and so give pocket money more as an allowance, or for any extra help given. Before your child is a little older, it may be difficult to know what will work best for you.

But the sooner you start introducing your child to the realities of money, the sooner they'll learn about financial responsibility and self-discipline.

▶ *Within reason, let them make their own mistakes – better they blow it all on a magazine and have to save a little longer for that DVD now, than that they splash out on a sports car and can't pay the mortgage later.*
▶ *As early as possible, explain the motivation behind advertising and the difference between 'want' and 'need'.*
▶ *Emphasize the link between working and earning, so they learn the difference between effort and entitlement.*
▶ *While still allowing some independence, discuss what it should and should not be spent on.*
▶ *Let them learn the value of saving, both in the short term and in the long term, and the importance of repaying borrowed money.*
▶ *When it comes to amounts, talk to other parents to avoid issues when your kids inevitably make comparisons. Alternatively, let them have what you can afford and feel is right, regardless of what their friends have – another valuable lesson.*
▶ *Be consistent in the amount and the timing of hand-outs.*

We gave Maddie a big, glass piggy bank when she was three so she could see the level grow as she saved. She's turned into a real little hoarder!

John, father to Maddie

For more on pocket money, go to
www.growingkids.co.uk/PocketMoneyAndAllowances.html.

10 THINGS TO REMEMBER

1 *Talk to your partner about your finances. Don't imagine it's your domain and therefore your problem any more than nappies are her domain and her problem.*

2 *As soon as possible, work out a comprehensive and honest account of your income and expenditure, including all debt.*

3 *Make sure you're claiming all the benefits to which you're entitled, and take as much paternity leave as possible – those early weeks can be critical.*

4 *Flexible working can be of enormous benefit to family life, and you've a right to request it and be taken seriously.*

5 *Making a will is a relatively easy way of having a huge impact on your child's future.*

6 *Get savvy when it comes to cutting back on your spending without limiting your lifestyle.*

7 *If you haven't got a pension, it's time to start one.*

8 *Be practical with your finances. Spending money doesn't make you a good parent.*

9 *As time goes on and you work your way up the career ladder, your finances should improve.*

10 *As in everything, your child will learn from you. So be mindful of how they see you handling money.*

11

Work and family

In this chapter you will learn:
* *how to find that crucial balance between work and family*
* *how to manage as a stay-at-home dad*
* *how to avoid the typical guilt of the working parent.*

The role of work

In more and more families, both parents work at least some of
the time, handing their children over to the care of others when
sometimes as young as three months. And the most common
reason is because they can't afford not to.

> *We rely on two incomes to meet the mortgage and all the
> other bills.*
>
> John, father to Maddie

Of course, leaving your child while you go to work is a necessary
part of meeting your responsibilities as a parent. But once you and
your partner have provided for the basics – once you've earned
enough to feed, clothe, shelter and educate your child, with a little
left over for leisure – then the link between earning money and
meeting your parental responsibilities begins to fade. Because many
of your responsibilities as a parent have nothing to do with your
income.

Insight

Studies show again and again that money doesn't equate to happiness. Once our basic needs are met, it's our connections with others that add real value to our lives. It is, therefore, possible to have enough money.

Your relationship with your child can be one of the greatest sources of happiness in your life. But your time together is limited and, no matter how much money you earn, status you gain or enjoyment you get from being at work, once that time has passed, you'll never get it back.

RICH CHILD, POOR CHILD

But time spent with your child is not only about your quality of life. More significantly, it's of fundamental importance to them. Studies have repeatedly shown that the amount of time you spend with your child will be one of the most reliable predictors of how they'll turn out as adults.

What will make your child someone to be proud of will not be their memories of another trip to EuroDisney or their mastery of the latest console game, paid for while you work all hours out of sight in a distant office, but the values that they exhibit as they grow older, in their attitude to themselves and the world around them. And no one is better placed to teach them those values than you, as their parent.

TEACHING THROUGH YOUR CHOICES

Don't underestimate how tuned in your child will be to your discussions, actions and lifestyle. If money and all it can buy play a large role in your life, they'll likely develop the same priorities. And your drive to work – however noble – risks being misconstrued, as though your priority is with your job rather than your family.

By turning away from a more materialistic approach towards demonstrating your recognition of the importance of connecting with others, you'll teach your child a far more enduring source of happiness through life.

Changing priorities

That value isn't always measured in financial terms is one of the most critical lessons you can teach your child. And recognizing it yourself can be the first step towards a reassessment of your own priorities. Once you and your partner are earning enough to provide your child with the basics, consider every additional minute at work in light of your commitment as a parent.

Insight
> There'll always be another step up the career ladder, but there may not always be another day when your child actively chooses to spend time with you.

CATCH 22

The pressure can be enormous. You may already be putting in long hours just to hang on to your job, let alone get a raise to meet your increased bills, and yet you're told at the same time to work less so as to spend more time with your child.

In some cases, it really is necessary to work all hours to put food on the table. Such parents need society's recognition and support. But before you classify yourself as one of them, just be sure you're approaching parenthood with realistic expectations.

Insight
> Is it reasonable to expect the same lifestyle now as you enjoyed before you became a parent? Or, now that you've a parent's responsibilities, shouldn't you make time with your
> *(Contd)*

child a priority, even if that means sacrificing some of the trappings of your lifestyle?

It might help to view that notorious issue of work–life balance more as a needs–wants issue instead.

> *The way I see it, I've a responsibility – on top of feeding, clothing, sheltering and educating Shona – to spend time with her as well. And you've got to put in the quantity to get the quality.*
>
> Iain, father to Shona

A NEW LIFE

If both you and your partner are working to the point that neither one of you spends much time with your child, consider doing something about it. If you can't live off the wages of one, change your life so you can. Ask about flexible working, going part-time, or working one day a week from home. And if your boss doesn't agree, think about looking for another job. If your mortgage or rent is tying you both to work, look for a smaller house. Holiday closer to home. Ask your family for help.

Insight
Do whatever it takes to allow you to spend as much time with your child as possible. Because this period won't last forever, and your family will be all the richer for it.

> *We moved to the country as soon as we could – mainly to give us a lifestyle that meant we could afford to spend time with our kids.*
>
> Michael, father to Amy and Tom

Working full-time and supporting your partner

Someone has to take on the essential role of working to pay the bills, and that someone might be you. You might feel a little guilty leaving your partner to manage alone, as perhaps you secretly consider yourself the lucky one, playing to your strengths in a predictable world you know well, with a commute, time off at lunch, and some adult chat.

But however willing your partner may be to play the role of housewife and manage all aspects of childcare and the home, don't imagine your life can simply continue as before.

AT WORK

I'm not nearly as productive at work. Things that used to take two hours now take a whole morning.

James, father to Adam

Returning to work after having a baby can reveal just how tired you really are, and how sluggish your brain has become. And because your friends and colleagues will ask about your baby – and probably reminisce about their own as they offer advice – you may find there's little respite from the baby stuff and little time to work.

So don't be too harsh on yourself. Be sensible about your workload and, bearing in mind the importance of spending as much time with your child as possible, look at alternative methods of managing your time:

▶ *Cut down on after-work socializing.*
▶ *Work through lunch to get away earlier.*
▶ *If distance allows it, head home for lunch.*
▶ *Claim your full entitlement to unpaid leave and holidays.*
▶ *Be reasonable with yourself – don't feel you have to give 100 per cent all the time if you can make it up later.*
▶ *Be methodical in your planning and focus on each task, without being sidetracked by phone calls, emails, colleagues or cups of coffee.*
▶ *Don't allow the unnecessary busyness to steal your time and keep you away from your family.*
▶ *Put all your child's important dates into a diary and at least try to treat them as unmissable.*

If your child's old enough, talk to them about your job, and let them see where you work. That'll help them picture where you are all day, understand more about you, and begin to appreciate the necessity and benefits of a work ethic.

And be prepared to receive many more phone calls from your partner than before. She may have no one else to talk to and just need to offload, or may want to share a worry or moment. Be patient, and be prepared, on some days, to hear only complaints.

> ### Insight
> It's natural to want to please your employers by accepting extra work. But remember that if your child could express their need for your time, they'd shout twice as loudly as your boss.

And don't think your work is only going to suffer from your new role. Many men cite the professional benefits of fatherhood, from a greater ability to communicate, make decisions and juggle conflicting demands, to an increased awareness of personal relationships.

AT HOME

For all the talk about work–life balance, the truth is that, for the average working parent, it's a work–life compromise. Torn between the office and home, you may find you're giving neither your best.

As far as possible, be firm with yourself about keeping the two apart. It may even be better to stay late at work if the alternative is distracted and perhaps even frustrated time with your family. And when you do get home, remember that your mobile phone has an 'off' button, and maximize on every moment. That doesn't mean trying to make up for lost time, at the risk of being over-controlling or hyper-stimulating. Nor need you do anything expensive or hugely memorable: consider a kick around, reading a book, a bath together, or cooking a meal, anything that lets you focus wholly on your child.

However exhausted I am by the time I get home, I'm very conscious of how Brooke perceives my willingness to play with her. I'd hate her to think I only give my best to my work.

Aaron, father to Brooke

And though life may settle back into a routine, it doesn't necessarily get any easier. You might find that the very thing that makes your partner's days more enjoyable – your baby developing and responding more and more – will make it harder and harder for you to leave each morning.

There's no doubt I've missed out on a lot – though some of it I've been glad to miss out on! But I've also got to appreciate the growing bond between Jess and Nathan, and there's nothing like it.

Oliver, father to Nathan

RESPECT HER ABILITIES

Another consequence of spending less time with your child is that you may have to be prepared to take the lead from your partner.

Because she's with your baby all day, she has more opportunity to learn their signals, be it a cry, an attempt at talking, or a pattern of behaviour. When it comes to responding appropriately, it's worth trusting her intuition, and respecting the skills she's gained.

....

Insight
Whoever's caring for the child the most is likely to have a better understanding of their wants and needs. Try to be respectful of that, without being jealous, and discuss ways to get more involved yourself.
....

A SENSE OF PERSPECTIVE

One huge benefit of being out at work all day can be the perspective you then bring home. After all, a large part of your life is continuing as before, giving you social interaction, the reassurance of familiarity, measurable achievements, and a life outside your own four walls.

It's easy enough for first-time parents to become engrossed in the world of their child, and for their every emotion to hang on each little smile or cough. But imagine that, at the same time, your fears and hopes have been hijacked by hormones, your body taken over and stretched out of shape. Imagine your nerves rubbed raw with the novelty and the enormity. Imagine that you've not spoken to anyone else all day, that you're utterly exhausted – perhaps still breastfeeding through the night – and maybe even recovering still from a difficult birth.

In such a state, it would be no wonder if your emotions swooped from high to low within minutes, and you saw the end of the world in one regurgitated feed.

> *The first time Amélie vomited back all her milk, I remember Anna wanting to rush her to hospital, even though she was still smiling happily and hungry for more. We both knew that it's normal for babies to posset, but it still took me half an hour to persuade Anna we didn't need a doctor.*
>
> Will, father to Amélie

As your partner's main support – and perhaps her main contact with the outside world – it's your job to be a rock, steady and calm through every storm, real or imagined.

So do what you can to share the benefits of that perspective. Give your partner time off to go for a walk or a drink with friends. Offer her the chance to reconnect with her old life and to burst the baby bubble, to allay any fears that life elsewhere is moving on without her.

In the wider context, one bellicose toddler or a rejected bowl of mushed chicken casserole – however lovingly prepared – doesn't signal a life-threatening disaster. But when your everyday world revolves around that toddler, the smallest of worries can grow out of all proportion.

PARENTING TOGETHER

Insight

The chances are that you're all too aware how hard your partner is working at home. But just in case you're not, don't for a second imagine you've got the more difficult job. You can at least leave the office.

> *When my wife left me at home with the kids, she was quite honest about it – she said returning to work was the easy option.*
>
> Chris, father to Rowen and Holly

At times, raising a child can be isolating, exhausting, tedious and never-ending. You may be the financial provider, but never lose sight of the fact that your partner is working as well, at all hours, seven days a week, and probably for a far more tyrannical boss. You have to value that, and do all you can to support her and show your appreciation.

So as well as offering her some perspective, do what you can around the home. And don't think that, just because you've left the office, your working day is over. The evenings and weekends are your chance to contribute, not to catch up with the telly.

> *It never stops. The moment I get back from work, I'm expected to take over the baby duty.*
>
> Sean, father to Becky

Being a parent isn't easy, whether you're working or not. However you manage, you'll wish you had at least 30 hours in each day. But the more you face parenthood as a team, the easier it will be. So avoid those 'I work harder than you' arguments – it's not a competition. It's about doing the best you can for your child, together.

That takes a lot of effort, and might take a lot of tongue-biting –
it can be all the harder to put yourself in her shoes when you're
tired. So be prepared to compromise and negotiate – alternate the
nights you deal with the baby, or agree to empty the bin if she'll
hang up the washing – and give yourselves common goals, whether
it's a Friday night out or just a takeaway. And in struggling to get
through the days, don't overlook the importance of spending time
together, as a couple.

Staying at home while your partner goes out to work

According to the Office for National Statistics, there are now more
than 200,000 men in the UK who've given up their careers to look
after their children – almost double the number there were in 1993
when official records began. And even more are opting to change
their work hours so they can play an increased role in raising their
children.

But despite the growing trend, it's still a minority role. And in
flaunting social conventions, you'll have to face not only the
problems that women have dealt with for centuries, but a whole
range of additional issues as well.

EXPECTATIONS

While women have struggled for – and are winning – their right
to be recognized as equals in the workplace, we men have still got
a long way to go when it comes to being a child's main carer. So
even if *you're* up to playing a role that's contrary to expectation,
others may not be so prepared.

> *I definitely get the sense that mothers are deemed capable
> of caring for children by virtue of being women, while men
> have to work harder to prove themselves.*
>
> Nathan, father to Bella

Others' expectations can be maddening, but they can also be advantageous. Clichés abound of dads who can't operate the washing machine or who put nappies on backwards.

Insight

However irritating, low expectations are easier to defy. And anything that relieves you of pressure only helps you relax and enjoy the role more.

LOSS OF IDENTITY

Since your occupation can play an enormous role in how you're perceived, you might begin to worry what others will think of you when you give yours up. You might even begin to question yourself.

> *I did worry what I'd talk to people about once I stopped working, like I'd develop more in common with mothers than other men.*
>
> Pat, father to Alex and Tyler

The threat to your identity is founded on the same misconception that threatens your self-esteem.

LOSS OF SELF-ESTEEM

Almost by definition, alpha males do not stay at home to look after the kids. And whether you actively choose to do so or are pushed into it by circumstance, it can be difficult losing your income and the other benchmarks of success offered by a job – particularly while your working friends will meanwhile be steadily climbing their own career ladders.

> *Some people seem to view the childcarer role as the default role, adopted for want of ability to do any better or anything else.*
>
> Raul, father to Ruben

And if it's your relative incomes that have dictated your new role while forcing your partner out to work, your self-esteem can suffer all the more.

But both the threat to your identity and the threat to your self-esteem are based on the same mistaken assumption, conscious or not, that staying at home to care for children is not a proper job. It's something housewives have had to deal with for generations, but they at least have the consolation of expectation.

The fact is that raising the next generation is one of the most important jobs you could have. The role is enormous in its influence and significance, and not just in how it impacts on your child. Because your parenting will directly affect how they raise their own children, you're indirectly responsible for generations. Not many jobs can claim the same.

ISOLATION

As a stay-at-home dad, you're a man in what's still predominantly a woman's world. Many mothers complain about the isolation of caring for their children but, when you're a man, the opportunities to find and integrate with a welcoming support network are all the fewer.

> *Waiting with all the mums to collect Leah from nursery, I do feel at times like I'm intruding. It was months before one of them even spoke to me.*
>
> Jamie, father to Leah

Linking with the outside world can be difficult. It can seem like every parenting event, be it in the local library or community centre, is – just like every baby-changing facility – geared towards mothers. But joining a social network with other stay-at-home fathers can be crucial to your sanity, and there are more and more of them out there. So throw off any inertia or awkwardness over a hunt for new friends, and get out there.

The internet's a great place to start. Go to the Forum at www.homedad.org.uk and you're bound to find others in your area. Knowing that you're not alone can make all the difference.

> *The radio was my only contact with the outside world until I tracked down my local dads group. It's been great, for me and for Keira. The support is phenomenal. And above all, fatherhood is now so much more fun.*
>
> Louis, father to Keira

THE JOB ITSELF

And then, on top of worrying about fitting in with the mothers, about being isolated and financially dependent, about the threat to your self-esteem and everything else, you've actually got to look after a young child.

> *I found it really, really difficult at first. It's messy and noisy and exhausting and often very, very boring. Sometimes the arrival of the postman was the highlight of my day, just for its unpredictability.*
>
> Raul, father to Ruben

Looking after a baby isn't easy – days filled with minimal stimulation after nights of sleeplessness and tears. There's no denying that the routine can be mind-numbing.

> *I had to stop lying on the floor to play with him, because I kept falling asleep.*
>
> Len, father to Dylan

Insight

The more you do, the more relaxed you'll feel, and the easier and more enjoyable it'll become.

And soon, as your baby becomes a toddler, your days will be less about looking after them and more about enjoying yourselves together, defined not by your focus on their needs, but on what fun activity you've chosen to pass the time. (See Chapter 8 for more on caring for your child.)

THE IMPACT ON YOUR PARTNER

If your partner is heading back to work – whether she's leaving you behind to care for your child or not – one of the strongest emotions she'll feel will be guilt: guilt over not being there for her baby, guilt that her absence will impact on your child, guilt that her mind's no longer so focused on her job, maybe even guilt at the pleasure of being at work.

Then there'll be the fear that, in handing over her child to another, she'll somehow be replaced and her relationship with her child impaired. Add to that the strains of restarting a job after time off and the physical aspect of either giving up breastfeeding or continuing to express, and you can appreciate the torrent of emotions.

> *Jen barely slept for two weeks before returning to work. She had panic attacks at all hours – something she'd never experienced before. It got better eventually, but she found that phase really tough.*
>
> Alastair, father to Iain

And it may only get tougher at first, as your baby develops and begins to respond and generally be more fun.

If your partner's finding it hard being back at work:

- ▶ *Make sure she realizes she's likely to be her greatest critic, and that her fear and guilt over the consequences of her return to work are likely to be far worse than any real consequences.*
- ▶ *Don't let her emotions impact on her interaction with your child, and make sure what time they do have together is undisturbed and focused quality time.*
- ▶ *Communicate regularly about your expectations and roles. For example, she may like to retain some form of traditionally*

maternal input by preparing the week's meals. And you have a
right to expect that same appreciation and help outside work
hours that you'd hopefully offer if the roles were reversed.

▶ *Emphasize the reasons for your choice of roles, and the*
subsequent positives: for example, the huge advantage of her
being able to work without worrying about who's looking
after her child, and how proud your child will be of their
mother's professional achievements.

THE IMPACT ON YOUR CHILD

More than how it'll affect you and your partner, you might worry
about how your role as principal childcarer will impact on your
child.

▶ *Will they be treated differently by others?*
▶ *Will they lack a necessary female influence?*
▶ *Or will they have too much of a masculine influence?*
▶ *Will they miss out on socializing because you can't invite other*
children home without sounding like you're trying to chat up
their mothers?
▶ *Will they get confused and think they have two mums?*
▶ *Or will they be ridiculed over what Daddy does?*

I'm not one for stereotypes, but I did worry for a while that
Megan would turn into a total tomboy from hanging around
with me all day. But in fact, if anything, she's more into the
girly things than her friends.

Alex, father to Megan

Before you worry that your child's a sociological guinea pig,
remember that they won't have any expectations based on gender.
Regardless of whether you're a man or a woman, they'll simply
look to you for love and security.

And when it comes to gender influencing, studies suggest that
the traditional divide between men and women in parenting style
narrows as men adapt to the role of primary caregiver – in other

words, you're likely to intuitively expose your child to qualities that would traditionally have been perceived as maternal anyway.

Not only that, but the bond between a mother and her child is better able to withstand the sort of distance imposed by work than the bond between a father and his child. So not only will your child benefit from close contact with you, but your partner's influence will still remain equally strong.

TIME FOR YOURSELF

If you possibly can, try to keep a slice of life for yourself, even if it's just an hour each week to get out of the house and have a drink with friends. That time can be crucial in refreshing your perspective, allowing you to reclaim yourself and, if you lack a support network of other parents, reminding you what it's like to have an adult conversation.

And it might be possible to use that time to maintain a skill or even gain a new one, to bolster your CV for the future.

> *I used what little spare time I had to go around the neighbourhood fixing computers. It helped to keep my brain engaged, stopped me deskilling, and even earned me a little money, which I found important for my self-respect.*
>
> Nick, father to Katriona

FLY THE FLAG

Staying at home to care for your child can be a relentless experience, especially in the early days when you're unsure and your baby's relatively unresponsive. But as your confidence grows with their ability to talk and play, you really will find it one of the most rewarding jobs you'll ever have.

You are no less capable of caring for your child than your partner. In fact, you may even come to consider yourself better suited to the stay-at-home role: more willing to manage the odd jobs around the home, and more appropriately built for hefting shopping in one hand and a growing baby in the other.

And however much you feel victim to a grinding routine, the time will pass, and quickly. The day will soon come when you're sending your child off to school, leaving you to re-evaluate, perhaps take up work again. Until then, relish the rare opportunity to play such a pivotal role in your child's life, to watch them develop, to teach them and to establish a relationship that should last the rest of your days.

Insight

Never feel as a stay-at-home dad that you need to justify your worth. The importance of your role is paramount, and the world is slowly changing to recognize that. Fly the flag with pride.

For more information and advice, go to www.dadathome.co.uk or www.stayathomedads.co.uk.

When you're both out at work

Somehow we've got ourselves into a world where it's often necessary for both parents to hand their child over to the care of another before heading out to work. In such cases, life can be all the more of a juggling act, both logistically and emotionally.

▶ *Make the best care arrangements for your child that you possibly can.*
▶ *Try to shake off the guilt by acknowledging why you're both working, and why that's the best option for your family.*
▶ *Find someone you can trust who can pick your child up from care if you're running late – an otherwise enormous source of stress.*

- ▶ *Get organized – prepare your child's clothes the night before, be aware what food's left in the freezer, establish a routine for getting things done, etc.*
- ▶ *Communicate with your partner – even if it's just through lists scattered about the house – to identify looming issues, and know where you'll both be at any given time.*
- ▶ *Make the most of willing family and friends, but don't exploit them.*
- ▶ *Be flexible – however organized, there might still be times when you have to drop everything to take your child to the doctor.*
- ▶ *As much as possible, try to make your time with your child quality time, even if that means keeping the household chores until they're in bed. Otherwise you risk further guilt that even your non-working hours are tainted.*
- ▶ *Focus on the benefits of your arrangement – what the income brings to your family, for example, or the increased confidence your child will gain from being at nursery.*

For information on your employment rights as a father, go to www.fatherhoodinstitute.org/index.php?id=10&cID=386.

THE IMPACT ON YOUR CHILD

The main worry for parents forced to work is often whether or not their arrangement will in some way emotionally or psychologically damage their child.

The answer is that it depends largely on the quality of your child's relationship with their caregiver, so do all you can to find them a secure and loving carer.

Insight

If both you and your partner work, make sure the emphasis is on quality time with your child, focused and engaged, and that they feel loved and valued in a secure environment.

Working from home

Undoubtedly, there are enormous benefits to working from home. You get to share far more time with your child, and can often fit your hours around their needs.

But don't be under any illusion that it's an easy option. Being constantly available can be a real hindrance when it comes to getting anything done, so either be ruthless in excluding yourself or prepare for regular intrusions.

> *Alicia would call me through at least once every hour, either to help her with a messy nappy or just to admire something Miles was doing. I'm glad I was involved, of course, but at the same time it was incredibly frustrating.*
>
> Dan, father to Tricia and Miles

And while being self-employed allows even greater flexibility, there's no paid leave and you might find you're expected to be astoundingly progressive when it comes to taking time off. So communicate with your partner from the start and, while emphasizing the benefits of your presence, don't be afraid to gently impose boundaries.

Guilt

Modern parenting often seems to be based upon guilt, especially if you and your partner are both working: guilt over not being with your child, and guilt that perhaps work isn't receiving the same level of dedication as before.

And of course it's simplistic to state that, since such guilt serves no purpose, you should shrug it off and move on. But because parenting can be difficult enough without carrying any extra weight, that's exactly what you have to do, for your child's sake as well as your own. The alternative is to taint every minute and risk a spiral that, at its most extreme, can push parents to actually distance themselves from their children just to reduce the emotional burden.

Before you slide into the guilt trap, talk yourself onto more level ground by reminding yourself that:

▶ *You've got the best childcare possible.*
▶ *You're exploiting the benefits and flexibility of modern working to the full, from flexible hours to working from home.*
▶ *When you are together with your child, you're giving them 100 per cent attention.*
▶ *More important to your child than your constant presence is a sense of stability and love.*
▶ *The benefits of your arrangement – the very reason why you're both working – outweigh any alternatives.*

Insight

If both you and your partner are working, it may take a little more effort to achieve the home environment you want. But with organization and recognition of the benefits of compromise, it really can be possible to get the best of both worlds, to have a rewarding job and quality time with your child.

10 THINGS TO REMEMBER

1 *You'll have the rest of your life to work, but your child won't be a child forever – make sure you're doing all you can to give yourselves time together.*

2 *By choosing to prioritize family over work, you're teaching your child the importance of values beyond the financial.*

3 *Even when your working day has ended, you've still got an important job to do in supporting your partner and caring for your child.*

4 *If working, you'll likely feel unable to give of your best to either the home or the office, so don't be too hard on yourself.*

5 *Recognize that, if your partner's spending more time looking after your child, she's likely to have a better understanding of their needs.*

6 *If you're at work while your partner's dealing with the baby all day long, share the benefits of your greater perspective to keep worries in proportion.*

7 *Stay-at-home dads face specific challenges on top of the usual ones of caring for a child. If you're in this category, reach out and get involved with others.*

8 *Raising a child is one of the most important jobs anyone could have – if you're your child's principal carer, don't ever sell yourself short.*

9 *If you and your partner are both working, do all you can to find your child a loving carer who'll provide security and stability.*

10 *Recognize the benefits of whatever childcare arrangement you choose, and refuse to let guilt impact on your time with your child.*

12

Childcare and schooling

In this chapter you will learn:
- *what childcare options are available*
- *what you need to know at this stage about schools*
- *how to fulfil your vital role in your child's education*
- *how to deal with bullying.*

With expectations of maintaining a two-income standard of living and with fewer families living close by to benefit from grandparents' help, more and more parents are handing their children over to the care of another at a very early age.

There can be considerable benefits – the early years are important when it comes to the development of social skills, for example, and it can give you as parents a much-needed break besides the opportunity to work.

But it can also be an incredibly emotional time for everyone, as you wrestle with the guilt of abandonment, and your child settles into a new routine. And because of the weight of tradition leaning on her to stay at home, it may be an infinitely more difficult time for your partner than for you.

> *I had to organize a later start at work each day because Sarah couldn't bring herself to do the nursery drop-off. Of course, she was more than happy to 'rescue' Adam at the end of the day.*
>
> James, father to Adam

Insight

It can be very hard on you both to recognize that your child's principal adult relationship is with someone other than you or your partner. But if you've done your homework and ensured your child's individual needs, strengths and weaknesses are recognized by all involved, then rest assured you're likely to find the process far harder than your child.

What type of childcare is best?

If you're working, you'll need someone you can rely on every single working day, someone you feel will take care of your child as if they were taking care of their own.

Insight

Your aim should be to maintain as much consistency for your child as possible, in treatment, routine and environment. And generally speaking, the more control you have over those aspects of childcare, the more expensive it will be.

Your own circumstances and requirements may limit your choice considerably, but there are a number of issues worth bearing in mind:

- ▶ *What can you reasonably afford and what are the payment options? Bear in mind the impact of having to remove a child once settled because you have to move to a different area or can't afford the fees – which may rise with depressing frequency.*
- ▶ *How old will your child be when you need a carer?*
- ▶ *Where will your child be cared for? If not in your own home, is it within walking distance? Is it on the way to work?*
- ▶ *What experience does your child have of socializing or being in a strange environment?*
- ▶ *How many days per week will you need childcare? And will it be just mornings or afternoons, or all day?*

- *Is there a waiting list for your chosen carer?*
- *How willing are you to compromise when it comes to the ratio of childcarers to children?*
- *What range of ages will your carer be looking after alongside your child?*
- *How easy will it be to request supplemental hours when required?*
- *What experience does your childcarer have?*
- *If a group setting, what is the staff turnover?*
- *If appropriate, is your childcarer registered? This is not only a requirement for some funding sources, but also a guarantee of a formalized structure to the care.*
- *What flexibility is offered if you're late returning from work?*
- *What's the policy when it comes to family holidays or national holidays?*
- *What will happen when you, your child or the carer falls ill?*

The Daycare Trust, a national childcare charity, can provide details on childcare options and the latest childcare news. Go to www.daycaretrust.org.uk or call them on 0845 872 6251.

For information about the availability of childcare in your area and the facilities on offer, contact your local family information service via www.childcarelink.gov.uk, or by phoning 0800 234 6346.

Based in Northern Ireland, Employers for Childcare is a charity that helps working parents, and their website offers information and advice to all: www.employersforchildcare.org or call 0800 028 3008.

IN-HOME CARE

What's good
Because your child is being cared for in your own home, you can be confident that they're in a safe environment, and one in which they feel comfortable. You can also have greater control over how they're fed and cared for.

A nanny can also offer far greater attention to your child than a nursery or childminder, and is likely to be more flexible when it comes to your requirements. For example, if your child falls ill, a nanny should still be able to care for them.

With luck, there's the potential to gain a real asset to the family who may remain in touch as a friend long after the official employment has ended.

What's not
In-home care is expensive – you pay for the benefits it brings, especially as your arrangement may involve covering tax, sick and holiday pay and National Insurance. Investigate sharing the nanny with another family to make it more economical.

And inviting a stranger into your home – especially if they're living in – could further disrupt an already unsettled family dynamic. Perhaps the last thing you'll want when you get in from work is to be sharing your home with an outsider. Alternatively, when you're under pressure and perhaps starved for sex, an attractive younger woman under your roof might be something you're at risk of wanting a little *too* much.

If you do decide to get a nanny, interview thoroughly and check all references, and consider drawing up a contract. Be clear from the start about expectations, and remember that a nanny has a life too.

For more about in-home care, including some suggestions for interview questions, contact the National Childminding Association on 0845 880 0044 or go to www.ncma.org.uk/nannies.aspx.

A CHILDMINDER

What's good
Childminders should be registered with their local authority and licensed to take children into their own home during the day. Cheaper than a nursery or nanny, they give your child the chance to mix with

a small number of other children in a homely environment, and can be more flexible than a nursery.

What's not
Because they're looking after a number of other children of differing ages, yours won't receive one-on-one care. Also, if one child has to be collected from school or dropped off elsewhere, everyone else has to be dragged along too.

Agree on a contract before you start. For more about choosing a childminder, go to www.ncma.org.uk/for_parents/choosing_a_childminder.aspx.

A DAY NURSERY

What's good
Many day nurseries operate all year round for a variety of ages, though some are open during school term time only, and often just for a morning or afternoon.

A nursery will allow your child to socialize with others of the same age in a carefully monitored environment. It can also offer the reassurance of a recognized curriculum designed to cover every aspect of your child's development. And, being more formal, the structured play can be a good preparation for preschool.

> *It was a bit tough at first, but since Dylan settled into nursery, his confidence has really grown. Now he loves it – he runs straight in without saying goodbye.*
>
> Len, father to Dylan

What's not
But because your child will only be one of many, they'll inevitably receive less attention, a fact that will only exacerbate your worries about leaving them. Another consequence of the greater numbers is a lack of flexibility – they'll likely charge if you're late for pick-up, for example – and if your child's ill, you'll be asked to keep them at home.

And because babies require more attention, some nurseries will only take them over a certain age – often two to three months – at which point the fees are higher than for older children.

> *We signed Freya up to three days a week, one of which was a Monday, completely forgetting about Bank Holidays. So we ended up paying for quite a few days when the nursery was closed.*
>
> Justin, father to Freya

For security reasons, it can be difficult to make an informal visit, but try to arrange a tour and be there to watch when children are dropped off – their reactions to being left can tell you a lot.

Try to get an idea of the prevailing atmosphere, the level of supervision and the range of activities and facilities and, ultimately, trust your own instinct.

You can search for a registered nursery near you at www.ndna.org.uk/parents, and the National Day Nurseries Association offers information as well as a factsheet for those considering a nursery: www.ndna.org.uk/parents/choosing-nursery.

For more information or to read the latest inspection reports, in England go to www.ofsted.gov.uk.

In Wales, go to the Care and Social Services Inspectorate Wales: www.csiw.wales.gov.uk/dataviewer/index.asp.

In Scotland, contact your local Childcare Information Service (ChIS), accessible through Scottish Childcare at www.scottishchildcare.gov.uk.

In Northern Ireland, go to www.nicma.org.

Different nurseries
Depending on location, you may not have any choice of nursery – not that choice is always a good thing.

Even at this stage, it feels like there's pressure to get
Zac into the right nursery, because that feeds the right
preschool which in turn feeds the right primary, then the
best secondary, which will – of course! – lead to a first class
honours degree at a venerable university and the highest
paid job. And he's not yet out of nappies!

Ross, father to Zac

As if location, price, availability and the question of feeding the right preschool weren't enough to worry about, there are different philosophies of nursery too.

MONTESSORI
Montessori aims to allow children to explore the world as they want and at their own pace, learning through interaction with specially chosen and placed items and equipment.

For more information, contact the Montessori Saint Nicholas Charity on 020 7493 8300 or go to www.montessori.org.uk.

STEINER
Steiner schools place great value on creativity, imagination and individuality. Teaching is by example rather than instructive, and abstract skills like reading and writing are introduced only once more social, emotional and physical skills have been mastered.

For more, contact the Steiner Waldorf Schools Fellowship on 01342 822 115, or go to www.steinerwaldorf.org.uk.

MAINSTREAM
These nurseries adopt the Government's formal statutory requirements introduced to ensure that all children receive a similar level of education by the time they start school.

A key principle of this approach is that children need a balance of adult-directed and child-initiated activities. For more on the Early Years Foundation Stage Curriculum, go to www.dcsf.gov.uk/everychildmatters/earlyyears/localauthorities/earlyyearsfoundationstage/efys.

FAMILY AND FRIENDS

What's good
The majority of parents rely on at least one grandparent at some stage to help out with the childcare, and for good reason. Not only will they be unlikely to charge you for their help, but you can trust them to have your child's best interests in mind. If you and your partner have to work, it can be of incomparable comfort to know your child is being cared for by someone who loves them almost as much as you do yourself.

Your own parents are also likely to share a similar childrearing approach and similar values – the very ones you'll want instilled in your child. They're also far more likely to be flexible when it comes to late pick-ups or changes to routine – another immensely valuable quality.

In addition, every minute your child spends with a grandparent is an investment towards their future relationship for life – not something you can always say of a nanny, childminder or member of nursery staff.

What's not
Although the benefits are many, relying on your own parents to care for your child can have its own unique drawbacks. Because you'll assume a certain amount of love and willingness, it can be easy to take their help for granted.

And when a problem does arise over one of the many aspects of caring for a child – and it's unlikely you'll agree on everything – it can be all the harder to address, not only because you're not paying them to take instruction, but because it's difficult to criticize your own parents, no matter how well-intended you both may be.

In such instances, discuss your approach beforehand with your partner, and communicate with diplomacy. And take every opportunity to voice and show your appreciation.

Without my in-laws, we just couldn't survive the way we do. Their support makes all the difference to my family.

Alex, father to Megan

See Chapter 3 for more on the role of grandparents.

Handing over your child

▶ *If possible, gradually build up the time that you and your child are apart, to settle them into any changes slowly.*

▶ *If they're old enough to understand, communicate with your child to prepare them, and return when you say you're going to return – a background of trust makes separation easier.*

▶ *Be aware how much your child can pick up from your anxiety – however emotional you are about leaving your child, don't share it with them.*

Schools

Though this book isn't intended to cover the school years, it pays to be prepared, so here's a brief outline of what you should know at this stage.

CHOOSING

The theory is that you have a right to choose which school your child goes to. In reality, for parents in rural areas, that choice is often limited to the one local school or a life in the car while, for those in busier areas where competition is fierce, exercising that right can be stressful and often frustrating.

And for those willing and able to go so far as to move home in order to exploit the catchment area rule – whereby children are given priority according to their proximity to a school – ensuring your child gets into your school of choice can also be very expensive.

Insight

It's only natural that you'll want the best for your child, and few things are more important than education. To avoid a panic, find out all you can about your local schools as early as possible.

To view inspection reports of schools in England, go to www.ofsted.gov.uk.

In Wales, go to www.estyn.gov.uk.

In Northern Ireland: www.denidata.nics.gov.uk/appInspRptsSearch/IRMain.aspx.

And in Scotland go to www.hmie.gov.uk.

For the Government's overview of schools and your child's learning, go to www.direct.gov.uk/en/Parents/Schoolslearninganddevelopment/index.htm.

Alternatively, for an independent outline of the many issues and choices, as well as parent reviews, try the Good Schools Guide at www.goodschoolsguide.co.uk. Access to some content requires subscription.

APPLYING

Once you feel you're ready to make an informed choice, check out your chosen school's application criteria, and ensure you meet the relevant deadline, often around the autumn term a year before your child's due to start.

For more on the application process, go to www.direct.gov.uk/en/Parents/Schoolslearninganddevelopment/ChoosingASchool/DG_4016369.

If your child's application is unsuccessful, it is possible to appeal: www.direct.gov.uk/en/Parents/Schoolslearninganddevelopment/ChoosingASchool/DG_4016309.

If your child isn't offered a place in your school of choice:

- *ensure their name stays on the waiting list*
- *keep in contact*
- *listen out for local authority policy changes when it comes to issues such as class sizes, siblings already in the school, and catchment area boundaries.*

GETTING INVOLVED

If, despite an appeal, your child still fails to gain the place you're after, it might be worth redirecting your efforts towards supporting and improving the school where your child ends up.

This needn't be mere consolation – one quarter of a school's governing body is made up of volunteer parent governors, there to represent parent interests. It's a key role, playing a critical part in maintaining and raising school standards and making a genuine contribution to not just your own child's education, but that of many others as well.

For more information, look at www.governornet.co.uk/publishArticle.cfm?&topicAreaId=2&contentId=254&pageStart=1&sortOrder=c.title.

PRIVATE SCHOOLING

One alternative to state schooling – especially if you're considering paying a property premium to move within a popular catchment area – is to put that money towards a private education instead.

> **Insight**
> Currently, 7 per cent of British children attend private – or independent – schools. And despite the notoriously high cost, competition can still be tight.

Common advice is to sign your child up as soon as you can for every school you're interested in – easy enough assuming you're happy to lose the many hefty non-refundable deposits necessary to secure just a place on a waiting list.

> *Dylan was three months old when I called up a local prep school to ask about a place for him when he was three. The secretary literally laughed at me, said I was far too late.*
>
> Len, father to Dylan

Obviously the cost of an independent education is a crucial factor: the latest survey found that the average cost is more than £12,000 per year. However, around one third of independent school pupils receive some form of financial assistance.

For more information on private schools, from inspection reports to details of open days, scholarships and bursaries, view the website of the Independent Schools Council at www.isc.co.uk.

Home education

As another option, you have a legal right to educate your child at home, without requiring any special qualifications or following a particular curriculum.

For more information on homeschooling in England and Wales, try www.home-education.org.uk. In Scotland, go to www.schoolhouse.org.uk, and in Northern Ireland try www.hedni.org.

Your role in your child's education

Even when your child is being educated or cared for by another, you still have an important support role to play that goes beyond the occasional glue-based activity or tricky piece of homework.

AUTHORITY AND RESPECT

In handing your child over to another, you're handing over some of your responsibility as a parent. And that responsibility is near impossible to meet without some of the same authority you hold as a parent.

We learn most from those we respect. So to support your child's development and education, you have to help foster and reinforce respect for their carers and teachers, avoiding any words or actions that risk undermining their authority.

KNOWLEDGE AND VALUES

> **Insight**
>
> While you can expect your child's teachers to dispense sufficient knowledge to allow your child to pass exams, don't rely on those teachers to do your job of instilling values.

Values are best learnt through example, so you and your partner are best placed to teach them, by sharing your values directly and communicating them through your actions. Without the opportunity to witness by your own demonstration the worth of your own values, it would hardly be surprising if they come to ignore – or even reject – those values themselves.

PRAISE AND CRITICISM

Your response towards your child's efforts to learn can have an enormous impact on their attitude towards education. Praise effort, avoid negative criticism and, when required, suggest alternative approaches to encourage them to develop self-motivation and be energized rather than overwhelmed in the face of difficulty.

For more on this, see Chapter 9.

Bullying

There can be few things more heartbreaking or likely to arouse anger than the realization that your child is being picked on or excluded, especially as, at this young age, they may lack the means to address the problem themselves.

If you suspect that your child is being bullied, discuss the issue with the adults in charge in as non-confrontational a manner as possible. Similarly, if you're concerned that your child is bullying others, it's important to address the problem early on.

For information and advice about all aspects of bullying, see the website of the national anti-bullying charity, Bullying UK: www.bullying.co.uk.

10 THINGS TO REMEMBER

1 *If you're forced to rely on childcare because you're both at work, recognize that – because of the traditional expectations according to which women stay home with the baby – it's likely to be a far more difficult, emotional time for your partner than for you.*

2 *Whatever form of childcare you choose, aim for consistency.*

3 *In general terms, the more attention you want your child to receive and the more flexibility you require, the more you can expect to pay.*

4 *Investigate your entitlements and options, from free early learning to childcare vouchers.*

5 *The person looking after your child will have an enormous influence on them, so do your homework and choose carefully.*

6 *The benefits of involving grandparents in the childcare are enormous, but discuss clear guidelines from the start to manage expectations – yours and theirs.*

7 *Introduce childcare gradually to give your child plenty of time to get used to it.*

8 *If you have any concerns over which school your child may attend, do your homework and start your investigations as early as possible.*

9 *Whatever form of education you choose for your child, remember they'll still learn more from you than from anyone else.*

10 *Give your child's teachers the respect they deserve, as befits the importance of their role.*

13

Relationship difficulties

In this chapter you will learn:
- *how to minimize the impact of relationship difficulties on your child*
- *how to put your child first if your relationship breaks down*
- *how to father from a distance*
- *how to cope with single fatherhood and stepfatherhood.*

Relationships can be demanding, even at the best of times. But with the additional pressures of a baby or young child – the fatigue and stress, the shifting dynamics and the lack of quality time to reaffirm the positives – it's perhaps no surprise that a large number of them break down entirely.

Insight

Unfortunately, all too often, it's a child's relationship with their father that pays the price – one in three children whose parents have divorced or separated over the last 20 years have lost contact permanently with their father.

The impact of such a separation on the child can be enormous. Surveys link a lack of domestic stability to an increased likelihood of a child turning to drink, drugs or crime, while almost a tenth of children from broken families are left suicidal.

Weathering the storm

No relationship is without some level of conflict. But if you as parents – and so responsible for more than just yourselves – find yourselves stuck in a destructive cycle, you've a duty to do all you can to break free of it. Identify the problems, and deal with them. And if you can't do it alone, get help.

For relationship counselling, try Relate at www.relate.org.uk or call 0300 100 123.

If your time as a family is suffering from a need to be at work in order to meet increased costs, Chapters 11 and 12 look at ways to reprioritize your life, whether through flexible working or reassessing your lifestyle expectations.

As parents, you should be prepared to do whatever it takes to provide your child with a loving and stable home to share with you both.

Of course, there may be circumstances in which you and your partner can best serve your child's interests by separating. But before you make a decision that will impact on their life forever, be sure that you've exhausted all other alternatives and that separation is a last resort.

> *We didn't get counselling until after we'd agreed to split up, but even then it helped us manage the process as amicably as possible. The counsellor really helped us focus on the relevant issues and consequences.*
>
> Will, father to Amélie

Insight

If you have to separate, do all you can to ensure you remain on good terms with the mother of your child. The more acrimonious your separation, the more drawn out, expensive and traumatic it's likely to be, and the greater impact it will have on the rest of your life – and your child's.

The impact on your child

Even the youngest of children will notice that one parent is no longer around as frequently as before. And the more aware they become, the more chance that their world will be turned upside down – and all through no fault of their own.

Children able to recognize what's going on may feel anything from denial or bewilderment to anger, shame or fear. Almost certainly they'll feel guilty, considering themselves in some way to blame for the break-up. And even if too young to vocalize their emotions, they'll likely express them in other ways, through anything from a stress-related illness to increased separation anxiety.

Whatever the reason for your separation and however tough you're finding it, both you and your partner owe it to your child to make them a priority. That might mean getting a grip on your own emotions as well, so don't be ashamed to seek professional help if necessary.

Insight

Above all, whatever additional pressures parenthood has brought, don't for an instant blame your child for the breakdown in your relationship. As adults, the responsibility lies with you and your partner – your child is an innocent victim.

For more about how to limit the impact on your children, go to www.resolution.org.uk/landing-three-cols.asp?page_id=179.

DON'T

▶ *Don't put your child in a position of having to take sides, for example by asking them who they want to live with.*
▶ *Don't use them to gather information on your partner, or ask them to act as confidant or ally – your child has a right to remain a child.*

- ▶ *Don't ever make them feel guilty about loving their mother, or effect petty sabotage of their relationship.*
- ▶ *Don't let them witness arguments with your partner, or hear you badmouthing her – even two-year-olds have ears.*
- ▶ *Don't give up on your relationship with your child, however hard it may seem.*

DO

- ▶ *Reassure your child every chance you get that, for all the upheaval, your love for them is constant.*
- ▶ *Answer any anger with demonstrations of love.*
- ▶ *Continue to provide for them.*
- ▶ *Identify the wide range of emotions they'll be feeling and look at ways to help them cope. If your child's too young to talk about it, get them to express their feelings in other ways, for example by drawing.*
- ▶ *Identify their needs, and discuss with their mother how best to meet them, from day-to-day responsibility and maintaining their standard of living to agreeing access and the important aspects of their upbringing.*
- ▶ *Reassure your child that they're not to blame.*
- ▶ *Maintain your connections with the wider family, not only to reassure them, but also to retain that element of stability in your child's life.*
- ▶ *Encourage contact with their mother, and continue to support her role and authority.*
- ▶ *Allow everyone involved – including yourself – time to adjust.*
- ▶ *Always communicate with your child.*

COMMUNICATE

A child's sense of security is shattered by the separation of their parents – to rebuild it, you need to regain and maintain their trust. That means treating them with honesty and, as far as they're aware, talking openly about what's happening and what's going to happen.

Sit down with your partner to explain the situation to your child
together. Be prepared not just for the awkward questions, but
also the more practical ones relating to the logistics of multiple
homes, such as where they'll sleep and keep their toys, and who'll
feed the dog.

Share your own feelings, ask them for their thoughts, listen to –
and look at – how they express themselves, and take every
opportunity to reinforce your love for them again and again.

As far as possible, keep all other aspects of their life unchanged.
Resettling them to be nearer to grandparents or any similar,
well-intentioned reaction may actually only steal from them the
last flotsam of stability.

For a guide from the Children and Family Court Advisory Support
Service on putting your children first, go to www.cafcass.gov.uk/
PDF/FINAL%20web%20version%20251108.pdf.

For a guide from the Department of Children, Schools and Families
about the impact of separation on your child, and for advice on
where to find support, go to http://publications.dcsf.gov.uk/default
.aspx?PageFunction=productdetails&PageMode=publications&
ProductId=DCSF-01051-2008&.

Child Support

Chapter 6 looks at whether or not you as your child's father have
parental responsibility. Either way, it's important to recognize that

parental responsibility is quite separate from your duty to provide for your child. Married or not, with parental responsibility or not, you're still legally obliged to pay maintenance to support your child.

For more information, go to the website of the Child Support Agency at www.csa.gov.uk.

Ending an unmarried relationship

If you and your partner are unmarried and separating, the best you can do is draw up what's called a separation agreement – a written document clarifying and confirming your agreement over various aspects of your child's future, from where they'll live to who'll pay for their maintenance. Without this voluntary agreement, you face the prospect of having to abide by a court's decision.

It's not necessary to involve a solicitor to draw up a separation agreement but, given the long-term implications for everyone, it's wise to get professional help, especially as that will help a court uphold the terms of the agreement should communication between you and your partner break down in the future.

For more information, go to www.adviceguide.org.uk/index/ f_ending_a_relationship_unmarried_couples.pdf.

Divorce

It's possible to informally end a marriage without ever going to court, in which case a similar separation agreement is recommended to that mentioned above. But if either of you want the separation to be formally recognized – for example, if one of you wishes to remarry – you'll have to apply to the courts for a divorce.

In such cases, the marriage – and the reasons for its breakdown – must meet certain criteria. Given that an amicable resolution is of paramount importance to your child's future, the best you can aim for is what's called an undefended divorce. This is when both parties agree to it, you've been separated for at least two years, and the court approves the arrangements made for your child.

For more on the process of divorce, go to www.direct.gov.uk/en/Parents/FamilyIssuesAndTheLaw/DG_4002976.

ARRANGEMENTS FOR THE CHILDREN

Before granting a divorce, defended or not, a court must be satisfied that you and your wife have made suitable arrangements for your child. This should be documented with the help of an experienced solicitor and include your plans for where they'll live, how they'll have contact with the other parent, and how they'll be provided for financially.

Remember, the court's fundamental priority should match yours – the best interests of your child – and will only intervene if you and your wife can't agree.

The specifics of divorce vary around the UK so, for details relevant to you, go to the Adviceguide website of the Citizens Advice Bureau at www.adviceguide.org.uk/index.htm and click on the relevant country.

ONE OPTION WORTH CONSIDERING

Other than in cases of adultery or unreasonable behaviour, a requirement of even an undefended divorce is that you and your wife be separated for at least two years. But if your principal aim is to minimize the impact of the break-up on your child, there's one option available that does just that while also allowing you to begin the process of separation.

Legally, as long as you each manage your own domestic chores and don't continue to eat or sleep together, it's possible to be officially separated while still continuing to share the family home. A signed deed of separation will start the clock ticking on the mandatory two-year period, yet still leave the door open to a future that causes minimum disruption to your child.

> *It's not easy at such an emotional time to keep a logical, calculating head. But it can make all the difference to everyone's future.*
>
> Jamie, father to Caitlin, stepfather to Florence and Rebecca

---

Ending a civil partnership

The process by which you bring about a formal end to a civil partnership is slightly different from that of a divorce.

For more information about ending a civil partnership, and for help filling in the necessary forms, contact your local Citizens Advice Bureau through their website at www.citizensadvice.org.uk.

A solicitor's role in your separation

Whether married or not, if you and your partner are separating, the chances are that solicitors will be involved at some point, simply by virtue of you being parents.

However, the more you can both agree voluntarily before legal professionals are involved, the less your separation will cost, and the sounder basis you'll have for a future relationship that continues to put your children first. After all, it's a solicitor's job to fight your corner, perhaps in an adversarial manner best avoided.

That said, before agreeing to any major changes to your family situation – for example, before leaving the matrimonial home – always get specialist professional advice on the possible implications.

For advice and help finding a solicitor in England and Wales, go to www.resolution.org.uk.

In Scotland, go to www.familylawassociation.org.

In Northern Ireland, go to www.nilsc.org.uk.

Mediation

Mediation is a confidential and impartial service for both married and unmarried couples, with the aim of helping everyone involved achieve an amicable end to the relationship. One or two trained workers will sit with you both and guide the discussion through the practical issues, giving priority to the welfare of your child.

Although still costly, mediators are cheaper than solicitors, and you may qualify for Legal Aid to meet their fees.

However, since a mediator can't advise on legal issues, it might also be worth running any agreements reached past a solicitor, especially if you or your partner are considering making the agreement legally binding.

In England or Wales, call the Family Mediation Helpline on 0845 6026 627, or go to www.familymediationhelpline.co.uk.

In Scotland, go to Relationships Scotland at www.relationships-scotland.org.uk or call 0845 119 2020.

In Northern Ireland, go to www.familymediationni.org.uk.

Help with the cost of separation

Even the most amicable of divorces costs money. And the drawing up of an agreement of separation, strongly recommended whether you're married or not, will likely involve solicitor's fees.

If you're on a low income, you may be able to get help with the legal costs.

In England or Wales, go to www.legalservices.gov.uk.

In Scotland: www.slab.org.uk.

In Northern Ireland: www.nilsc.org.uk.

For more about help with legal costs, go to www.adviceguide.org.uk/index/your_rights/legal_system/help_with_legal_costs.htm.

Informing the authorities

Whether married or not, if you and your partner separate, you have a legal responsibility to notify various parties, from your local council to your local benefits office if you're receiving any welfare payments.

For advice on who to notify, contact your local Citizens Advice Bureau at www.adviceguide.org.uk.

For information on how your new situation might affect your tax credits, go to www.hmrc.gov.uk/taxcredits/keep-up-to-date/changes-affect/family-change/partner-change.htm.

The mother of your child

Insight

One of the greatest influences on how your child copes with your separation will be how well you and your partner get along afterwards.

Whatever happens, she'll always be the mother of your child, crucial not just to them, but also to how easy it is for you to be involved in your child's future. If only for that reason, you need to make your continuing relationship with your partner a priority, and limit the damage as far as possible.

As soon as you can, agree not to allow emotions to rush you into an acrimonious separation – the result will only be worse for everyone. Instead, focus on that vital area of common ground – your child's needs, from the practical to the financial. And if you can't talk face-to-face, find another way to communicate that works.

After the separation, remember her vital role in your child's life, and show her appropriate respect. Support rather than undermine her – even defend her if necessary. And if there really is a serious problem, talk to her about it, not to your child, with an aim of resolving all conflicts as early as possible.

Be fair with her, and respectful of her time with your child, just as you'd wish her to be of yours. That means keeping your appointments, and being clear what commitments you've made. The more you communicate, the more you'll both give your child the structure and consistency they need.

Communication is perhaps all the more important if you begin a relationship with someone new. In such a case, it's diplomatic to at least attempt to discuss the situation with your child's mother, perhaps even write a letter outlining your approach. For example, she'll be reassured to hear that your child will always take priority, that you'll continue to reinforce her importance, that your child won't be subjected to a string of one-night stands, and that your child's feelings towards your new partner will be respected.

> *Strange though it sounds, when I started seeing more of Sam and her kids, I made sure my ex-wife was quite closely informed. I wanted her to be comfortable with the impact of any new arrangements on Jenny.*
>
> Florian, father to Jenny, stepfather to Julia and Brendan

Insight
Be flexible – separation is a process, not an event. Don't expect instant and satisfactory change from all involved.

For more on the importance of your relationship with your child's mother, go to www.dad.info/separation/making-it-work/communicating-with-your-childs-mother.

Fathering from a distance

Insight
Studies reiterate again and again the importance of a father's influence – children growing up in fatherless homes are far more likely to struggle through life with poor self-esteem, poorer academic achievement and an increased likelihood of involvement in drugs and crime.

Your role in your child's life is vital. So if you find yourself fathering from afar, it's all the more important that you seize every opportunity to be involved – especially if you and your child's mother are estranged, in which case the odds are depressingly high that you'll lose all contact entirely.

My main priority is to be actively involved in Josh's life in any way I can. Because as much as I miss him, I know he misses me more.

Pete, father to Joshua

The isolation that can result from being apart from your child can be difficult to deal with, so allow yourself time to adjust and, if necessary, get professional help.

For advice and support, try Families Need Fathers on 0300 0300 363, or go to www.fnf.org.uk.

Alternatively, look at www.separateddads.co.uk.

SHARED PARENTING

If circumstances allow, it might be possible to come to an arrangement where your child splits their time between you and their mother. In comparison to a full custody and visiting rights arrangement, the advantages are numerous and the situation beneficial for all.

For more information about shared parenting, go to www.spig.clara.net.

WHEN YOU'RE WITH YOUR CHILD

- ▶ *Be consistent with your visits – short and regular is better than lengthy but infrequent.*
- ▶ *Let your child know what to expect of your time together and time apart, and maintain their trust by keeping to arrangements.*
- ▶ *Leave any negative emotions resulting from your broken relationship at the door.*
- ▶ *Give your child undivided attention and allow them the opportunity to express their feelings – but don't force it.*

- Engage with their interests and their everyday world – even if just by going to places they like to go, from the park to their bedroom.
- Introduce a structure to your time together – with consistency comes stability.
- Don't try to make up for lost time by overdoing it, for example, with extravagant presents or lax discipline. You still have to enforce the old boundaries and be a parent.
- Make it clear whenever possible that you'd rather be with them.
- Accept that perhaps you'll have to focus on quality fathering rather than quantity.
- However distant, you are still your child's principal male role model. In all your contact, be the person you'd want them to be.

WHEN YOU'RE APART

- Do whatever it takes to prove your determination to be involved in your child's life.
- If the option exists, cut back on work to see more of your child. You may bring home less money, but the time spent together is an investment as well.
- Remove any excuse for your partner to limit your time with your child, for example, by keeping your home clean and ready for their visits.
- Maintain contact with the other adults in your child's life, from nursery staff to grandparents.
- If necessary, get professional advice, especially before agreeing to any significant change to the status quo.
- Maintain regular contact with your child as much as possible. With all the options available, there's no excuse for losing touch.

Phone calls

If at this young age conversation is a problem or you risk competing for attention, try to set up a routine. Schedule the calls with your ex, and do more than just talk to your child – watch a programme together or share some other activity. And as soon as they're able to use a phone, make sure your number's on speed dial and they know they can call you at any time.

Letters
Even if your child can't read, they'll still love receiving pictures and other reminders through the post. If your relationship allows, ask your ex to read out what you write, from accounts of your day to short stories. And enclose a stamped addressed envelope – that way you'll encourage your partner to help your child respond.

> *Every few weeks, I record and post a new CD of me reading a bedtime story. Emily loves it, and I like the idea that she falls asleep listening to my voice.*
>
> Rick, father to Emily

Email
With the right equipment, you can send not just emails, but sound recordings and video footage. You and your child can even see each other as you chat, with free services like Skype (www.skype.com). And it's ever easier for even relative technophobes to set up their own websites for their children to visit.

Insight
At this young age, don't expect too much in return, but know that you're laying the foundations for future reciprocal communication.

In sight, in mind
As well as communicating directly, there are other ways to play a role in your child's life while you're apart, especially if you're prepared to get creative – print up photos of yourself onto T-shirts and placemats, spray your aftershave onto an item of clothing for them to keep and then wear it when you're together, create a display in their room of activities you enjoy doing together, and so on.

For more on staying in touch at a distance, go to www.divorceinfo .com/kidsacrossmiles.htm.

Single fatherhood

Whatever the reason for you parenting alone, you have an enormously difficult role to play, dealing not only with the emotions of your circumstance but also the everyday issues of raising a child alone.

On top of that, you may have to deal with society's too frequent suspicion that, as a man, you're incapable of caring for your child by yourself (see Chapter 11 for more about being your child's main carer).

Communicate with your children by discussing your feelings and allowing them to talk about their fears. Be open and honest about the changes required to make a new life – you'll likely be surprised by their adaptability and resourcefulness.

REPRIORITIZE

If you find yourself as your child's only remaining parent, you face a tough decision, and one that should be based upon how you can do the best for your child. Is that by turning with confidence to a professional world you know well so as to pay another to care for your child? Or by stepping back from your career to be more directly involved yourself? Or would the best be a mixture of the two?

> *After Siobhan died, I instinctively felt I should be around more. But staying at home with Lizzie and Jem left me so isolated, I soon began to struggle. Now I'm confident that I can give them my best through being back at work.*
>
> Hugh, father to Lizzie and Jem

However you choose to handle the situation, in order to give your child the time with you that they'll need, you'll inevitably have to reshape areas of your life. And because yours is the only parental time your child receives, it's important to engage fully on those occasions you are together.

Insight

Don't feel that, because your child lacks a mother, you have to adopt that role as well. It might be that you'll instinctively assume some of the traditionally maternal qualities without even knowing it. Either way, parent as you feel comfortable – be yourself, and do what you do best.

SUPPORT

If you're finding your circumstances overwhelming, it's imperative that you take control of the situation before your involvement with your child ceases to be anything other than positive.

Stave off isolation by reaching out and getting involved with others in a similar position. Try www.lone-parents.org.uk, or contact your local Family Information Service for details of support and activities in your area, either by calling 0800 234 6346, or going to the Sure Start Childcare website at www.childcarelink.gov.uk.

Gingerbread, the national charity for single parents, also offers a wealth of advice and support. You can contact them for free on 0808 802 0925, or go to www.gingerbread.org.uk.

Alternatively, try the Single Parent Action Network at www.spanuk .org.uk, or www.onespace.org.uk.

Financial help

Take up whatever financial help is available towards childcare costs (Chapter 10), and get advice on topping up your salary.

If you're a widower, you may be eligible for additional financial assistance: www.direct.gov.uk/en/Governmentcitizensandrights/ Death/WhatToDoAfterADeath/DG_066810.

Your family

However young your child, don't overlook their role in pulling your family through. Often what makes life challenging – juggling the role of two parents and perhaps holding down a job as well – can be what ultimately provides a sense of stability and improvement.

> *We're definitely a team. I might be in control – most of the time! – but my kids are partners and increasingly play their part.*
>
> Shal, father to Alim and Mazhar

Take time to remind yourself what it is you're struggling for. Your child can help, often in practical ways as well as simply boosting morale.

Stepfatherhood

If you've been lucky enough to establish a new relationship with someone who has children of her own, it can be notoriously tricky to integrate the two families, and a never-ending exercise in diplomacy.

While differing ages and characters dictate different approaches, there are a few generalizations to bear in mind.

As much as they're able to understand the situation, your stepchildren are likely to feel a range of emotions, from guilt and fear to jealousy and grief. But as the adult in the relationship, it's your role to act like one – ignore any hostility, and control your own emotions and preferences.

Insight
Whatever your personal feelings, your ultimate aim – when your relationship has developed sufficiently to allow it – should be to show total equality between your own child and your stepchildren.

> *While I've always tried to act like a father to my stepchildren, they call me 'Uncle', rather than 'Dad', and I think that's*

important. I'd hate my biological children to resent another child trespassing on their territory.

Jeremy, father to Evie and Dan, stepfather to Pete and Trish

MEETING YOUR NEW PARTNER'S CHILDREN

▶ *The more you know in advance about your partner's children, the better you'll be able to relate to them, even if that just means swatting up on their favourite television show.*

▶ *Remember that few children meeting their stepfather for the first time will share your goal of a happy new family. So expect to be tested, and respond with consistency.*

▶ *Don't try to buy popularity, or act like their father no longer exists. Just take your cue from them and be yourself, treating them with the same respect and affection you show your own child.*

▶ *Children are amazingly adaptive, but they need stability and they need to trust you, both of which require time.*

It's a tightrope between trying to guide them and play a paternal role, while not looking like you're trying to replace their real dad.

Paul, father to Yvonne, stepfather to Rob and Kyle

INTRODUCING YOUR CHILD TO YOUR NEW PARTNER

In this scenario, all the above applies, though in reverse. What's more, with your ability to better read your own child's reactions, you should be prepared to guide the pace of their relationship with your new partner.

INTRODUCING YOUR CHILD TO HER CHILDREN

▶ *Choose a neutral area, ideally somewhere familiar – though be wary about hijacking places that might normally be exclusive to just you and your child.*

- ▶ Keep initial meetings short but regular, based around an activity that gets them playing alongside each other naturally, without the pressure of anything too structured – the aim is to keep it relaxed and simple, an enjoyable time that ends too soon rather than an over-ambitious outing that stretches everyone.
- ▶ Do what you can afterwards to reassure your own child of their place in your affections, with some quality one-on-one time. Having lost the stability of their own home, they may well fear losing you to others.
- ▶ Be realistic about your expectations – you can't force everyone to like each other, and perhaps they never will. All you can do is encourage the possibility, and allow things to develop at their own pace.
- ▶ As time goes by, don't beat yourself up if you feel unable to love your stepchildren as you do your own. It's not uncommon to have favourites, even amongst biological children. The important thing is never to show it, or give one cause to feel jealous of the other.

White lies can be useful in planting the seeds of their relationship. For example, I'd casually mention how I'd heard my stepson complimenting my daughter, or vice versa. Children remember these things – it helps to overcome the natural jealousies that always exist.

David, father to Wilf and Ursula, stepfather to Nicholas

LIVING WITH YOUR STEPCHILDREN

- ▶ Whether or not you're moving into your partner's home, you have to respect the fact that you're merging with another family dynamic. That means being tolerant, and not forcing change in the name of a fresh start.
- ▶ Leave your partner to discipline her own children until you can confidently say you've gained their acceptance.
- ▶ Show consistency – not just between your own child and hers, but also between your home and that of any other parent involved in the children's care. Wherever possible, discuss issues beforehand with all involved adults.

- *Whether you're divorced, separated or widowed, your child and hers will be grieving the loss of the stability they knew before. Accept that, and accept that their grief may be expressed in challenging behaviour.*
- *If possible, encourage easy access for all children to the other parent, supporting their involvement in their children's lives.*
- *Establish routines or rituals to foster a sense of cohesion.*
- *Spend as much time together as possible, but take it slowly. Accept them for who they are, and show them the same respect you'd expect in return.*
- *If their age allows, discuss the situation openly, acknowledging that you're not their father but that you want to do your best for them.*
- *Without flaunting the physical aspects, remember that the quality of your relationship with your new partner is important to them. After the separation of their parents, they need to feel secure.*
- *Even once you've established a good relationship with your stepchildren, never take it for granted – it will always need to be treated with sensitivity.*

Insight

As stepfather, you're not the main parent. You begin as your partner's supporter, and grow over time only as you win her children's respect and earn equality of responsibility.

For more information and support, see the website of Care for the Family at www.careforthefamily.org.uk/stepfamily.

Alternatively, contact Parentline Plus on 0808 800 2222 (www.parentlineplus.org.uk) for confidential advice on step-parenting.

Moving forward

It's too easy to let the past taint the present – especially when you're reminded of it every day. But whoever's to blame for your current situation, you have to do your best – for the sake of your child's future – to leave negative emotions in the past. However you've arrived where you are, you still share responsibility for their happiness and wellbeing.

So hold fast to the positives – whether it's your increased confidence and the tighter bond that results from being more involved with your child's care, or the benefit to them of being exposed to two differing, yet equally loving, households.

And if you find you could do with a little help and support, don't be reticent about asking for it, either from friends or from professionals. Try Relate at www.relate.org.uk or give them a call on 0300 100 123.

It can take years and a lot of effort to carve something positive from the devastation of a broken relationship. But think of the child you've gained, and keep fighting to make it work – there are hundreds of thousands of people around the country who have proved that it's possible.

10 THINGS TO REMEMBER

1 *You and your partner should be willing to do whatever it takes to give your child the best chance of a stable and loving home with you both – if your relationship breaks down, they will be the greatest victim, affected for life.*

2 *There is help available at every stage, whether it's to patch up a faltering relationship, or to ease your separation. Professionals can help minimize acrimony and ensure the focus remains on your child's best interests.*

3 *Take every chance you get to reassure your child that they're blameless for the separation and that, whatever the upheaval, your love for them is constant and unconditional.*

4 *Don't ever use your child as a pawn.*

5 *Be wary of responding to the breakdown of your relationship by imposing dramatic – and potentially traumatic – further changes on your child's routine.*

6 *If you're separating, married or not, it's worth getting a solicitor's help with drawing up an agreement outlining your mutual assent over various important aspects of your child's future.*

7 *Do your utmost to remain on good terms with the mother of your child – the better you get on, the less the separation will cost and the easier it will be to remain involved in your child's life, for their and your benefit.*

8 *If you're forced to father from a distance, do all you can to beat the odds and remain involved in your child's life.*

9 *If you're raising your child alone, your time with them will be that much more precious, so be sure to engage fully whenever you can.*

10 *As a stepfather, act like the adult you are – ignore hostility, show sensitivity and patience and, as far as possible, treat any stepchildren as you do your own.*

14

Enjoying fatherhood

In this chapter you will learn:
- *how to get the most out of being a dad*
- *how to help yourself through the transition into fatherhood*
- *how being a dad can influence almost every aspect of your life for the better.*

A brief window

Life as a parent can be hectic – there's no easy way through it. You'll frequently feel you're short-changing everyone, at work and at home. But don't kid yourself that a slower day will come when you'll finally be able to sit back and give your child the time they deserve.

These early years are precious and intense – and brief. Your child won't always be so willing to share their time with you and soon, with the start of school and their life beyond, they may not be able to. So try to limit your use of words like 'later' and 'tomorrow' – when it comes to your involvement with your child, you're setting a pattern for the future *now*. So weigh your values, and ration your minutes accordingly.

If you have to, carve out the time – refuse to accept that you can't. Let that list of endless little jobs wait for another day, and see if the sky really does fall on your head as a result. Time spent with your child will never be wasted.

A sense of humour

There's something about the awesome responsibility of being a father that leads some – particularly those lacking confidence – to assume that the greater part of a dad's day should be spent in stern seriousness, as though putting on funny voices or making up nonsense songs is somehow contrary to the dignity of the role.

And while it's true that your aim is to raise an adult, not a child, no adult should be without a sense of playfulness. Those fathers who clown around with their children, tumbling on the floor or playing out childish games of make-believe regardless of what others will think, can do so precisely because they're comfortable in their role. And because they recognize what fun it can be.

Insight

There's no wisdom in stealing from yourself the chance to share your child's pleasure in the simpler things. So let them reconnect you to the enjoyment of being silly – pull faces, surprise them, tickle them constantly. We all have opportunity enough to cry together, so don't ever forget to laugh together as well.

Looking after yourself

With your partner undergoing all the physical changes, it's easy to overlook how widely the process can impact on you.

THE TRANSITION

To me, the word 'son' suggests youth, inexperience, perhaps even impetuousness. By definition it implies the existence of a parent, someone older, more capable, hopefully wiser and more responsible. And simply by virtue of getting our wives or partners pregnant, we're expected to jump overnight from one role to the other. The mere thought can be enough to get your heart beating faster.

But, of course, you don't stop being the person you always were just because there's now a child in the house. It might take time to adjust, but you'd be wrong to think you've suddenly got to be a whole new person. It's not about your identity changing, but about your identity growing.

COMING TO TERMS WITH FATHERHOOD

Before I became a father, I had no idea what to expect. And without having witnessed someone close making that same transition, you may be surprised by the emotions it can arouse.

You may feel marginalized, no more than a spectator in your own home. You may feel isolated, trapped, exhausted, angry, out of control, or just utterly bored with all the baby chat. You may resent the continual sacrifice, the lack of money, and the lost time and lost intimacy with your partner. You may feel your real friends are edging out as your in-laws are edging in. You may wonder how many of the recent grey hairs can be directly attributed to your child.

Sometimes fatherhood can seem like a lifetime of opposing emotions that threaten to tear holes in places you never knew you had. You want to provide comfort, but you want your child to be independent. You want to show them a world full of nothing but happiness, yet not be hurt by the harsher reality. You want so much for them without dictating what they'll want for themselves.

And it's a 24-hour job – you can't forget parental worries just because you're at work, and there's certainly no returning afterwards to an idyllically peaceful home, your pipe and your slippers.

So respect the demands of the role, and respect your own importance. For everyone's sake, you need to keep your head above water as you try to be all things to all people. That means considering your own needs, and taking responsibility for meeting them. After all, if you're stressed or miserable, that only impacts negatively on everyone else around you, including your child – consider it your paternal duty to be happy.

STRESS

Stress is typically caused by one or more of a number of issues: finances, work, illness, unemployment, children or personal relationships. Since fatherhood has the potential to introduce you to almost every one of those, it's completely normal to have moments when you feel close to breaking.

Since becoming a dad, I've certainly felt my emotions lurking closer to the surface. Sheer physical exhaustion alone can leave you feeling permanently raw, and the psychological demands can be crushing. Sometimes it's all you can do to get from one day to the next.

> *If I get anything wrong, it affects the people for whom I most want to get it right. And yet I'll never discover where I've gone wrong until it's too late. There's no structured feedback, no rolling review.*
>
> Christian, father to Adrian, Kelly and Alice

How to cope
- *If you're feeling overwhelmed, try to identify the specific issues bearing down on you, and prioritize them. Draw up a list, and deal with one thing at a time.*
- *Be prepared to put some aspects of your own life on hold – they'll still be there when any opportunity to kick a ball around or play hide-and-seek has long gone.*
- *Acknowledge that parenthood isn't easy – it doesn't mean you're doing anything wrong if you're finding it hard.*
- *Don't forget to exercise regularly – you really will feel better for it. As stress levels rise, fitness levels sink, so the sooner you get started the better. Not only does exercise help you burn off*

stress, but it'll give you the increased stamina to get through the days and nights.

▶ *Learn to distinguish the achievable from the ideal – you can't always juggle every plate at once, so be easy on yourself.*

▶ *Recognize that it's perfectly acceptable to make mistakes, as long as you learn from them.*

▶ *Eat healthily.*

▶ *Give yourself credit for – and take comfort from – the things that are going well and those qualities that are contributing positively to your role.*

▶ *Take up a new hobby, something that can occupy your mind and allow you a little time alone without your problems.*

▶ *Face up to any decisions that have to be made rather than letting them linger over you.*

▶ *Get all the sleep you can (see Chapter 5).*

▶ *Take time off, whether it's a weekend, an evening, or just a half-hour break.*

▶ *Alternatively, keep things as normal as possible – routine and structure can prop you up through the day.*

▶ *Cling to your sense of humour – even if it's only as a drowning man clings to a lifebelt.*

▶ *Never be ashamed to talk about your feelings and, if need be, ask for help.*

Even when I'm utterly exhausted I find myself staying up late, not because I want to watch whatever rubbish is on telly, but because I'm determined to reclaim just a few minutes for myself.

Oliver, father to Nathan

Don't stop communicating

> **Insight**
> The days of the stiff upper lip are past, so don't bottle up your feelings, no matter how much pressure you feel to soldier on. We all need to offload now and again.

- ▶ *Talk to your partner – communication is the glue that holds relationships together.*
- ▶ *Talk to friends and family – especially if they're parents themselves.*
- ▶ *Talk to your doctor, a local support group, or a parenting advice line (see 'Taking it further' at the end of the book).*
- ▶ *If they're old enough and it's appropriate, talk to your child – get them onside as part of the team, rather than being a source of friction or worry.*
- ▶ *Reach out to local dad networks and, if there isn't one, develop your own.*

There's nothing like recounting a bad experience to encourage others to share their own. You'll soon find you're not the only one feeling as you feel.

Don't ever blame your child
Needless to say, however stressed or out of control you feel, never take it out on your child, even if they seem the specific source of your difficulties.

It's unfair to judge them as you would an adult – with limited control over their circumstances, limited understanding of what's going on around them, and a limited ability to manage their emotions, the real wonder is young children ever exhibit balanced personalities.

Think of all those contradictions they're forced to navigate in these early years. We wake them when they're sleeping, then send them to bed when they're awake. We act as though nothing in the world is more interesting than their shit and their piss, then want nothing more to do with it. We encourage them to talk, then tell them to be quiet.

....
Insight
It only takes a moment's thought to appreciate the potential for blameless confusion, and recognize how wrong it would be to hold your child responsible for your frustrations.
....

MEETING THE CHALLENGE

It's hard work being a parent, with potential for pain and worry like nothing else. It's utterly disruptive, messy, noisy, exhausting, scary, frustrating, and a whole lot more. It's an endless juggling act.

Living it every minute, it's easy to lose perspective, and be swamped by the latest issue. And often it seems like you've only just overcome one problem when the next crops up – or several more. But that's how it should be, as your child grows and develops. And you, too, will grow and meet each new challenge as a more experienced, more capable parent.

> **Insight**
> It's no small achievement to be able to say that all you do for another is out of love. And if your child is happy and healthy, then whatever you're doing is right.

It takes time to regain the equilibrium of your pre-child life, and perhaps you never will. But then you may never want to, either – the hardest challenges really are the most rewarding.

What's in it for you?

Most of this book is about what you as a father can give to your child, but it wouldn't be complete – or fair – if I made out it was all a one-way street.

INCREASED HEALTH

Studies show that the more involved and active you are as a father, the lower your risk of suffering from stress, depression or substance abuse. You're also less likely to be admitted to hospital, or to die prematurely or through accident. And hard though it is to believe when I see how my grey hairs are threatening to take over, fathers in stable relationships actually live longer on average than single men without children.

PSYCHOLOGICAL WELLBEING

The vast majority of fathers agree that nothing brings more happiness or fulfilment in life than children, and that a crucial ingredient of success isn't income or status but the solidity of the parent–child relationship.

There's also the satisfaction of knowing that you've made such a pivotal and positive difference to another's life, and the justifiable pride that comes from the accomplishment. And there's nothing like being needed and loved and, ultimately, irreplaceable to massage the ego.

Another oft-cited benefit is how fatherhood can bring a greater sense of purpose to your days. For a life that might feel otherwise adrift, a family can bring identity and stability, acting like a rudder to provide direction, and ballast to help weather the storms.

> *On a purely evolutionary level, as long as I can keep Becky alive, I'm a success! I've passed on my genes – I've fulfilled my role on this planet. And I'm still in my thirties!*
>
> Sean, father to Becky

A NEW PERSPECTIVE

One consequence of being forced to view life through your child's eyes can be a renewed appreciation of things around you. Their instinctive curiosity, amplified by their often infectious enthusiasm, can reveal something fresh and colourful in what long ago became faded and mundane, whether it's riding a bus or walking through fallen leaves, giggling at a strange noise or recognizing again the forgotten magic of Christmas.

And almost every parent can quote a memorable comment or question prompted by their child's honest and appealingly simplistic outlook.

We were camping last summer when my daughter pointed to a corner of the tent. 'If spiders can't swim,' she said, 'why has that one come on a beach holiday to Italy?'

Nathan, father to Bella

CONSOLATION

Particularly in the early years, much of parenthood is a conflict between pride in your child's development, and a strong desire to put them on ice and so retain their enchanting innocence forever – it's a bittersweet moment to find your child's favourite teddy sitting forgotten on the shelf.

In the same way, as you're forced to witness one generation giving way to the next, children can provide a consolatory sense of balance to the loss, and an understanding that decline is a natural partner to growth.

IMPROVED RELATIONSHIPS

You can't fully understand an equation if you only know half of it. So given that the parent–child relationship is fundamental to every person on this planet, it's easy to see how becoming a parent yourself can offer enormous insight, and make a positive impact on almost every relationship you have.

Most immediately, parenthood can give you a greater appreciation of all your own parents did for you. It can also strengthen your bond with your partner – and not just through a determination never to separate for fear of being granted sole custody. At the end of the day, nothing else has the power to bind two people together like the shared trials and pleasures of parenting.

Now that I'm a parent myself, I've got a whole new respect for single parents doing it all alone.

Simon, father to Alex and Emily

NEW SKILLS AND QUALITIES

Fathers quote numerous skills they've been forced to learn and qualities they've developed through raising their children.

▶ *From managing children – especially toddlers – you learn patience and tolerance.*

▶ *From the inevitable time constraints, you learn self-discipline, a greater recognition of your own limitations, and an ability to prioritize.*

▶ *Forced to focus beyond yourself, you develop greater empathy, and an awareness of the world your children will grow up in. Consequently, many parents are driven to better it, whether it's through championing the environment or joining a school committee.*

▶ *Having not only survived the many dramas and imagined emergencies but actually produced a healthy, happy child as well, your self-confidence soars.*

▶ *The unpredictability develops flexibility and a knack for contingency planning.*

▶ *While an utterly dependent child can force you to grow in maturity, they can also keep you young, expanding your own world through theirs as you get involved in new activities, develop new interests and stay connected with the next generation.*

▶ *An understanding of your own child allows you to relate to, and communicate with, others – even if it's just through correctly naming their favourite blob-like CBBC character.*

SUPPORT

Insight

Families provide the strongest and most important support network a person can have. And a child doesn't have to be capable of discussion to provide comfort or reassurance – two little arms around the neck can often be enough.

Just as I taught my parents how to operate their video recorder, we'll have a resident techno-expert on hand to guide us through the challenges of modernity.

Giles, father to Edward and Lara

A NEW IDENTITY

However nostalgic you may be for aspects of your life before – or however far away that life now seems – your new identity as a father, and your ability to meet the responsibilities required, should only be a source of pride.

LOVE

If love is something that grows in the sharing, you're only going to have more and more. And though every relationship has difficulties, at its heart will always remain an oasis of pure, unconditional goodness.

A LEGACY

Whatever your religious beliefs, with a child comes the opportunity to feel that when it's over, it's not entirely over.

THOSE INCOMMUNICABLE PLEASURES

Before I became a father, I'd watch scenes in films or TV shows where a child's in danger, and I'd scoff at the obvious attempt to manipulate my emotions with something so trite. Now, though the stories remain just as clichéd, I sit on the sofa and sniff pathetically, an easy victim.

It's as though in becoming a dad I've developed a whole new internal organ, of embarrassing sensitivity, that makes me a complete sucker for any story involving any child suffering. Because suddenly it seems real.

In the same way, it's near impossible to communicate the many pleasures that come from parenthood to those who haven't got children without sounding just as trite. I would never have imagined how special that moment can be when your child falls asleep on your chest or leans in for a cuddle, when they giggle or call for you that first time, or reach for your hand and lead you somewhere they want to be. They're pleasures I would never have understood before.

I'm just looking forward to the time when, thanks to Father's Day, I'll never have to buy another pair of pants again.

Jason, father to Jack and Daisy

Into the future

In many ways, the first few years of fatherhood can be the hardest. In those very early weeks it may be all about your partner, but every passing day brings more opportunity for you to enjoy your child's company, until soon you'll face the appealing prospect of being not only a father to your child, but a friend as well.

Every present is heavy with potential for the future, so start building the foundations now. The more time you spend with your child when young, the more they'll want to share with you as they grow older. And one day they might even choose you a good retirement home.

Conclusion

There can be no greater responsibility than caring for and guiding a child through their first years. As each little development rouses a disproportionate sense of pride, you get to watch them – and help them – develop from total dependence into a chattering, laughing, playful child. But it doesn't stop there – your every interaction shapes their future as an individual, and influences how they, in turn, will relate to their own children.

It's an incredible privilege, not only to be the one to whom they turn for help, comfort and advice, but to be the primary representative of half the world's population.

A strong, loving relationship with your child can help them grow into a healthy and well-balanced individual, equipped with the skills to not just stand alone in the world, but to be happy in it as well.

Insight

In any relationship, the more you give, the more you receive in return. But unlike any other relationship, being a father to your child demands so much more. As a result, it has the potential to offer more pleasure and more satisfaction than anything else.

10 THINGS TO REMEMBER

1 *The time you spend with your child now will set a pattern for the future – don't imagine you'll ever be able to make up for lost time.*

2 *Try to maintain a sense of humour.*

3 *Becoming a father isn't about losing or changing your identity, but about growing it.*

4 *Be forgiving of yourself – few things in life have the potential to shake your foundations as much as new fatherhood.*

5 *It's normal at times to feel overwhelmed by the pressure to please work and family – it doesn't mean you're doing anything wrong.*

6 *Look after yourself – eat healthily, exercise and, if possible, keep a little part of the week for yourself.*

7 *Keep communicating with your partner.*

8 *Don't lose perspective – as long as your child is happy and healthy, the chances are everything's going okay.*

9 *Never be ashamed to ask for help if you need it.*

10 *There can be few things in life requiring more responsibility than the raising of a child – and few things in life that can give you the same amount of pleasure and fulfilment.*

Taking it further

Books

Down to Earth with a Bump, Andrew Watson, Book Guild, 2011 – My own personal diary of first-time fatherhood, from conception to my daughter's first birthday.

The Expectant Father: Facts, Tips, and Advice for Dads-to-Be, Armin A Brott and Jennifer Ash, Abbeville Press, 2001; *The New Father: A Dad's Guide to the First Year*, Armin A Brott, Mitchell Beazley, 2005; *The New Father: A Dad's Guide to the Toddler Years*, Armin A Brott, Abbeville Press, 1998 – Authoritative and informative month-by-month handbooks covering all aspects of fatherhood.

Fatherhood Reclaimed: The Making of the Modern Father, Adrienne Burgess, Vermilion, 1997 – An exploration of modern fatherhood, based on sociological, anthropological and historical research.

New Toddler Taming, Dr Christopher Green, Vermilion, 2005 – A common-sensical approach to dealing with the wide range of toddler issues.

The Sixty Minute Father, Rob Parsons, Hodder & Stoughton, 2009 – A brief but heartfelt book about the importance of spending time with your children.

Your Pregnancy Bible: The Experts' Guide to the Nine Months of Pregnancy and the First Weeks of Parenthood, Anne Deans, Carroll and Brown, 2007 – The sort of authoritative reference book that no new parent should be without.

Websites

www.awwa.co.uk – My own website, where you'll find details of my books and other parenting projects.

www.babycentre.co.uk – Detailed information and advice for expectant and new parents.

www.childalert.co.uk – A website dedicated to child safety and wellbeing.

www.citizensadvice.org.uk – Specialist advice from the Citizens Advice Bureau.

www.dad.info – A site dedicated to providing dads with information and support.

www.dadtalk.co.uk – Social network and parenting discussion forum for dads.

www.direct.gov.uk/parents – A gateway to governmental advice and support on all aspects of parenthood.

www.familiesonline.co.uk – A website by parents for parents, with local resources around the country.

www.fatherhoodinstitute.org – Collates research and promotes paternal involvement.

www.homedad.org.uk – A support group dedicated to stay-at-home dads.

www.home-start.org.uk – A national support network for parents struggling to cope.

www.moneysavingexpert.com/family – Financial advice tailored to parents.

www.nct.org.uk – Nationwide support for parents, including courses, from the National Childbirth Trust.

www.nhsdirect.nhs.uk – The NHS Direct online portal for health information.

www.parentlineplus.org.uk – A national parenting charity.

www.patient.co.uk – Comprehensive health information as provided by GPs.

www.workingfamilies.org.uk – Information and support to help parents juggle work and family life.

www.yourfamily.org.uk – Information and advice for parents of young children, from the National Society for the Prevention of Cruelty to Children.